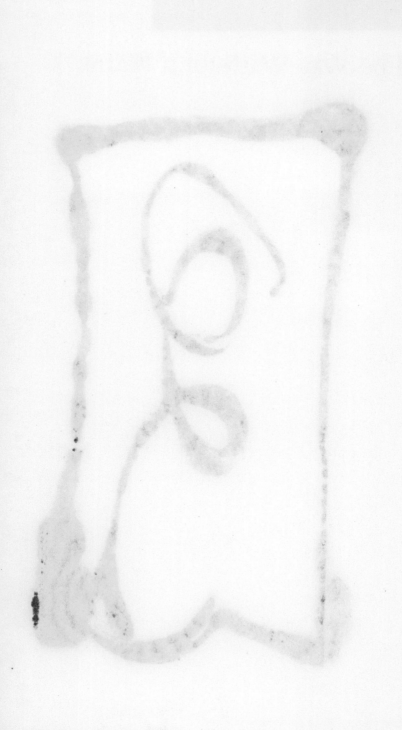

The War Without a Name

JOHN TALBOTT

The War Without a Name
France in Algeria, 1954–1962

 ALFRED A. KNOPF   NEW YORK   1980

Copyright © 1980 by John Talbott

All rights reserved under International and Pan-American Copyright Conventions. Published in the United States by Alfred A. Knopf, Inc., New York, and simultaneously in Canada by Random House of Canada Limited, Toronto. Distributed by Random House, Inc., New York.

LIBRARY OF CONGRESS CATALOGING IN PUBLICATION DATA

Talbott, John. (Date)
The war without a name.

Bibliography: p.
Includes index.
1.   Algeria—History—Revolution, 1954–1962.
2.   France—Politics and government—1945–
I.   Title.
DT295.T25   1980   965'.04   80–344
ISBN 0–394–50909–9

Manufactured in the United States of America
First Edition

To Dave Pinkney
and Gordon Wright

Le pays descend un degré de plus, les yeux fermés, dans une guerre qui ne dit pas son nom.

PAUL MUS

Contents

Acknowledgments

Research for this book was begun in the Bibliothèque Nationale, continued in the Fondation Nationale des Sciences Politiques, and completed at the Hoover Institution on War, Revolution and Peace. Interlibrary Loans brought to Santa Barbara many books I was unable to read elsewhere. The Class of 1931 Bicentennial Preceptorship of Princeton University permitted me to spend 1970–71 in France; a Social Science Research Council travel grant paid my Atlantic crossing. National Endowment for the Humanities grant #FC-10503 enabled me to begin writing the manuscript at the Institute for Advanced Study, oasis of conviviality and solitude, during the academic year 1975–76. The Committee on Research of the University of California, Santa Barbara, supported research trips to Paris and Palo Alto and underwrote such far from incidental expenses as photocopying. I am grateful to these institutions and organizations for their assistance.

I want to thank the editors of *Armed Forces and Society, Contemporary French Civilization,* and *The Virginia Quarterly Review* for permission to include in this book material that first appeared in these journals in somewhat different form.

I am obliged to all those who were willing to talk with me about the Algerian war, and to Pierre Vidal-Naquet, who read the manuscript. Thanks to Chris Atkinson, Helena Kirk, and Darcy Ritzau, who typed and proofread the final draft. Thanks to Ashbel Green, my editor, for finding so many better ways of saying what I meant. Thanks to Felix Gilbert, helpful to more historians in more ways than he can ever know. For mistakes that remain, I alone am responsible. For innumerable kindnesses done me since my days as a graduate student, I am grateful to Alfreda Birmingham and the late Earl Birmingham.

JOHN TALBOTT

Santa Barbara, California
June 1979

Preface

This book is about a war of shattering divisiveness. In late 1954 a government that had but recently negotiated an end to the war in Indochina replied to an insurrection against French rule in Algeria both with armed force and with a sweeping program of reform. This policy of repression and reform, pursued in various guises from the beginning of the war nearly to its close, came under attack in the most diverse sectors of mainland opinion. Once a huge conscript army had been committed to carrying out the policy, divisions of opinion deepened.

For nearly eight years, the Algerian war dominated French public life. On more than one occasion this last bloody step in France's retreat from empire seemed to threaten the nation with civil war. The present work deals mainly with those Frenchmen whose convictions on the Algerian question impelled them to take action. Before the tricolor had been struck in North Africa for the last time, a number of French citizens found themselves either conspiring against their government for the sake of *Algérie française* or lending aid to the enemy on behalf of an *Algérie algérienne*. Some stopped at nothing in furtherance of their cause. Some paid for their devotion with prison and exile, some with their lives. The chief actors in the story are army officers and politicians, antiwar activists, colonial leaders, writers on all sides of the question—and Charles de Gaulle, who abandoned the policy of keeping Algeria French, entered into negotiations with the Algerian revolutionaries, and relieved France of a ruinous obsession.

The War Without a Name

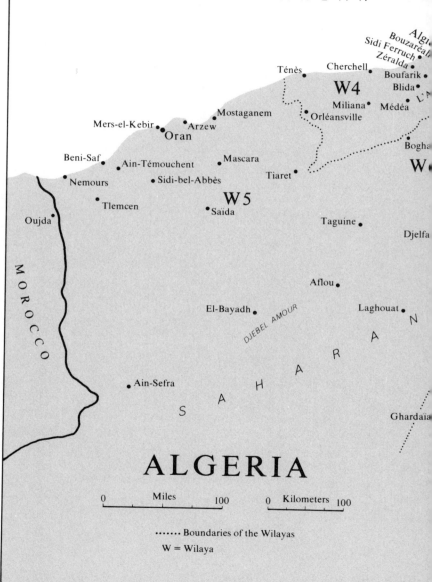

MEDITERRANEAN

Alg...
Bouzaréah
Sidi Ferruch
Zéralda
Ténès Cherchell Boufarik
W4 Blida
Miliana Médéa
Orléansville
Mostaganem

Mers-el-Kebir Arzew
Oran
Bogha

Beni-Saf Mascara W
Ain-Témouchent Tiaret
Nemours Sidi-bel-Abbès

Tlemcen W5 Taguine
Saïda Djelfa

Oujda

MOROCCO

Aflou

El-Bayadh Laghouat
DJEBEL AMOUR N

Ain-Sefra A R

S H Ghardaïa

ALGERIA

0 Miles 100 0 Kilometers 100

······ Boundaries of the Wilayas
W = Wilaya

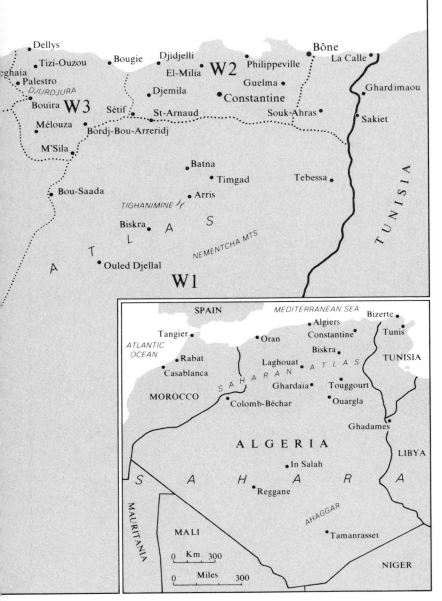

SEA

Dellys
Tizi-Ouzou
Bougie
Djidjelli
Bône
La Calle
eghaia
Palestro
El-Milia
W2
Philippeville
Ghardimaou
DJURDJURA
Djemila
Guelma
Bouïra W3
Sétif
Constantine
Mélouza
St-Arnaud
Souk-Ahras
Sakiet
Bordj-Bou-Arreridj
M'Sila

TUNISIA

Bou-Saada
Batna
Timgad
Tebessa
Arris
TIGHANIMINE
Biskra
L A S
A T
NEMENTCHA MTS
Ouled Djellal
W1

SPAIN
MEDITERRANEAN SEA
Bizerte
Algiers
Tangier
Oran
Constantine
Tunis
ATLANTIC
OCEAN
Biskra
TUNISIA
Rabat
Laghouat
A T L A S
Casablanca
S A H A R A N
Ghardaia
Touggourt
MOROCCO
Colomb-Béchar
Ouargla
Ghadames
ALGERIA
LIBYA
In Salah
S A H A R A
MAURITANIA
Reggane
AHAGGAR
MALI
Tamanrasset
0 Km. 300
0 Miles 300
NIGER

1 French Algeria

Armistice Day, November 11, 1954: A battalion of French paratroops parades through the streets of Algiers. The soldiers belonged to a larger force that Pierre Mendès France had dispatched from the mainland a week earlier. The prime minister had acted immediately on getting word that armed disturbances had broken out all over Algeria in the early morning hours of November 1.[1] "In official circles," *Le Monde* reported, it was believed "that these attacks are part of a well-organized plot of the nationalists."[2] By November 13 the paratroopers found themselves chasing these elusive "nationalists" through the rugged defiles of the Aurès mountains. But first they went on parade, resplendent in their red berets and green camouflage battle dress, proof of the French government's resolve to keep Algeria French. Their berets identified them as "colonials"—professional soldiers, defenders of the Empire, seasoned guerrilla fighters. To the settlers lining the sidewalks it was a reassuring sight indeed. "The settlers believed we had just returned from Indochina," one young paratrooper recalled, "and they applauded wildly, with all their hearts." In fact, these formidable-looking warriors were all green troops, fresh from mainland training camps.[3]

The settlers' mistake was understandable. Soldiers such as these had spent the past eight years in Indochina. Sent to reestablish French rule, the expeditionary corps wound up conducting a crusade against communism. Draftees never set foot in Southeast Asia; this first Indochina war was the task of a professional army. In the course of the conflict, many Indochina hands came down with *le mal jaune*—army lingo for the spell Vietnam cast over them. They fell in love with Vietnamese women, they immersed themselves in the culture, they fell captive to the landscape, they swore they would never leave. And when they did leave, traces of *le mal jaune* lingered on, in their peculiar vocabulary and in their tendency to interpret all events in the light of their Asian experience.[4]

Their years abroad (many had already spent most of World War II overseas) made the Indochina hands strangers to their homeland. And the war estranged them from it. The first Indochina war did not arouse the fierce passions of the second. Public indifference in France to events in Southeast Asia left the expeditionary corps with the feeling that it had been abandoned to its fate. Deepening the army's sense of estrangement was the French Communist party's aggressive opposition to the war. Reports had reached the soldiers of longshoremen, at the party's behest, refusing to load ships bound for Southeast Asia; of hospitals, at the party's insistence, promising blood donors that their contributions would never run in the veins of members of the expeditionary corps.[5]

The army did not stint in spilling its own blood. Between 1945 and 1954, according to one estimate, ninety-two thousand members of the expeditionary corps were killed, one hundred fourteen thousand were wounded, and thirty thousand taken prisoner.[6] Enough officers were killed every year to fill a class at the military academy of Saint Cyr.[7] Surviving classmates did not easily forget the tales they had heard of promises made to blood donors.

In the spring of 1954, the siege of Dien Bien Phu recapitulated in eight weeks the main themes of the war. At last France paid attention. Fashioning a noose around the French fortress, the Vietminh doomed not only its defenders but the French presence in Indochina. The army preferred to think that conniving politicians, selfish and fainthearted civilians, a traitorous Communist party, had stabbed it in the back. Younger officers believed that the army's own high command had held a hand on the dagger. The captains and majors who had done the fighting held in contempt the politicians and generals who had shared the planning. Years of living by their wits gave them a warlord's disdain for the traditional chain of command.[8]

As the soldiers weighed anchor for France, Vietnamese whom they had promised never to abandon lined the shore in silent reproach. Many swam to the departing ships and begged to be taken aboard. Those who stood watching them swore that never again would they be brought to such a pass. In his *Portrait d'un officier,* the novelist Pierre-Henri Simon captured their anger and remorse:

> What ate into us like acid was the look of despair and contempt of men whom we had engaged ourselves to defend, of the Christians of the North cooped up in camps, of those who had lost everything for being faithful to us. We had fought decently enough; we had nothing to reproach ourselves for, as far as courage is concerned; and yet we were ashamed of this pointless and ignoble war the leaders of our country had obliged us to make. . . .[9]

Many officers believed they had been betrayed; many also believed they had fought the wrong kind of war. They agreed with the assessment of the commander of the Vietminh army. "The Vietnamese people won," Vo Nguyen Giap explained, "because its war of liberation was a people's war."[10] In the aftermath of Dien Bien Phu, French military writers turned to explicating the mysteries of a people's war. The French were the first of a generation of Western military writers to fall under the spell of guerrilla warfare. The French army, the writers announced, had to learn to conduct what they called *guerre révolutionnaire.* What the West had

most to fear, they urged, was not consumption by holocaust
—the vision of the nuclear strategists—but asphyxiation by
brush fire, the metaphor of guerrilla war.

The French theorists saw in the Vietminh a Marxist-
dominated revolutionary party that had made itself the expression of the yearnings of the Vietnamese to be rid of
foreign rule; a party that had by coercion and persuasion
shaped such yearnings into a political movement, that had by
means of ancient military techniques conducted a successful
war of liberation. Marxism, nationalism, and the war of the
guerrilla: here were the ideas, the motive forces, and the
methods behind the Vietminh's victory. That not all nationalists were Marxists, that not all wars were wars of liberation
or wars of the guerrilla, that not all liberations had, or would,
come about by means of war—such considerations as these
the theorists of *guerre révolutionnaire* put aside. They were
not interested in history lessons, in the peculiarities of the
struggle that drove them from Southeast Asia. They were
looking for generalizations that could be put to use elsewhere. The theorists made the Indochina experience the very
model of modern warfare.[11]

"The people is to the army as the water to the fish" became their chief maxim. Any soldier who had ever fought
against irregulars knew that guerrillas raise recruits, find
shelter, get supplies, gather intelligence from their own
people. Geronimo employed the same tactics in his war
against the United States army as had Jugurtha in his
war against the Romans. Twentieth-century guerrillas
pressed ancient techniques into the service of revolution.[12]
Defenders of the established order would not succeed
against revolutionaries by holding their supporters and
sympathizers at gunpoint. They also had to capture popular loyalties. The French, the theorists went on, had failed
to convince the Vietnamese that French rule held any advantage worth staking their lives on. This political failure
had as much to do with the outcome of the war as
France's military reverses.

Elaborating the virtues to be found in the Vietminh's political and social organization drew attention to vices the theorists had discovered in their own. The Vietminh's unified civil-military command had enabled it to organize the population in pursuit of aims from which it brooked no dissent. French soldiers and politicians, by contrast, had worked at cross-purposes, and in the civilian population the treachery of a few had gone unpunished amidst the indifference of the many. The Communists and dissenters at home, the theorists concluded, were as dangerous as their guerrilla-allies in the bush. In the face of such treachery, the army's tradition of political neutrality was as obsolete as the red breeches it had worn to war in August 1914.

In October 1954 General René Chassin, one of France's ablest military writers, declared in an army journal that "it is time the army stopped being the great mute. The time has come for the free world, if it does not want to die a violent death, to apply certain of its adversary's methods. One of these methods—and undoubtedly the most important one—resides in the ideological role that, behind the iron curtain, has fallen to the military forces."[13] Chassin stood Clemenceau's famous aphorism on its head: Politics, he announced, was too important to leave to politicians.

Writing impassioned articles for army magazines was, however, a far cry from meddling in politics. And the musings of a coterie of military intellectuals were a far cry from official army doctrine. Many officers, especially in the senior ranks, could not have been pleased to hear their methods and traditions, their conception of the army's place in state and society condemned as hopelessly out of date. Many officers dismissed the new theory as medicine more dangerous than the ills for which the doctors of *guerre révolutionnaire* presumed to prescribe.[14]

Had peace followed the war in Indochina, talk of *guerre révolutionnaire* might have remained a diversion of Indochina hands, a means of whiling away long evenings in mainland garrison towns. But war sent the Indochina hands to

Algeria, and with them they took their resentments, their sense of estrangement, their memories of their dead, and their lessons from Southeast Asia.

Pierre Mendès France had more to do than any other French politician with disengaging France from Indochina; he was made prime minister precisely for that purpose. He also had more to do than any other French politician with committing France to putting down the insurrection in Algeria. Indochina cast him in the role of the providential man, but in dispatching paratroops to Algeria he simply did what any other French prime minister would have done. For one million well-established settlers of European origin looked to France for protection, and neither Mendès France nor his successors could escape the moral obligation of protecting them. Arguments for keeping Algeria French abounded, but none save the presence of the settlers was compelling enough to be enforced with an army of a half-million men.

Until the close of the nineteenth century, however, a scarcity of settlers had given French rule a look of impermanence. In an age of imperialist expansion this had been the cause of much worry and regret. Algeria was no El Dorado; in the early years of the French occupation it was not even an inviting land. Settlers risked being shot by Algerians, bullied by the army, swindled by land speculators, ruined by drought, killed off by disease. Such a prospect limited settlement to "immigrants of crisis"—victims of hard times, political repression, and war. Of those who made the trip against their will, such as the political exiles of the Second Empire, few stayed. Settlers who did remain tried one crop after another—sugar cane, cotton, tobacco, tea, mulberries—and all of them failed. Wheat did well, but not well enough to enable growers to undersell competitors in the world market.[15] Fortunes were struck in Algeria only when misfortune struck France.

In the late 1870s the phylloxera, a plant louse that attacks the roots and leaves of grape vines, devastated the vineyards of France. In the ruination of French vintners the European settlers of Algeria found their salvation. Wine rescued them from bankruptcy and collapse, just as tobacco saved the settlers of colonial Virginia.[16] Bankers once stingy with credit were suddenly eager to thrust money into their hands. New roads and railroads drove into the interior from expanded port facilities on the coast. And the proliferation of the vine brought an upsurge in the pace of settlement. Between 1872 and the outbreak of World War I, the European population of Algeria grew more rapidly than in any other period in the history of French rule, increasing from two hundred eighty thousand to seven hundred fifty-two thousand. In the four decades from the Great War to the outbreak of the insurrection, immigration dropped off sharply and the settler birthrate declined.[17]

In their frenzy to cash in on the wine bonanza, the settlers scanted other crops. They went on planting vines as if the mainland would never conquer the phylloxera. But in the 1880s Louis Pasteur found the remedy (grafting American vines onto French root stocks), the French industry recovered, and, as the years passed, shipping Algerian wine to Marseilles more and more resembled carrying coals to Newcastle. After 1935, especially, the wine trade stagnated. The glutted market forced some settlers under and encouraged others to turn to growing wheat, alfalfa, citrus fruit, and vegetables—crops that accounted for such increases in agricultural productivity as took place in the last years of French rule.[18]

Still, wine growing and trading remained Algeria's biggest industry. Organized not to benefit a majority of the population but to enrich the European minority, the wine trade epitomized Algeria's classic colonial economy. The settlers' vines carpeted the Mitidja, the central plain between the mountains and the sea. Some grew on corporate *latifundia* employing hundreds of field hands, others on properties taking on a few hired men at harvest time. Agribusinessmen and family vintners alike drew their labor from the sea of Algerian peasants whose tiny patches of land fringed the European enclaves. Nothing more vividly demonstrates the dualism of colonial society than comparing the holdings of the European growers with those of their Algerian workers. European settlement had on the Algerian countryside the same impact as Clifford Geertz has described in a case study of Indonesia: "a radical segregation of modern and traditional economic, social, and cultural systems into sharply distinct, contrastively organized sectors."[19]

The dualism so vividly displayed in the contrast between traditional and modern agriculture also manifested itself in the social and economic inequalities of the cities and towns. From the 1880s on, many European smallholders gave up the struggle against more efficient, better-financed growers and moved to town; newly arrived settlers put urban skills to work in urban settings; and by the 1950s, 80 percent of the Europeans resided in cities—half of them in Oran and Algiers. Living with their backs to the hinterland, they engaged in trade with the mainland, they worked for the state or in a handful of small industries, they sold goods and services to each other.

The Algerians were late arrivals to the towns (even in the 1950s, 80 percent continued to live in the countryside); until 1930 Algiers, Oran, Constantine, and Bône were all preponderantly European. But native population growth put on the land more mouths than subsistence farming could feed, and a rural exodus began. By 1954, two-thirds of the inhabitants of the four major cities were Algerians. One in three squatted in shanty towns, squalid encampments patched together from odds and ends other people had thrown away.[20]

In Algiers in the 1950s, one-quarter of Algerian males worked as unskilled laborers. Only one European in a hundred had to settle for such work. Each community had the same proportion of skilled workers (25 percent) and shop-keepers (12 percent), but many of the Algerian "shops" were one-man stalls that barely kept their owners alive. More than a third of the settlers in Algiers worked in white-collar jobs, but only 6 percent of the Algerians. Algerian doctors and lawyers were as rare as European day laborers. The Algerian entrepreneurial class made up only a thin slice of the statistician's pie. Fully one-quarter to one-third of Algerian males crouched in their shanty towns, down if not out, unable to find work. Every European who wanted a job had one. The few Algerian women working outside their households were employed in domestic service, keeping the houses and minding the children of Europeans.

Dualism did not run to residential segregation. Except for the richest quarters and the shanty towns, Algerians and Europeans shared neighborhoods. Bab El Oued, for instance, an important working-class section of Algiers—and a stronghold of diehard settler activism—had a sizable Algerian population.[21]

The settlers of Bab El Oued shared their Algerian neighbors' social class and economic condition. With the European owners of the great *latifundia* they had in common an ethnic identity—and little else. But when the chips were down, and the ascendancy challenged, ethnicity prevailed over differences among the settlers in wealth, status, and power.

Alexis de Tocqueville would have been disappointed. He had returned from his travels in America to make himself an expert on Algeria—and an enthusiastic advocate of French settlement. In 1837 he wrote: "It is not enough for the French to put themselves alongside the Arabs if they do not succeed in establishing a lasting bond with them, and at length in forming from the two races a single people."[22] Tocqueville got the settlement he wanted, but not the single people. The French lived not intermingled with the Algerians, however things looked in Bab El Oued, but adjacent to them.

This lack of social contact manifested itself in countless ways. One of the most telling was the absence of intermarriage between Europeans and Algerians. Such liaisons took place at the rate of fewer than 100 per year.[23] If marriages were rare, illicit relationships were unheard of. Half-castes were remarkably scarce. Sexual encounters between Europeans and Algerians were limited to the furtive meetings of homosexuals and the commercial transactions of prostitutes.[24]

In colonial Algeria, linguistic, religious, and racial differences ran parallel along either side of one vast cultural fault, Algerians on one side, Europeans on the other. No institution served, at any point in the society, to join the two sides of the fault together: "Neither the school, nor the army, nor any other factor succeeded in melding into a harmonious society groups thus juxtaposed. Social relations were reduced to their simplest expression: people intermingled to the degree that economic relations dictated. . . ."[25]

Two cultures inhabited the same soil in the relation of conqueror and conquered, occupier and occupied. "This inequality that no one challenges," the noted Arabist Jacques Berque remarked, "works to the profit of the French establishment, legitimizes it in the eyes of its beneficiaries and even, to a certain extent, in the eyes of its subjects, who are also its 'object.' "[26]

Elsewhere, of course, Europeans lived as removed from the non-Europeans they had subjugated as they did in Algeria; the white settlers of North America pushed the Indians aside and kept them at arm's length. But between North America and North Africa there was an enormous difference. The Indian population covered North America in a thin veneer. By 1866 settlers in the West already outnumbered Indians ten to one.[27] Algeria in 1830 had a native population of roughly 2.5 million. By 1954 Algerians outnumbered settlers by at least nine to one.[28]

Some observers had expected the native population to diminish on contact with the settlers, as happened elsewhere in the course of European expansion. In the decades of the conquest the French army and disease killed Algerians by the thousands. After 1870, however, improved sanitary conditions and the spread of European medicine reduced the death rate, disrupting the mechanism that kept a peasant society from outstripping its material resources. For though the rate of mortality fell, the fertility rate stayed high, and the Algerian population commenced to increase rapidly. Over the years, the tempo of growth accelerated, doubling in the half-century between 1896 and 1948, promising to double again in the next twenty-five years.[29]

As the number of mouths requiring feeding multiplied, the yields of peasant holdings declined. By the thousands, Algerian peasants were forced to the road, and many drifted into the cities. Others went to France in search of work. From the turn of the century on, young men traveled northward and their postal money orders southward in steadily increasing numbers. By the 1950s more than three hundred thousand Algerians worked in French factories, fields, and construction sites and huddled together in French slums.[30]

While the native population of Algeria grew, the number of Europeans scarcely rose at all. The settlers found themselves a shrinking minority. For decades this was a source less of anxiety than of self-congratulation on the beneficence of European medicine and of satisfaction at the effect on native wages of an expanding labor pool. In the years before the Great War, especially, the French of Algeria were too confident in the promise of the future to read ill portents in the increase of their workers and servants.[31]

After the turn of the century, native-born settlers outnumbered immigrants. They thought of France as the Old Country, an ancestral homeland, but not home. Besides, many settlers were not French in the first place, but Spanish, Italian, or Maltese. And those who were French by virtue of having French parents or grandparents did not feel the same about Montpellier and Besançon as they did about Bône and Constantine. Some settlers might take vacations and visit cousins in France, but many never set foot on the mainland. Algeria was where they buried their dead.

The settlers looked on mainlanders as meddlers who understood nothing of local conditions. Paris, they believed, imposed on them all sorts of ridiculous rules and regulations —with respect to the wine trade, for instance—while denying them any voice in the conduct of their own affairs. They whistled the same tune American settlers had whistled for English ears. At the turn of the century, they talked of secession. But they never came to issuing a declaration of independence, for Paris granted much of the internal autonomy they had been seeking. Secessionist talk died away, to be revived only as an insane last hope by the desperadoes of the OAS.[32]

Had the settlers made good on their threats, the mainland might have experienced a happier fate. Cutting their ties with France, the settlers would have resolved the Algerian problem, insofar as it was a French problem, at a stroke. The mainland French could have withdrawn their garrison and their economic support and left the settlers to fend for themselves. Set loose from France, however, the settlers might have drifted in the same direction as their counterparts at the opposite end of Africa. Unable to get help from across the sea, released from the restraints imposed on them by membership in a large liberal democracy, they might have been tempted to compensate for their numerical inferiority by some scheme similar to *apartheid*. In this event, the day of reckoning between them and the Algerians might have been even worse than it was.

In the 1930s Algerian Algeria began encroaching on French Algeria. Some forms of this encroachment were visible and dramatic: Algerian peasants crowded into cities once over-whelmingly European. Other aspects went unnoticed: in 1930 the birthrate in the Casbah of Algiers exceeded the deathrate for the first time.[33] Traditional agriculture decaying, life winning over death in the depths of an urban slum—such forces as these ground with glacial slowness against the moorings of the settler ascendancy.

The pace of political events was swifter, their impact more immediate and noticeable. In the 1930s the number of voices speaking the language of Algerian nationalism increased, and so did the number of listeners. One rabble-rouser, whom the French frequently locked up, had already raised the demand for Algerian independence.

For the better part of fifty years, up to the very eve of the insurrection, the dominant voice of Algerian nationalism remained that of the liberals. Accommodating men of infinite patience, they wanted nothing better than to work out with the settlers some kind of modus vivendi. Indeed, the liberals resembled the settlers more closely than they did their fellow Algerians. In French schools they learned to believe in the idea of progress, equality before the law, careers open to talent. They sought to work within the framework of parliamentary institutions, confident that their program of political emancipation and economic modernization could be carried out under French sovereignty. Already assimilated themselves, they were prepared to lead the assimilation of the Algerian masses. They placed their hopes in the French nation of their ideals because they did not believe an Algerian nation had ever existed or would ever come to pass.[34]

In 1936 Ferhat Abbas, pharmacist of Sétif and outstanding liberal of the generation come of age between the world wars, expressed this doubt about the possibility of an Algerian nation. Neither the settlers nor mainland politicians nor nationalist opponents ever let him forget it. Abdelhamid Ben Badis, a founder in 1931 of the Association of Ulamas, or religious teachers, had an answer for Abbas. The association was a movement of Muslim puritans who sought to restore Islam to its ancient rigor without turning away from the modern world. Ben Badis held that the purification of a return to religion would bring in its wake the revivification of politics, culture, and society. Algeria, he insisted, was a nation in being, a nation without a state. Moreover, "this Algerian nation is not France and does not want to be France."[35] But neither Abbas nor Ben Badis was ready to abandon the path of legality for the sake of achieving his aims.

Both Abbas and Ben Badis believed themselves to be expressing popular hopes, but neither man spoke in the popular idiom of a poorly educated ex-soldier named Messali Hadj. A spellbinding orator in both French and Arabic (a language Abbas and many other liberals could not speak), a skillful organizer, a fearless, vain, and strikingly handsome man, Messali had no stomach for the politics of accommodation. From the outset he aimed for an independent Algeria. Pursuing it landed him behind bars as often as a vagrant looking for a warm place to sleep. His politics were revolutionary, and his following proletarian.[36]

In 1927 Messali took over in Paris the Etoile nord-africaine, a newly formed association of Algerian workers having rather vague ties with the French Communist party. In 1929 he called for revolt against French rule in North Africa. The French government promptly dissolved the Etoile nord-africaine and put Messali in jail. The formation of an organization, public agitation, dissolution, imprisonment, underground activity, reorganization under a new name, public agitation again—such was the cycle within which the Messaliste movement contrived to exist for the next quarter-century.

In the 1930s Messali was estranged from the Communists when he gave nationalism precedence over the proletarian revolution. When the Etoile nord-africaine, dissolved yet again in 1937, reemerged as the Parti populaire algérien

(PPA), Messali made much greater play of the nationalist impulses that such men as Ben Badis had already detected in Islam. In 1939 the PPA had no more than three thousand dues-paying members, most of them in the Paris region, its stronghold to the end. Still, the historian Charles-André Julien thought it was "by far the most popular party, the one whose action best translated the aspirations of the native masses."[37]

Had French officialdom listened to one of the more moderate voices of the Algerian political awakening, might French Algeria have avoided a violent end? Would the political and economic reforms for which Ferhat Abbas called have reconciled settlers and Algerians? Might coming to terms with the Ulamas, unyielding in their cultural nationalism but open to political compromise, have permitted a measured and peaceful surrender of French sovereignty? Had the French greeted Messali Hadj with respectful attention instead of arrest warrants, might he have moderated his demands and become, under French sponsorship, the father of his country? Or were Europeans and Algerians fated to end their long encounter by slaughtering each other?

Some observers have seen in the history of French Algeria a history of lost opportunities. Mainland governments, they suggest, let chances to set Algeria on a new course slip by them. Their sins, according to this view, were sins of omission: failing to discuss the future with such Algerians as were willing to talk about it; refusing to award Algerians political rights without demanding they surrender their personal religious status; neglecting to carry out timely economic and social reforms; ignoring the seriousness of the nationalist challenge; and so on.[38]

Proponents of the lost-opportunities thesis, however, fail to reckon with the settlers' control of the political, administrative, and judicial apparatus in North Africa. The history of the American South from the end of Reconstruction to the 1950s, for instance (not to mention that of the American colonies on the eve of the Revolution), shows how easy it is for officials on the periphery to evade and obstruct the directives of the central government. It seems doubtful that a mainland government could have forced the settlers to live under reforms the settlers said they would rather die than accept. Moreover, it is not at all clear that French governments ever had the will, or even the inclination, to make the settlers listen to reason; the structural weaknesses of parliamentary democracy, Third Republic style, may have been sufficient in themselves to prevent action on Algeria. What is certain is that a great many deputies saw no reason to act. Some simply took no interest in Algeria; some believed as strongly in the settler ascendancy as the settlers did.[39]

In any event, native liberals advocating reform lost out to radicals preaching revolution, and French rule in Algeria ended as violently as it began. The Second World War sealed the fate of the settler ascendancy, as it ended European dominance of the world. In the absence of the war, it is impossible to imagine such a sudden transformation of the political geography of Asia, Africa, and the Caribbean.

No European empire felt the impact of war more profoundly than the French. In 1940 France suffered the worst defeat in its modern history. With the French army shattered, the Third Republic set aside, and half the country occupied, an old field marshal and his former protégé disputed between them the right to speak in the name of France. From London Charles de Gaulle denied the legitimacy of Philippe Pétain's rule at Vichy. To all intents and purposes, the war cut European France off from the empire. Parts of it rallied to de Gaulle, parts of it to Pétain; parts of it fell to the Japanese. Everywhere, French authority either collapsed or dwelt for a time in confusion and disarray.[40]

Such a spectacle convinced nationalists throughout the empire that the liberals' patient sapping techniques, their burrowing away at the foundations of European dominance, were a waste of time. The war exposed the vulnerability of the fortress and invited a rush at the gates.

The rush came sooner in Southeast Asia than in North Africa. Nevertheless, the war accelerated the tempo of political change in Algeria and decisively altered the balance among factions of Algerian nationalism. On February 10, 1943, Ferhat Abbas, the liberals' leading spokesman, issued the Manifeste du Peuple Algérien, announcing the death of Algerian support for assimilationism. Abbas called instead for home rule and loose federal ties with the mainland. He refused any longer to be satisfied with reforms carried out within the structure of the existing colonial system.[41]

Late in 1943 Abbas met for the first time with Messali Hadj, another sign of his moving toward the left. In 1944 the Messalistes and the Ulamas discovered they had fewer differences with Abbas than formerly thought, and they joined his Amis du Manifeste et de la Liberté.[42] This display of harmony among Algerian political factions was unprecedented. It did not endure, but it signified agreement on the need for Algerians to take their own political future in hand. There remained great disagreement about what this meant and how it could be achieved, but henceforth Algerian politicians concurred: to be Algerian was not to be French.

Abbas remained far more cautious with respect to tactics than Messali and the hot-blooded young men around him. He feared that the PPA had greatly exaggerated the extent to which the war had disarmed the settlers. He was convinced that the Messalistes were playing into the hands of diehards itching for an excuse to put the Algerian political movement out of business altogether.[43]

Certainly, the Messalistes did not go out of their way to avoid trouble. Feeling between the nationalists and the police was already running high when on May 8, 1945, news of the German surrender arrived. May Day demonstrations in Oran and Algiers had taken a violent turn, leaving dead in the streets. Nevertheless, the authorities issued permits for parades celebrating victory in Europe—and nothing else.

In Sétif, Ferhat Abbas's hometown, it was market day, and

the streets were jammed with people. Members of the PPA showed up waving nationalist placards and shouting for the release of Messali, who had been jailed once again. A police officer tried to wrest a poster from a demonstrator; they scuffled, and shots rang out. In a fury, the Algerian demonstrators surged through the town, setting upon whatever Europeans were in their way. By the end of the day, at least twenty-one had been killed—beaten, shot, or hacked to death.

Violence spread to the countryside. Algerians fell upon isolated farms, sometimes attacking Europeans they had grown up with. On May 10 and 11, French military units went into action; by May 12 mob attacks had subsided. But military action continued. Shorthanded, fearful that the disturbance in Sétif presaged the general rising of which army intelligence had warned (there is evidence that the PPA was trying to provoke such a rising), the authorities called for air support and bombardments from naval vessels lying offshore. For days the army hunted down suspects, taking prisoners by the thousands, tracking some to hiding places in the mountains, shooting others out of hand—a task in which a vengeful settler militia participated.

Estimates of how many died in Sétif range from the French government's low of fifteen hundred to the nationalists' high of fifty thousand. An American reporter put the number somewhere between seven and eighteen thousand. On the basis of documents he saw in the governor-general's office, Charles-André Julien narrowed the figure to between six and eight thousand.[44] As is usually the case in such affairs, no one really knows.

The consequences of the Sétif massacre are less open to question than the number of its casualties. It was the bloodiest encounter between Europeans and Algerians since the insurrection of 1871, the episode that marked the close of the era of the conquest and the onset of the settler ascendancy.[45] Both risings broke out in the same place and at the end of

European wars that had left France defeated. In hindsight, the second rising can be seen to have closed the parenthesis —the era of unchallenged French rule—that the first opened.

Sétif was the recurrent settler nightmare come true. For a few days the settlers had found themselves nearly helpless in their homesteads, at the mercy of sickle-wielding natives who in some cases turned out to be their own farmhands. After the first Sétif uprising, Algeria had lived in the same atmosphere C. Vann Woodward found hanging over the American South in the same years, thick with "flying rumors of plot and counterplot, of bands armed with icepick and switchblade knife, or . . . conspiratorial societies, and subversive . . . agitators."[46] The settler and native communities of Algeria retreated further within themselves.

If some of the settler leadership saw Sétif 1945 as sounding "the hour of the gendarme,"[47] liberal politicians on the mainland read the insurrection as warning of the necessity of reform. In 1945 Algeria was essentially governed as it had been at the turn of the century, when the secessionist impulse had run strong. Executive authority remained in the hands of a governor-general named by the French president on the recommendation of the prime minister. The French National Assembly still made laws for Algeria as well as the mainland, but not all French laws applied to Algeria. The settlers enjoyed certain tax and tariff privileges not available to the mainland French. A quasi-parliamentary body, the Assemblée financière—formerly the Délégations financières, and the main concession to secessionist sentiment—decided how to spend the money the mainland parliament allocated to Algeria. Local government was divided between the European *communes de pleine exercice,* complete with mayor and town council, and the native *communes mixtes,* whose affairs were in the hands of a French administrator. The civil bureaucracy in North Africa was as rigorously centralized as its counterpart on the mainland.[48]

These formal arrangements did not take into account the

settlers' lobby in Paris, nor the pressures the settlers could bring to bear on governors-general, nor the enormous influence the association of Algerian mayors exerted on local government. Nor did civil-service manuals reveal how short-handed the administration was, how badly underadministered large stretches of the interior were. Many Algerians rarely saw the face of French authority.

In 1947 the new Fourth Republic moved to replace the collection of ad hoc measures by which Algeria had always been governed with a single statute, an undertaking most mainland deputies greeted with total indifference. The government, presided over by the Socialist Paul Ramadier, faced the nearly impossible task of balancing concessions to the Algerians with reassurances to the settlers. In the end, the statute preserved many of the old institutions; most of the administrative and financial ties with the mainland remained as they had been. On paper the statute extended numerous civil and religious liberties to Algerians, but in order to be put into effect these reforms required the approval of two-thirds of the Algerian Assembly, and this they never received.

The assembly, which was the Assemblée financière renamed, became a device for thwarting majority rule in internal Algerian affairs. During World War II, General de Gaulle's provisional government had extended the right to vote to all Algerian males over twenty-one. The statute established two electoral colleges, one for Algerians and one for settlers. Each college elected sixty representatives to the Algerian Assembly. A limited number of select Algerian officials, war veterans, and university graduates were assigned to the European college. The result was that eight million Algerians had sixty representatives in the assembly; one million settlers also had sixty. Any issues likely to divide the assembly along factional lines—such as putting into effect the statute's provisions on Algerian civil liberties—required a two-thirds majority. No issue on which the settlers chose to stick together would ever pass.[49]

At first, diehard settlers denounced the statute as yet another of the mainland's attempts to shove a dangerous and unworkable reform down their throats. Presently they came to see its virtues and became as intent on maintaining the separate electoral colleges as were segregationist Southerners on maintaining separate school systems. In each case, separateness came to seem the last guarantee of a way of life. On the other side, to all but the most cautious liberals among Algerian activists, the statute offered too little, too late.

How wide the rift between settlers and Algerians had grown became apparent in the municipal elections of 1947. Algerians newly enfranchised since the war voted for the first time, their numbers swelling the hitherto modest group of eligible native electors. The majority of seats on the town councils went to the extremists in each camp: the Union Algérienne, a coalition of diehard settlers, unwilling to yield an inch to any nationalist demands; the Mouvement pour le triomphe des libertés démocratiques (MTLD), the latest incarnation of Messalism, as intransigent as ever in its demand for independence. This demand the MTLD expressed in a hair-raising electoral slogan offering the settlers a choice between "the suitcase or the coffin." The Messaliste success at the expense of Ferhat Abbas and other moderate nationalists alarmed the government into postponing further elections until the following spring.[50]

Late in 1947, a handful of Messalistes, bent on forcing the settlers to the choice their party had brandished in the elections, founded the Organisation Secrète. The OS rehearsed guerrilla warfare in the mountains and held up the Oran post office, but in March 1950, the police arrested some of its membership and put the rest on the run. From its ranks came much of the early leadership of the Algerian Revolution.[51]

For all its menacing talk, the MTLD was not prepared to break with the legal order. The older Messali Hadj got, the more jealous he became of his own authority, the more convinced of the soundness of his views, the more impatient with criticism. His critics believed the long years of prison and exile had put him out of touch with conditions in Algeria. In the postwar years he became the main cause of dissension within the movement he had founded. His irascibility, his insistence on the correctness of his own judgment, his intolerance of dissent alienated much of the party leadership.[52]

Messali's adversaries, led by the party general-secretary, Hocine Lahouel, organized their opposition to him in a group they called the Central Committee. Messali kept the loyalty of the rank and file, but the Central Committee controlled the party treasury. In 1953 or 1954 an open break took place between Messalistes and Centralistes. In a July 1954 meeting in Belgium, the Messalistes read the Centralistes out of the party. In August the Centralistes in Algiers excommunicated the Messalistes.

Former members of the OS tried to patch the splits in radical nationalism. The name of the group they founded declared their purpose. The Comité révolutionnaire d'unité et d'action (CRUA) meant to reunify radicals by means of revolutionary action.[53]

The organizers covered their tracks so well that opinions still differ as to when the CRUA was founded and who belonged to it. Sometime between January and July 1954, or perhaps in the fall of 1953, from four to nine men met in Switzerland, France, or Algeria and organized the new group.[54] This handful drew two dozen more into their planning. A conspiracy against the settler ascendancy was now reality.

The thirty revolutionaries had little in common with the liberals. They were younger than the men of Abbas's generation; most were in their twenties and thirties and had had little or no experience of prewar politics. More than half of them had grown up in the small towns and villages of the Constantinois, scene of the Sétif rising and the insurrection of 1871. Most had committed themselves to underground politics long before 1954, and when they met in the summer of that year, most were wanted by the police.

The radicals were far less well educated than the liberals. Only four of them had gone beyond secondary school. They had held jobs as agricultural and industrial workers, shop-keepers and clerks, petty trade-union officials and school-teachers. Many had been frustrated in early political ambitions. At least a dozen were failed candidates for local office, the victims of official election-rigging. But the commonest denominator among them was service in the French army. Some had liked the army well enough to think of making it a career. As matters turned out, however, they put what they had learned in the army to use against it.[55]

Their having much in common does not explain why they became revolutionaries. Young army veterans of modest origin, modest education, modest jobs, and modest prospects— Algeria in the early 1950s was filled with such men. There was not among them a charismatic leader like Ho Chi Minh or Mao Tse-tung, Nasser or Sukarno, Washington or Bolívar. They had no striking ideas. They did not interpret the world in the light of any systematic ideology, and this may have spared them quarrels over the meaning and require-ments of a revolutionary faith. They opposed French rule in Algeria, and their willingness to take the risk of ending it by violence is what distinguished them from thousands of other Algerians.

In June or July 1954 a "Committee of 22"—five members of the CRUA and seventeen trusted confederates—met in Clos Salembier, a suburb of Algiers. They pledged them-selves to a fight to the finish. From their own military expe-rience and from the printed works of Colonel Passy and Colonel Rémy, legendary heroes of the French Resistance, they drew up plans for the organization of the Algerian Resistance.[56]

Later that summer the CRUA agreed that November 1, All Saints' Day on the French calendar, should be the day for the rising. At the same meeting, perhaps, the committee adopted a new acronym: FLN—Front de libération nationale—a movement eager to welcome anyone willing to fight for independence. All other ambitions were to be subordinated to this end.[57]

What did the French authorities know about the CRUA? An official report of May 1954 described the new organization as "a truly revolutionary instrument," but the writer mistakenly regarded this instrument as a tool of the MTLD. Another report, dated October 23, 1954, suggested that French police intelligence in Algeria knew about the CRUA's existence, knew of its violent intentions, knew it was composed of former members of the Organisation secrète, but were unaware of their identities and their hiding places. The chief of intelligence in Algiers considered the report sufficiently important to be forwarded to the ministry of the interior in Paris, where it was filed away unread.[58]

The FLN chose the Aurès mountains as the best spot to strike first. For centuries the Aurès massif, scattered with stands of pine, live oak, and cedar, had been the refuge of men fleeing invaders or the law. Some of the poorest peasants in Algeria lived in its mud-daubed villages, eking out an existence from sheep, fruit trees, and sometimes a little banditry. What especially recommended this wild and inaccessible place to the planners of the rising was that there were only seven gendarmes in charge of maintaining order over its considerable expanse.[59]

Pierre Mendès France was forty-seven when he took office, on the youngish side for a French prime minister. He was a veteran politician, however; in 1932 he had been the youngest deputy elected to the Chamber. As one of the reform-minded Young Turks of the Radical party, which had otherwise become a "machine for the occupation of power," Mendès quickly established a reputation as an economic and financial expert. In 1938 Léon Blum made him an adviser to his Popular Front government. In 1940 the Vichy government jailed Mendès for trying to continue the war from North Africa (desertion was the formal charge), but he escaped, made his way to England, and joined the Free French air force. De Gaulle reassigned him from carrying out bombing raids on the continent to conducting economic planning for postwar France. At war's end he and de Gaulle parted company over the general's refusal to accept his recommendations for stringent monetary reform. Mendès returned to parliament and took up his role as a Cassandra.[60]

His entire public career, then, down to his becoming prime minister, coincided with a protracted national crisis. To the debilitating effects of the Great War—an enormous loss of life, physical destruction, financial instability, hidden psychic wounds—the Great Depression, striking on the eve of Mendès's first electoral victory, added chronic economic weakness and new sources of political division. The Third Republic never recovered from the blows it suffered in the wake of the Depression. Whether the republic was the victim of poor leadership, as some have maintained, or of circumstances beyond anyone's power to master, as others have argued, it was weakened by domestic turmoil and overwhelmed by challenges from abroad. And whoever was to blame for the calamitous defeat of 1940—fingers have pointed in all directions—the republic did not survive.

France emerged from four years of Occupation as a nominal member of the victors' camp. But the French contribution to the Liberation, for all its heroism, was nevertheless slight compared to the efforts of the British and the Americans. To fervent French nationalists, this was galling enough; but the wartime divisions between Vichy and the Free French, between Vichy and the internal Resistance, lingered into the peace. The knowledge that countless Frenchmen had collaborated with the Germans added to the sense of national humiliation. If losses of French lives had been far

smaller in this war than in the previous one, material destruction was substantial and industrial production was
badly disrupted.

France in the forties and early fifties was widely regarded
as the new sick man of Europe, its life as a liberal democracy
sustained only by massive transfusions of Marshall Plan
money. Observers gathered at the bedside offered no end of
diagnoses as to what ailed the patient. Some stressed political
and economic debilities; others blamed psychosociological
sources. The paralytic state of parliamentary politics came in
for mention in most accounts, sometimes as the cause of the
country's difficulties, sometimes as only a symptom of deep-
er-seated ills.[61]

Certainly, the high hopes for parliamentary reform were
not realized. Constitution-makers had been determined to
fashion a Fourth Republic cleansed of the vices of the Third,
but they wound up with a parliamentary system that, in
practice, pretty much resembled the old one. That practice
was one of ministerial instability and vulnerability to the
threats and blandishments of pressure groups, of which the
Algerian lobby—the settlers' deputies and their friends—
happened to be among the most powerful. No element in the
multiparty system could elect enough deputies to dominate
parliament. So well dispersed were the seats, and so incompatible the major parties on certain issues, that resolving a
series of problems required finding a series of different
majorities. And so remote seemed the likelihood of dissolution that party leaderships, except for the Communists', had
little means of exerting discipline over their members. Once
safely elected, many deputies felt themselves answerable only
to their constituents, not to the party leaders. The ceaseless
changes of ministries and consequent lack of effective political action earned the National Assembly a reputation as a
"tragic circus."[62]

Some Frenchmen found solace from this discouraging domestic situation in contemplating maps of the empire. All

those rose-colored swatches of territory proclaimed that France was a nation of grand accomplishments, a world power still to be reckoned with.

What might be called the compensatory argument for imperialism was older than its adherents may have realized. In the nineteenth century, France's population and economic and military strength declined while those of other powers rose. Some politicians and journalists began to argue that control of overseas territory would compensate for the loss of preeminence on the continent. The obverse of the argument was, of course, that to surrender such territory would be to surrender great-power status. Alexis de Tocqueville took this view. As long ago as 1841 he wrote, "If France ever gives up Algeria, it is evident that she can only do so at a moment when we will see her undertake great things in Europe, and not in a time such as ours when she seems to descend to the second rank and would appear to be resigned to allowing the direction of European affairs to pass into other hands."[63]

France was hardly in a position to undertake great things in Europe in the postwar era. Beholden to the Americans for economic and military assistance, convinced that the Russians posed an expansionist threat to the West, the leadership of the Fourth Republic was constantly reminded that *la grande nation* inhabited a world dominated by two superpowers. From what else but the remnants of its empire, proponents of the compensatory thesis asked, could France salvage a claim to greatness?[64]

Mendès France regarded the empire not as an asset but as a liability. Chief among the difficulties besetting France, he believed, were economic backwardness and financial instability. "Mendesism" was less a specific program than a strategy of governing, a demand for giving priority to the resolution of these economic problems. Mendès called for the state to become the generator of economic expansion, by devising means of stimulating private investment, reforming state-owned enterprises, finding ways of remedying the structural deficiencies of agriculture and small-scale industry. A dynamic neocapitalism was to be the engine that would haul the nation from the mire of permanent crisis.[65]

As a chief critic of successive governments of the Fourth Republic, Mendès championed the view that economic modernization at home would put France in a much stronger position to resolve its problems of empire. But when he finally reached office, he had to conduct himself as if he believed the contrary, as if he were convinced that liquidating the imperial problem would clear the way for economic reform.[66]

Mendès became prime minister in the first place only because of the long parliamentary tradition that the main antagonist of a defeated government be given the chance to show whether he can do better. He was chosen not to reform the country but to get it out of a jam. Mendès took office on June 20, 1954, a few weeks after the disaster at Dien Bien Phu had all but rendered untenable the French position in Indochina. Having declared he would resign if within a month he had not reached a settlement, he made good on his race against the calendar. In the early morning hours of July 21, after "eight years of war, four hundred thousand dead, three months of negotiations," the delegates to the Geneva Conference signed a handful of documents signifying the end of French control of Indochina.[67]

As remarkable as was Mendès's achievement, the war's end was something almost everyone in France welcomed. By 1954 the struggle in Indochina had become unpopular in the country at large, and when Mendès offered the deputies in parliament a choice between supporting him in the Geneva negotiations and sending conscripts to Southeast Asia, they had little trouble making up their minds. The settlement received the overwhelming support of the National Assembly; even his parliamentary opponents had to recognize that he had rid them of a burden. The aim of reestablishing

French rule in Indochina had long since been given up, but the expeditionary corps fought on, less in pursuit of any compelling national goal than as an American proxy in a global war against Communism. The judgment the Swiss journalist Herbert Lüthy delivered shortly after the war's end has stood up well: "What came to grief in the spring of 1954 was a foreign policy of power and prestige for which any real basis was lacking, a policy based on borrowed resources and a juridical scaffolding that was more ingenious than solid. The principle of the policy . . . was that France was a World Power with important European, Atlantic, African and Asian interests and prerogatives on all of which she insisted, preferring to risk losing them all rather than abandon any single one."[68] Even those who continued to believe that France must continue to play a role as a world power were willing to concede that Indochina was not the place in which to play it, and Mendès was the beneficiary of this concession.

The prime minister also benefited from the absence of a powerful mainland lobby for Indochina. A handful of Frenchmen administered Vietnam, and another handful turned a tidy profit from such ventures as the rubber plantations, but their compatriots never settled there in any numbers.[69] But the moment Mendès turned to areas in which considerations of national prestige intermingled with the anxieties of French settlers, he ran into trouble.

Tunisia, where a nationalist movement had been agitating for independence, was just such an area. Mendès went to work at the same speed that had characterized his search for a negotiated settlement in Indochina. He flew to Carthage in the company of Christian Fouchet, his minister for Moroccan and Tunisian affairs, and Marshal Alphonse Juin, known as a champion of the empire. On July 31, with Juin at his side, Mendès made a speech promising Tunisia home rule. This was short of what the Tunisian nationalists wanted, and short of what they eventually got. To the European settlers and their friends on the mainland, however, the promise of home rule was an outrage. Many who had written off Indochina as a lost cause could not bring themselves to do the same with Tunisia. Applauded from nearly every bench in the Palais Bourbon for making the best of a bad situation in Southeast Asia, Mendès was henceforth to be execrated as "the empire-wrecker."[70]

The French had originally occupied Tunisia in large part to protect the eastern flank of Algeria, just as the protectorate over Morocco had been established in 1912 with an eye to safeguarding its western approaches.[71] On August 10, 1954, General Aumeran, a right-wing deputy and member of the Algerian lobby, issued in parliament a French version of the domino theory: "I wish you would realize that any mistake made in Tunis will have disastrous repercussions throughout the whole of North Africa, especially in Algeria and Morocco, because the seditious men to whom you are about to hand over Tunisia are carrying out precisely the same policy as the equally seditious leaders in the other two countries . . . Only the solemn reaffirmation that France intends to exercise her authority over the whole of North Africa can allay fears, restore order and reassure our friends. You must say clearly where you stand: we stay in Africa or we go. We can't stay and go away at the same time."[72] Aumeran and his friends regarded home rule as merely a way station on the road to independence. This being the case, they preferred defending the status quo—by force, if necessary—to making concessions in the vain hope of preserving the connection between North Africa and France. Nevertheless, Mendès carried the day; his liberal Tunisian policy won the approbation of the National Assembly.

But the days of such an unorthodox prime minister were numbered. His rushing to and fro on errands of foreign and colonial policy distracted him from the issues of domestic reform that were the main object of Mendèsism. The attempts at reform he did make met at every turn the opposi-

tion of interests big and little, private and public, indu
and agricultural, all of them united only in their devot
the status quo. It is probably true, as the political scientist
Stanley Hoffmann has remarked, that "what Pierre Mendès
France wanted to accomplish in French society could not be
done by a man of the left within the French parliamentary
system."[73] Once he extricated the politicians from the Indochina tangle, his usefulness to them rapidly diminished. By
the time the insurrection in Algeria broke out, it was plain
that the end of the Mendès France experiment was near.

Yet his regime cast a long shadow over the Algerian war.
Mendès's call for France's renovation attracted a youthful
and varied following: technocrats who heard in his appeal for
government efficiency echoes of their own thoughts; left
Catholics disappointed in the reformist performance of
Christian democracy; resisters expecting the fulfillment at
long last of their wartime hopes for reform; Gaullists who
saw how neatly some of Mendès's aims coincided with some
of theirs; like-minded Radicals; the more undoctrinaire Socialists; intellectuals unattached to any political party. Insofar as this motley band shared anything in common, it was
the habit of reading—and writing for—the magazine *L'Express*. Founded in the spring of 1954 by Jean-Jacques Servan-
Schreiber, *L'Express* quickly became a kind of house organ
of Mendesism—more Mendesist, indeed, than the prime
minister himself. From the outset the magazine opposed
colonialism as vigorously as it agitated for reform. When the
experiment it did so much to proselytize failed, its anticolonialist stance persisted. *L'Express* became the most important
forum of liberal opposition to the war in Algeria.[74]

Mendès France was fond of saying, "To govern is to
choose."[75] In early November 1954, he chose to meet with
force the armed challenge to French rule in Algeria and to
call for the major reforms in Algerian politics, society, and
economy that had been so long advocated on the mainland
and so long resisted in North Africa. Eighteen months and

two governments later, he broke with Guy Mollet's interpretation of the policy of repression and reform and himself became an opponent of the war in Algeria. Six years further on, Charles de Gaulle ceased resisting the FLN's demand for Algerian independence and withdrew from North Africa the forces Mendès had dispatched. The time had come, he said, to undertake the renewal of France—just what Mendès had been saying in 1954.

2 The Military Buildup

A tract discovered on the body of a terrorist killed in the All Saints rising read: "As thou canst observe, under colonialism Justice, Democracy and Equality are only a snare and a delusion designed to deceive thee and plunge thee day by day into the poverty thou knowest only too well."[1] This could have been the work of any enemy of French rule; such scraps of intelligence were not much for the authorities to go on. In the absence of hard information on the instigators of the rising, the French police acted on hunches and assumptions. They assumed the MTLD—Messali Hadj's wild men—was behind the outburst of violence. They were half-right. For the organizers of the FLN had indeed sprung from the Messaliste organization, but they were dissidents who had broken with it, and they had not involved the established leadership (which was itself being bitterly contested) in their plans. Acting on their educated guesses, the police wound up doing the FLN a favor. They jailed Messalistes who were also mystified by the events of November 1. In Algeria and in France the police seized party files and banned further publication of Messaliste literature. The drive against the MTLD left the FLN with a monopoly on radical nationalism, with FLN agents free to proselytize while their rivals languished in prison.[2]

How many men were involved in the early morning attacks of November 1 remains a mystery. Estimates of the charter membership of the FLN range from fewer than seven

hundred to about three thousand.[3] The journalist Yves Courrière, who in the early 1960s conducted interviews with former guerrillas, puts the figure at eight hundred.[4] Philippe
Tripier, who served during the war in the intelligence-coor-
dinating service of the ministry of national defense, estimates
the revolutionaries to have been no more than seven hundred. Five hundred of them waited in the Aurès for word to
strike, two hundred more in the Djurdjura, the highest chain
of mountains in Grand Kabylia.[5] Whichever estimate is correct, their numbers were extremely small, and had they
failed, their revolutionary enterprise would have looked foolhardy in the extreme.

The FLN was more impoverished in weapons than in
manpower. If Courrière is correct, only half of those who
took part in the All Saints rising were armed.[6] A French
army doctor later reported that most of the wounds he
treated in the early months of the war had been inflicted by
hunting rifles and shotguns.[7] Most of the bombs exploded on
All Saints' Day were homemade gadgets fashioned locally by
inexpert artisans. Only months after the rising did gunrunners begin bringing military weapons across the frontiers
from Tunisia and Morocco in any quantity.[8]

General C. A. de Cherrière, commander in chief in Algeria, led some fifty-four thousand troops, the vast majority
of whom were far from combat-ready. Most of the army's
experienced guerrilla fighters were either still in Indochina or
on their way home. Many of the latter had recently been
released from Vietminh prison camps and were in no condition to do any fighting. Cherrière estimated he had only
thirty-five hundred usable combat troops on hand. No real
air support was available.[9] For transport the French possessed eight old Junkers, relics of the Second World War.
There was only one helicopter in all of Algeria.[10]

But Mendès France lost no time sending reinforcements.
By December 31 the government had dispatched some
twenty thousand additional troops and twenty companies of

riot police, one-third the mainland force.[11] On November 26 an enormous *ratissage*—essentially a search-and-destroy operation—got under way with air and artillery support. With the Aurès and Grand Kabylia swarming with French troops, terrorist actions against Europeans fell off as suddenly as they had begun. Between November 2, 1954, and the fall of Mendès's government in early February 1955 not a single settler was killed.[12] What did go on, however, was terrorism against Algerians—the means by which the FLN aimed to show what lay in store for "collaborators," to establish by fear its authority among Algerians, and to coerce them into supporting the revolution.

Mendès France backed up his forceful actions with forceful words. The first parliamentary debate on Algeria after the outbreak of the insurrection came on November 12. Answering critics who blamed the rising on his Tunisian policy, Mendès warned, "Let no one expect of us any circumspection with respect to the sedition or any compromise with it. We don't compromise when it comes to defending the internal peace of the nation and the republic's integrity. The departments of Algeria are part of the Republic, they have been French a long time. Between it [the Algerian population] and the mainland, no secession is conceivable. . . . Never will France, never will any parliament nor any government, yield on this fundamental principle."[13] François Mitterrand, the minister of the interior, was equally adamant. "Algeria," he said, announcing the theme to be sounded endlessly in parliament and press, "is France."[14]

Neither Mendès nor Mitterrand believed Algeria could remain French without drastic changes. Mendès left office three months after the outbreak of the insurrection, but he had time to establish the policy whose outlines each of his successors followed until September 1959. The plan called for simultaneously repressing the rebellion and carrying out reforms in the Algerian economy and society, in internal Algerian politics, and in the political relationship between Algeria and France. If ever a policy was more easily said than done, this was it. For Paris had to overcome not only the military resistance of the insurgents but the political resistance of the settlers. As the insurrection spread and the settlers organized in defense of the status quo, the balance shifted away from reform and toward repression. The failure of this policy in all its guises—or its abandonment—meant the end of French Algeria.

No one was more closely identified with the reform side of the policy, with remaking Algeria in order to keep it French, than Jacques Soustelle, whom Mendès France named governor-general on January 25, 1955. A decade later, at a time when Soustelle could not set foot in France without risking arrest for his activities as a diehard of *Algérie française,* Mendès remained convinced he had made the right choice.[15]

Soustelle's was an extraordinary political odyssey, even for a nation that had undergone the vicissitudes of twentieth-century France. Like Jean Jaurès and Édouard Herriot, he was a phenomenally successful scholarship boy who had made his way in politics. Among the youngest and brightest of the bright young men admitted to the École normale supérieure, before 1945 the most prestigious school in France, Soustelle quickly established a reputation as one of the leading ethnographers of his generation (to which Claude Lévi-Strauss also belonged). His first taste of political activism came at age twenty-six, when he helped his patron, Paul Rivet, director of the Musée de l'homme, organize the Vigilance Committee of Anti-Fascist Intellectuals, an important early component of the Popular Front.

After the defeat of 1940, Soustelle made his way to London and became one of de Gaulle's most trusted lieutenants. As director of the Free French propaganda service and later of Intelligence and Counter-Espionage, he acquired a taste (or revealed a talent) for intrigue and the shadowy arts of secret-police work. After the war his energy and organizational flair earned him the secretary-generalship of the Gaullist Rassemblement du peuple français (RPF). That exercise in constitutional revisionism ran out of steam in the early 1950s, but Soustelle remained the parliamentary leader of the dwindling band of Gaullist Social Republicans, a party the general had washed his hands of.[16]

Perhaps what most recommended Soustelle to Mendès, aside from sheer intelligence, was his reputation for being both a tough administrator and a man of liberal imagination and temperament. Not all of Mendès's colleagues were happy with his choice; some mistrusted Soustelle as a Gaullist.[17] *L'Express,* however, welcomed the appointment as symbolizing the awakening of the liberal conscience on the question of Algeria.[18]

His reputation guaranteed Soustelle a chilly and suspicious reception from the settlers.[19] In truth, in his ceremonial governor-general's uniform this pudgy and bespectacled figure looked more like a band director than a man about to take in hand the struggle against the insurrection. Some of the people who arrived on the scene with Soustelle intensified the settlers' suspicions. One such person was the well-known anthropologist and liberal political activist Germaine Tillion, who had spent the prewar years in field research among the villagers of the Aurès mountains and the war years in a German concentration camp.[20] As his military adviser Soustelle chose Major Vincent Monteil, an Arabist well acquainted with conditions in Algeria. To the settlers the sympathies of such people seemed to lie with the wrong community.

Soustelle was hardly at a loss for proposals for Algerian reform. The statute of 1947 stood as a dead-letter reminder of the fate of the most recent and most ambitious of such attempts. Soustelle did incorporate some of its provisions into his own reform scheme. In the end, though, the Soustelle Plan was far more ambitious in scope than the statute, and very different in intention.

The provisions of the statute, Soustelle believed, opened the door to home rule, and beyond that door lay independence. In order to arrive at this conclusion one had only to be able to count. If Europeans and Algerians belonged to the same electoral college, as an early draft of the statute proposed, then the electorate would be overwhelmingly Algerian, and so, in all likelihood, would any assembly elected by their votes. What were the odds on such an assembly's being content to leave Algeria's external affairs in the hands of the French? And what were the chances, under such a scheme, that the minority so long in the ascendancy would get a fair shake?[21]

Soustelle came up with a proposal that in his view would give political rights to the Algerian majority without endangering the rights of the European minority. He proposed the "integration" of Algeria into France. The Soustelle Plan provided for increasing Algerian representation in local government, extending the vote to women, providing schooling in Arabic, just as the statute had done. But instead of increased autonomy in fiscal and administrative affairs, Soustelle proposed replacing the governor-general with a minister for Algeria, concentrating administration in three "super departments," and absorbing all state services into the relevant ministries in Paris.[22]

The key passages of the Soustelle Plan dealt with political arithmetic. Soustelle called for eliminating the dual electoral college in favor of a single body mixing Algerians and settlers together. But one million settlers would not have to fear being swamped among eight or nine million Algerians. Integration would include Algerians and settlers together in a political entity composed of nearly fifty million mainland French. A majority in North Africa, the Algerians would be a minority in a Greater France stretching from Dunkirk on the North Sea to Tamanrasset in the Sahara.

Soustelle always insisted that he had meant integration to cover only politics, public administration, and the economy. Algeria's native culture and its Islamic religious personality would be not only preserved but encouraged to flower. Becoming a French citizen did not require becoming a Frenchman.

Despite his efforts at explaining himself, Soustelle found his intentions bitterly disputed. "Integration" became a political catchword meaning exactly what adversaries over Algeria chose it to mean. Some of Soustelle's critics on the left saw in integration a futile attempt to resurrect the assimilationist policy of the early Third Republic. Others considered it a political shell game, a sleight-of-hand trick aimed at preserving the status quo. The army interpreted integration as assuring it a role in the economic and social reform of Algeria. The settlers made it a synonym for *Algérie française,* which in turn meant maintaining their ascendancy.[23]

Putting the political arrangements of the Soustelle Plan into effect required getting the insurrection in hand; they were a promise to be made good in the future. But social and economic reforms were a means of combating the insurrection. The policy-makers' tactics betrayed their conviction that poverty breeds revolution.

This conviction found characteristic expression in a book Germaine Tillion published after she broke with Soustelle. Returning to the Aurès in 1954, Tillion had been astonished to see how drastically an already impoverished peasantry had declined in the fifteen years since she had done field research there. The peasants, she wrote in *L'Algérie en 1957,* were undergoing *"clochardisation"*—being reduced by overcrowding to the circumstances of rural derelicts, skid-row bums of the countryside. Far from exploiting them, colonial rule ignored them, and neglect exacerbated their plight. In the Aurès, Tillion had found "a school without a teacher . . . not a doctor, nor a nurse nor any kind of emissary of civilization."[24] The peasants cast their lot with the FLN, she claimed (without saying how she knew), because they thought independence would mean land and bread, jobs, schools and houses.

France now had to provide what the revolutionaries could

only promise for a distant day: the modernization of native agriculture, industrialization, housing, schooling, medical care. To these ends the Soustelle Plan, and each of its successors, called for pouring huge sums of money into the Algerian countryside. Algeria must be reconquered—indeed, vast areas where the French had seldom set foot must be conquered for the first time—the revolutionaries defeated by force of arms, and the populace won over by the benefits of modernity.

As a catchphrase, *clochardisation* caught on. The view that poverty breeds revolution—and its corollary, that eradicating poverty will snuff out revolution—received wide currency, not only in government circles but on the moderate left as well. *L'Express,* for instance, subscribed to this notion, long after Soustelle and most of its writers became enemies. French liberals were not alone in thinking that overcoming misery would be an effective means of combating revolutionary nationalism, as two decades of American involvement in Indochina attest.

The desperate poverty of the Auresian peasants may have encouraged them to throw in with the FLN. What did they have to lose? But the urban Algerian poor were as impoverished as their compatriots of the mountains, if not more so; they lived in much closer proximity to the French, on whom the FLN blamed all their woes.[25] Nevertheless, the urban poor were much later recruits to the cause. And in the Casbah of Algiers, they were as much terrorized into lending support to the revolutionary organization as they were converted to its side. As for the members of the revolutionary leadership itself, none of them came from a poverty-stricken background.[26]

If the poverty thesis had shortcomings as an explanation of why the FLN won adherents, supplying money for social and economic reform projects was bound to have limitations as a strategy for winning the Algerians back. The strategy failed to address itself to the political side of the revolution—the side that was paramount. Ending French rule, dismantling the French administrative apparatus, expelling the French army and police were the overriding goals of the revolutionaries. Independence came before well-being on their list of priorities. Reforms the French undertook in behalf of the Algerians were still *French* reforms, and the FLN would not allow anyone to forget it. Banishing foreign rule was its only war aim; banishing poverty could wait.

Appointing Soustelle governor-general was one of Mendès France's last acts in office. For some time it had been obvious that his days were numbered. He had made too many enemies over too many issues to be able to keep his majority together. His burying of the European Defense Community (EDC), a scheme for a multinational military force (and in some eyes a Trojan horse for a European common market) had angered the Socialists and the Mouvement républicain populaire (MRP), the two main pillars of his parliamentary support. Soustelle's appointment was too much for the right. *L'Aurore,* among the big metropolitan dailies the one most sympathetic to the hard-line settlers, complained about naming this "*crypto-progressiste* [crypto-fellow-traveler]" to such a sensitive post.[27]

A debate on the government's North African policy furnished the occasion for bringing Mendès down. The Independents, a coalition of conservative farmers and businessmen, blamed the rising in Algeria on his efforts at reaching a Tunisian settlement. The settlers' staunchest mainland friends, they had never been part of Mendès's majority. But more than twenty deputies of his own Radical party deserted him, which sealed his fate. René Mayer, Radical deputy for Constantine, a powerful member of the Algerian lobby, and himself an ex-prime minister, set the tone: "I don't know where you're going, and I can't believe that a policy of change can find a mid-point between immobilism and adventure."[28]

Resentful of Mendès for pulling France out of the Indochina quagmire it had helped lead the country into, disgruntled by his treatment of the EDC, the MRP chose North Africa as the best ground on which to abandon the prime minister—despite its approval of his policy. The Gaullist Social Republicans' pleasure at the appointment of Soustelle did not overcome their displeasure with Mendès on other counts. The Socialists stuck by him, but their numbers were insufficient to save his government. The Communists, who had never forgiven Mendès for spurning their proffered support at the time he formed his cabinet, joined the conservatives, and all seventy-three MRP deputies, in defeating him. On February 5, 1955, his government was overturned by a vote of 319 to 273.[29]

Edgar Faure, Mendès's archrival within the Radical party, succeeded him as prime minister. Finance minister in the previous two governments, foreign minister toward the end of the Mendès France experiment, Faure differed from his predecessor more in style than in policy. He took pleasure in the parliamentary wheeling-and-dealing that Mendès disdained. His talents as a conciliator enabled him to obtain the National Assembly's approval for the agreements on Tunisian devolution that had brought Mendès down. In Algeria he continued the same mixture of repression and reform that had been the announced policy of the previous government.[30]

Jacques Soustelle embodied the continuities on Algerian policy between the two governments. He stayed on as governor-general for a year after his sponsor's departure. During most of 1955 he worked on his reform plans, and in September he presented to the government a document outlining his intentions. He even succeeded in pushing the beginnings of his program of administrative and social reform through the Algerian Assembly. But he later wrote that he never felt sure of Edgar Faure's support; he did not believe Faure's heart was in the Soustelle Plan.[31]

The forcefulness of the French response to the events of November 1 took the revolutionaries by surprise. For a time, the revolution risked petering out in confusion.[32] In the summer of 1954, the leadership had divided Algeria into six military-political districts, or *wilayas,* each under the head of a district chief. For at least a year after All Saints' Day, three of the district chiefs had almost no followers or weapons at their command. Violence was confined almost entirely to the three *wilayas* of eastern Algeria, from the outskirts of Algiers to the Tunisian frontier. The western *wilayas,* from Algiers to Morocco, were for months nearly as peaceful as Paris on Sunday morning. For most of the war the Sahara saw more oil prospectors than guerrillas.[33]

By the end of 1955, most of the founders of the FLN had been killed or arrested. New leaders took their place, but their right to give orders was contested. The FLN had little success winning from abroad the aid and recognition needed to raise it to the status of a revolutionary movement.[34]

But the FLN's internal problems—most of which the French government remained unaware of—did not keep political violence from spreading. In the early weeks of 1955, a guerrilla band of about two hundred appeared in the hills bordering the main road between Constantine and Philippeville, the first armed force of any size seen outside the Aurès mountains. In March 1955, acts of terrorism were committed for the first time in the towns of Bône and Philippeville and in the countryside north of Souk-Ahras, along the Tunisian frontier. Outbreaks of violence moved in a southeasterly direction along the Nementchas massif toward Tunisia, the favorite route of gunrunners. By the end of the summer of 1955, the hitherto isolated guerrilla bands of the three eastern *wilayas* made contact with each other. Not daring to roam about in daylight, rarely traveling in units larger than company size, or roughly eighty men, the guerrillas nevertheless made the settlers of eastern Algeria think twice about driving the roads unarmed and unescorted.[35]

In western Algeria, in Algiers and Oran as well as in the countryside, life went on much as before. But as the first anniversary of the revolution approached, violence broke the settlers' tranquillity. Actions averaged 200 a month in April 1955 (an "action" included everything from isolated attacks on persons and property—shooting a constable, sawing down a telephone pole—to a skirmish with the French army); they soared to 900 in October, 1,000 in December, 2,624 in March 1956.[36] In the course of 1956, guerrillas began drifting into western Algeria from across the Moroccan frontier. Some crept along the Tellian Atlas, the coastal chain of mountains in the thickly populated north, from Oujda to Tlemcen to Saïda and finally to Orléansville. Others made their way along the Saharan Atlas, the parallel chain running farther south, to Colomb-Béchar, the peaks of Ksour, Djebel Amour. By the end of 1956, these guerrilla bands had made contact between the parallels on the high plateau between Saïda and Tiaret.[37]

At the beginning of 1957, then, the forces of the revolution had insinuated themselves into every corner of Algeria save Wilaya VI, at the desert's edge. The size of these forces remains open to question. For one thing, opinions differ as to what a revolutionary was. Jacques Soustelle, for instance, estimated the FLN had between fifteen thousand and twenty thousand members at the end of 1955, but this figure included auxiliaries—part-time guerrillas who never carried a weapon.[38] Philippe Tripier, the former intelligence expert, thinks the Armée de libération nationale (ALN), the FLN's armed force, numbered about six thousand "regulars" at the end of 1955 and about twenty thousand at the end of 1956, the year of its most rapid growth. The revolutionaries never had enough weapons to arm every man, but gunrunning across the Moroccan and Tunisian frontiers succeeded as well in the course of 1956 as recruiting did. The French shortly brought the arms traffic nearly to a halt, but by the end of 1956 the ALN had at its disposal about thirteen thousand weapons, chiefly automatic rifles and pistols.[39]

Twenty thousand guerrillas raised from a population of nine million hardly amounts to a nation in arms. A countrywide version of the Sétif riots of 1945 was out of the question. The Algerians were not going to push the French into the sea. And the experience of the first two years of revolution ended dreams of bringing off another Dien Bien Phu. Scattered in their mountain hiding places in bunches of fifty to a hundred, the guerrillas were capable of carrying out deadly skirmishes against the French. But destroying a sizable part of the army was beyond them.

Nevertheless, raising and arming twenty thousand men from a population indifferent to revolutionary exhortations,[40] erecting a workable politico-military network over such a vast terrain—these were considerable achievements. The revolutionaries could not have carried them out without successfully terrorizing their own people. Winning a decisive military victory was beyond the reach of the FLN, but not losing seemed well within its capacities.

With one exception, the FLN confined itself during the first year of the revolution to the kind of hit-and-run terrorism that French editors took to burying on the inside pages of their newspapers.

On August 20, 1955, in the area around Philippeville, ALN regulars pushed before them several hundred peasants whom they had convinced the hour of deliverance lay at hand. Armed with axes, knives, sickles, and such firearms as were available, the peasants set upon settlers and Algerians alike. The most horrifying scenes took place at the little mining village of El Halia. Algerian miners slaughtered the European overseers and their families. Some they hacked to death; others they disemboweled; they slit the throats of still others. At least fifty-two Algerians and seventy-one settlers were killed in these attacks. French army units, chiefly the Foreign Legion, arrived in the midst of the carnage. In reprisal they killed more than twelve hundred Algerians, many of them women and children, and made prisoners of as many more.[41]

El Halia was the settlers' worst nightmare come true: death at the hands of one's own workers. Miners docile and deferential one day had become brutal assassins the next. Settler vigilantes rode out to teach a lesson to the field hands down the road, just as had happened in the aftermath of Sétif. Vincent Monteil, Jacques Soustelle's erstwhile military adviser, writing under the pseudonym "François Sarrazin," assessed in *Esprit* the consequences of the Philippeville massacre: "Now the breach is yawning, the two communities are drawn up against each other, race war, war unaccountable and merciless, is at our doors."[42]

Fears that Philippeville was just the start of things proved groundless. For the governor-general, however, one such massacre was enough. Soustelle flew to El Halia to view the hideous spectacle for himself. *L'Express* later described him as a man obsessed with the affair, unable to resist injecting the incident into the idlest conversation.[43] Perhaps what he saw caused him suddenly to lose heart for reform; perhaps the butchery merely pushed him farther and faster in a direction he was already taking. By the end of 1955, Soustelle was telling the New York *Herald-Tribune* that "the rebels represent anti-western totalitarian fanaticism. . . ."[44] He was now difficult to distinguish from the hard-line settlers who had become his friends.

The settlers complained that the French military buildup was too small in numbers and too slow in coming. Soustelle, they grumbled, gave time to devising reforms that he should have given to repressing terrorism. Some journalists and historians have agreed.[45] True, an early application of overwhelming military force might have crushed the revolution. But whether ruthlessness could have preserved French rule, the conviction behind the settlers' complaint, is another question. A new version of Sétif might only have postponed the day of reckoning between Algerian nationalism and the settler ascendancy.

Besides, times had changed drastically since 1945. A reenactment of Sétif might have brought on the French government unbearable pressures to negotiate with the FLN, precisely the outcome the settlers wanted to avoid. In any event, neither the governor-general's reforms nor the French government's fear of international opinion slowed the military buildup as much as deciding what kind of war to fight and who was going to fight it.

The government had maintained that France faced a rebellion of French citizens. Rebelling against their own government put these citizens *hors la loi.* They were outlaws, persons beyond the law yet at the same time subject to it. The government, according to this view of the matter, had sent troops to restore order in North Africa, just as it might dispatch police to quell a riot in Brittany. In Algeria the army was not fighting a war but conducting "operations for the maintenance of order."[46]

There was more at stake than terminological niceties. The fiction that France was not at war lessened the likelihood of foreign intervention; reestablishing order was strictly an internal affair. No international law kept a government from suppressing a rebellion or gave a foreign state the right to intervene in one. Still, the question of whether the conflict in Algeria was internal or international was never as clear-cut as the French tried to make it.[47]

At any rate, French attempts to seize the initiative from the FLN belied the official claim that the nation was not at war. In early April 1955, the government, with parliamentary assent, declared a "state of emergency" *(état d'urgence)* in Algeria.[48] A state of emergency curtails civil liberties but falls short of martial law *(état de siège)* by leaving the civil authorities in control over the military. In the spring of 1955, the Faure government was reluctant to give the screw of repression more than a half-turn at a time.

A state of emergency was designed to deprive the revolutionaries of free run of the land. The law restricted daytime movement and established a nightly curfew; gave the authorities power to close whatever public places they saw fit; sanctioned twenty-four-hour searches (French law ordinarily permitted only daytime searches); established a vaguely worded "control of the press"; enabled the police to expel from Algeria any person held to be a threat to public order; permitted the administrative internment of suspects against whom insufficient evidence existed to press charges.[49]

Soustelle immediately proclaimed a state of emergency in the areas of the most intense violence: in the Aurès and Grand Kabylia, the arrondissements of Tizi-Ouzou and Batna, the countryside around Tebessa, Biskra, and El Oued. Extending the state of emergency to an ever larger area was the same as acknowledging the spread of insurgency. The paratroops and legionnaires early on the scene doused fires here and there, but there were too few of them to keep the flames from spreading. Soustelle repeatedly called for more troops. He complained of a shortage not only of soldiers capable of hunting down the insurgents but of men able to protect lives and property and to provide logistical support.[50]

Short of calling up reservists, additional hands for Algeria could come only from stripping other garrisons and converting units organized for one task into performing another. In the spring of 1955, the army command transferred troops from Morocco and Tunisia to Algeria. The Second Division of Motorized Infantry was shipped to North Africa from its garrison at Nancy. Two more infantry divisions followed.

Later the Seventh Mechanized and the Fifth Armored divisions withdrew from West Germany and sailed for Algeria. These moves angered France's NATO partners and French officers who had painstakingly assembled these divisions for the purpose of fighting in Europe. Their fancy heavy equipment was almost useless for chasing guerrillas in the Algerian back country.[51]

Such juggling and shuttling could not go on for long. The government knew how many troops it had on hand; it evidently concluded in the early spring of 1955 that they were not enough to master the insurgency. Only by calling up reservists and postponing the return to civilian life of draftees already in service could the manpower pool be much expanded.

In May 1955, the Faure government took the step every cabinet responsible for the Indochina war had avoided. It recalled eight thousand active reservists and announced plans to delay releasing from service one hundred thousand draftees. In August the Philippeville massacre precipitated call-ups the authorities might otherwise have spread over many months. On the 22nd the Faure government recalled sixty thousand reservists. A week later it announced that one hundred twenty thousand conscripts scheduled for discharge would be kept under arms. On August 30 Soustelle extended the state of emergency throughout Algeria.[52]

Except for those excused by virtue of physical disabilities or of some other special status, or deferred for educational purposes, all French boys went under the colors for eighteen months in the year of reaching their twentieth birthday. They were obliged to serve three years in the active reserves. Most of the men Faure recalled on August 22 were twenty-three years old. Many were married, some had families, most had begun careers.[53]

August 1955 was a far cry from August 1914, when men well along in middle age had joined the young in defending *la patrie*. In 1955 *la patrie*—one's own backyard—was not being defended, no matter how much the government claimed that Algeria was part of France. "Operations for the maintenance of order" looked for all the world like a colonial war. Never before had a conscript army gone overseas when the mainland was at peace.

The government's misgivings about calling up reservists were soon confirmed. On September 11, at the Gare de Lyon in Paris, some four hundred air force reservists shouted antigovernment slogans. By pulling the emergency brake handles and other means, they tried to keep their trains from leaving the station. A similar incident took place at the Gare de l'Est. On October 7, at the Richepanse barracks in Rouen, about six hundred members of the 406th Artillery Regiment rioted against their officers—according to one account, ten thousand workers joined in—and the police had to restore order. Toward the end of November, a group of draftees retained beyond their expected date of release mounted a demonstration on the Champs-Elysées. Protests against the call-up took place in Vincennes, Nantes, Valence, and Marseilles.[54]

The authorities quickly learned to remove the emergency brake handles from trains carrying troops to Marseilles. CRS, the tough riot police, rode aboard the trains and lined rights-of-way when they passed through towns.

One antiwar activist remembered that like-minded friends of the Catholic and Socialist left had tried to coordinate and organize these demonstrations, but for the most part they looked spontaneous and were probably not politically motivated.[55] Resentment at being torn from homes and jobs, not opposition to the government's Algerian policy, lay behind the disorders.

Resentment boiled over into rage—into repeated incidents of near-mutiny and, in at least one instance, a riot—when the reservists arrived at their camps; neither in 1955 nor in the spring of 1956, when another huge call-up took place, did the military and civilian authorities make adequate preparations for accommodating so many additional soldiers at once. On the mainland the reservists were jammed into cold, drafty, and disused barracks, poorly fed—often on American C rations dating from World War II—and left with nothing to do. In Algeria they found themselves in equally wretched surroundings.[56]

Calling up reservists was a stopgap measure. From 1957 on, first-time draftees made up the rank and file of the new Army of Africa. For many twenty-year-olds, saying goodbye to farmyards and hometowns was the beginning of an adventure. The army offered an escape from too familiar places, tiresome relatives, narrow horizons, and dreary jobs.

In the course of 1955 the number of French troops in Algeria more than doubled, from seventy-five thousand in January to one hundred eighty thousand in December. And at the end of the year rumors circulated of the government's planning to send sixty thousand more.[57] Already in October 1956, a third of the nation's armed forces were on duty in North Africa. In November the government advanced the reassuring thesis that larger numbers of troops in Algeria would mean less fighting there. Sending more soldiers by the hundreds of thousands was also bound to have a drastic effect on the character of the war. After 1955 Algeria was no longer the war of professionals that Indochina had always been; this meant a profound change in the mainland's relation to the conflict. Major Marcus, a career soldier figuring in Jean-Jacques Servan-Schreiber's *Lieutenant in Algeria,* put his finger on the difference: "No, this time it's not at all the expeditionary corps of Indochina —this time it's the nation."[58]

3 Pacification

Mendès France and each of his successors, including Charles de Gaulle, announced his plans for putting down the rebellion in Algeria, modernizing the backward Algerian economy, and remaking the political system. On the face of it, the strategy for keeping Algeria French scarcely varied from one government to the next. Nevertheless, shifting the emphasis from one element of the strategy to another amounted to reshaping Algerian policy. In the early months of 1956, crushing the insurgency had precedence over political and economic reform. Men who had run for office as peacemakers made the decisions that pulled France deeper into war and the Fourth Republic deeper into trouble.

On November 29, 1955, Edgar Faure lost a vote of confidence. The prime minister seized this opportunity to dissolve the National Assembly and call for new elections. A parliamentary dissolution had not taken place in France in eighty years. By advancing the elections six months, Faure aimed to increase and solidify his Center-Right majority. He also hoped to catch his opponents by surprise and cut short their attempt to organize a "new left" coalition. The election campaign was short and bitter.[1] In mid-December, *L'Express* published a public-opinion poll showing that the Algerian war had become the most important issue facing the nation.[2] But parliamentary elections are rarely referendums on single issues; the election of January 1956 was no exception.

Opposing Faure was the hastily contrived Front Républicain. Even as left-wing electoral coalitions went, the Front did not amount to much. Pierre Mendès France, leader of his own wing of the Radical party, worked out an agreement with Guy Mollet, secretary-general of the Socialist party (SFIO); they were joined by Jacques Chaban-Delmas of the Gaullist Social Republicans and by François Mitterrand of the UDRS, a party of former members of the Resistance. This rickety contraption had no common program, or even a statement of what its partners promised to do if they won. The Front, as Jacques Fauvet, editor of *Le Monde,* put it, was mainly "an advertising slogan."[3]

Mendès himself campaigned on the imperative need to find a rapid solution to the Algerian problem.[4] But even in his own party's program, Algeria was relegated to an unimperative fourth place. Except for the Communists, who called for bringing home the draftees and negotiating with the FLN, all other parties gave priority in their formal statements to domestic affairs.[5]

The left did well in the elections, but not as well as it had hoped to do. The big surprise was the success of Pierre Poujade and his followers, who managed to get more than fifty of their number elected to parliament. Poujade's tax revolt thrust him into prominence overnight as a passionate defender of a declining way of life at home and of every square meter of French territory abroad.[6] The Republican Front commanded no more than 160 to 170 seats, not enough to rule without help from the MRP and a couple of left splinter groups.[7] The Socialists, with ninety-five sure votes, held the key to putting together a majority. No government of the left could survive without them.[8] Their leader, Guy Mollet, became prime minister.

It is tempting to think that things might have turned out differently in Algeria had Pierre Mendès France and not Guy Mollet become prime minister. For Mendès had already successfully defied North African settlers and their friends for the sake of a liberal policy in Tunisia. Finding a way out of the Algerian crisis required the same energy, imagination, and nerve he had displayed in ending the war in Indochina. Instead, he joined Mollet's cabinet, as minister without portfolio, a post of little influence—left with plenty of chances to say how he would have done things differently, but never given an opportunity to do them.

Guy Mollet presided over the Fourth Republic's longest-lived government. Like Lyndon Johnson, Mollet became identified with a war policy that ultimately divided the country, tore apart his own party, and earned him the enmity of erstwhile political allies. An owlish-looking former lycée professor from the Pas de Calais, a stronghold of the SFIO, he had been secretary-general of his party since 1946. Anticlerical and anticommunist, an advocate of European economic and political unification, supporter of NATO— save for his doctrinaire Marxism, Mollet would have been quite at home among the cold-war liberals of Americans for Democratic Action. He had never previously been prime minister.[9]

In a campaign speech in Marseilles, Mendès France had suggested that the new prime minister go to Algiers, to show that Algeria was his government's paramount concern.[10] Mollet took up the idea, making plans to install in office his own choice as head man in North Africa, the mildly liberal arabophile and octogenarian General Georges Catroux. The elevation of the governor-generalship to a resident ministry gave the office cabinet rank and enhanced its powers. Already alarmed by the Republican Front's electoral victory, the settlers interpreted Catroux's appointment as the first step of a sellout, and they prepared a special reception for Mollet.[11]

On February 6, 1956, having made his investiture speech to the National Assembly, the new prime minister flew to Algiers. The historian André Mandouze had warned Mendès France that trouble was afoot in the city. Mendès urged Mollet to make the trip before the settlers got themselves organized.[12] But Mollet refused to hurry, and when he arrived, they were waiting for him. A crowd of several thousand had gathered at the War Memorial for the obligatory wreath-laying ceremony. In response to warnings of trouble, several companies of riot police had been flown in from Paris. As soon as the band struck up the "Marseillaise," a chorus of boos greeted Mollet. The settlers pelted the prime minister and his entourage with rotten tomatoes, clumps of grass, clods of dirt, chunks of dried horse manure. They roared for Catroux to be sent before a firing squad. The riot police responded with tear gas. Having laid the wreath, a shaken Mollet beat as dignified a retreat as circumstances allowed.[13] The mob got what it wanted. That evening, Catroux asked that his appointment be withdrawn, and Mollet agreed.

February 6 was obviously no spontaneous outburst. Behind the demonstration, which reporters on the scene compared to a lynch mob, was a then shadowy outfit calling itself the Action Committee of Defense, a coalition of patriotic organizations, veterans' associations, clubs of reserve officers and noncommissioned officers—activist Algiers in embryo. The army took no part, but in the days following, contacts between settler activists and army activists began to be made.[14]

Having parted with Catroux, the symbol of a liberal Algerian policy, Mollet parted with the policy as well. The prime minister's change of mind has ever since been interpreted as a change of heart. The decisions escalating the war have been traced by many accounts to the psychological impact of February 6 on Mollet. According to this thesis, the trip to Algiers was in the nature of a revelation. Mollet had expected to meet the *Colons* of Socialist myth: a class of rich and greedy planters grinding their boots in the faces of the Arab poor. Instead, he found a North African version of the Socialist voters of his home town of Arras—postmen, school-teachers, hairdressers, electricians, garage mechanics, office workers, minor civil servants—their faces contorted in rage and fear.[15] It was the sight of such faces that caused Mollet to abandon his liberal intentions in Algiers and return to the mainland bent on taking a hard line.

This view may exaggerate the impact of a barrage of fruit on the course of the war. For the Algerian question looked different from the prime minister's office than it had looked from the campaign trail. Mollet took office, it will be recalled, in the midst of the troop buildup Faure had already begun. He could not have stopped the flow of reinforcements, or have refused requests for still more soldiers, without exposing himself to the charge of abandoning the settlers to the mercies of FLN terrorists. Weighing the insubstantial electoral promises of the Republican Front against the political and military realities of the war, Mollet might well have turned his back on the promises without ever having gone to Algiers.

Shocked to discover that the settlers closely resembled the clientele of the SFIO, Mollet chose as Catroux's successor a man who resembled the settlers. Robert Lacoste, who had the squat and beefy look common to Algiers activists, became resident minister. His credentials made him seem the right man to carry out a liberal policy: a good Resistance record, high standing in the Socialist party, enthusiasm for the reformist ambitions of Mendesism, a reputation as a tough administrator. But he also had a weakness for bluster, some of the instincts of a bully, little knowledge of the Algerian problem, and no experience in dealing with the wide range of civil and military questions that came under the purview of the resident minister.[16] He soon fell under the spell Algiers had cast over so many of his predecessors; before long he came to see things as the settlers saw them.

The Mollet cabinet was from the outset divided between doves and hawks. Gaston Defferre, Socialist boss of Marseilles, minister of colonies, and the prime minister's main rival for the party leadership, joined Mendès France in think-ing the government ought not to put any conditions on hold-ing talks with the FLN. The minister of defense, the Radical Maurice Bourgès-Maunoury, Lacoste, and Mollet all took the view that reestablishing order should precede attempts at negotiation.[17] The hawks prevailed. Their position came to be embodied in the policy of "pacification," a euphemism old as the conquest of Algeria for the application of military force.

Nothing better expressed the new ordering of priorities than the Special Powers Law of March 16, 1956. This en-abling act handed the executive virtually unlimited powers, and was to the Algerian war what the Tonkin Gulf Resolu-tion of 1964 was to the American war in Vietnam.[18] French parliaments had frequently resorted to enabling acts in the declining years of the Third Republic, when a Chamber of Deputies too divided to make a decision, or too fearful of the political consequences of making one, allowed the govern-ment to act in its stead. The National Assembly followed the example of its predecessor. By increasing the government's responsibility for conducting the war, the assembly dimin-ished its own.

The Mollet government acted as a sorcerer's apprentice, for the Special Powers Law had the effect of placing immense power in the hands of the army in Algeria—more power than the republic found itself able to control.

That the government submitted its bill to the parliament soon after February 6 suggests that it was the events in Algiers that precipitated the law. But Mollet might have brought in such a bill even without overt pressure from the settlers. From the beginning of the insurrection both the army and the police had incessantly complained of the legal obstacles in the way of their hunting down the insurgents.[19] Such complaints could be translated into the political charge that they had not been given the tools for the job.

Both Mollet and Lacoste presented the Special Powers Bill to the assembly as an attempt to strike a delicate balance between repression and reform.[20] The Special Powers Bill did include a list of reforms taken over wholesale from the Soustelle Plan, but its key passage was article five, which gave the government "the most extensive powers for undertaking any exceptional measure required by circumstances with a view to the reestablishment of order, the protection of persons and property and the safeguard of the territory."[21]

Such opposition to the bill as existed arose mainly from conservatives who believed it carried reform too far and repression not far enough. Expressing alarm at the dictatorial powers the bill gave the resident minister, and declaring their sympathy with the revolution, the Communists nevertheless supported the government. They did not want to give offense to the Socialists. They hoped to end their political isolation by establishing a coalition of the two parties, an ambition in which they persisted long after the war. They were also eager to please Mollet on the eve of the Soviet leadership's visit to France. The Communist voting on the Special Powers Bill made plain the party's refusal to allow the Algerian question to take precedence over other concerns.[22]

Article five cleared the assembly by a vote of 455 to 76— not quite so overwhelming as the near-unanimous support the U.S. Congress gave the Tonkin Gulf Resolution, but certainly enough to allow successive governments to claim that their actions with respect to Algeria expressed the national will.

Expanding the army's authority in Algeria presaged increasing its numbers. In April 1956 Lacoste asked for another one hundred thousand men; there were rumors that the cabinet was discussing even larger figures.[23] The government intended not only to draw reinforcements from the pool of eligible reservists; it also planned to call for volunteers for service in North Africa. The steady buildup of troops, and Lacoste's requests for still more, soon made duty in Algeria nearly every draftee's fate.

The troop buildup helped destroy the remnants of the spirit of the Republican Front. The war was beginning not only to disrupt political alliances but to strain the principles of the liberal state. Two incidents of early April 1956 marked the onset of the government's harassment of critics. On a charge of "undertaking to demoralize the army," police arrested and jailed overnight Claude Bourdet, editor of *France observateur*.[24] Police ransacked the apartment of the historian Henri Marrou, who had published an article in *Le Monde* critical of the government's Algerian policy in general and the army's conduct in particular.[25] The authorities never said what they were looking for in his apartment; perhaps they hoped to find evidence linking Marrou to the FLN. No doubt they meant to warn other critics of government policy that their turn for a police visit might come next.

The Mollet government accepted the political risks of sending vastly greater numbers of troops to Algeria in the hope of crushing the insurgency. By the end of 1956, France had committed more than four hundred thousand men to North Africa—perhaps as many as twenty soldiers for every FLN guerrilla in the bush.[26] Less than 10 percent of this force did much fighting. The main task of the majority was to protect the persons and property of settlers and Algerians, to keep the main roads and railroads open and travelers safe from ambush, to protect from sabotage such strategically important installations as port facilities, power stations, telephone and telegraph exchanges. These troops were spread out in a *quadrillage,* the same term as applies to the ruled squares in a schoolchild's notebook. The job of the remainder of the army—between thirty thousand and forty thousand men— was to hunt down the guerrillas of the FLN, or—to borrow again from the lexicon of the Indochina war—to engage in "search and destroy" missions.[27]

Draftees maintained the *quadrillage;* professional soldiers and volunteers chased the guerrillas. Considerations of military efficiency played some part in this distribution of responsibilities. The professionals, especially the Foreign Legion and paratroops, had already acquired vast experience in counterinsurgency warfare. But *quadrillage* was a lot safer than combat: standing watch over a settler's farm involved far less risk than playing hide-and-seek in the mountains with an armed guerrilla band. The troops of the *quadrillage* belonged to an army of occupation, the combat troops to an army at war. The government did what it could to preserve the differences between them.[28]

Assigning draftees to the army of occupation and professional soldiers to the army at war may have been in some respects a politically wise decision. But in one important respect this division of military labor was a mistake. The combat troops were designated "units of intervention." It was the paratroops, more than anyone, who quickly came to be identified with this role, who received more attention from the press than any other soldiers in Algeria (despite their being only 3 percent to 5 percent of the forces on duty there).[29] It was the paratroops, roaming the length and breadth of Algeria, often carried to the assault in helicopters, who fulfilled the romantic image of war as an enterprise of danger, of continuous movement and action. And it was they who identified most closely with the diehards of French Algeria, who in the course of the crisis gave the designation "units of intervention" ironic overtones.

The paratroops were already closely identified, both in the public eye and in their own minds, with the loss of Indochina. They had contributed the one dash of gallantry, at least as their actions were reported in the newspapers, to a distinctly ungallant war.[30] And they were more associated with the theory and mood of *guerre révolutionnaire* than other outfits in the army. Haunted by the memory of the Vietnamese allies they had abandoned, they arrived in Algeria determined to stay.[31]

Still, if the paratroops came to think of themselves as special soldiers with special obligations, they did so with the encouragement and assistance of governments of the Fourth Republic. Bastille Day parades provide evidence of this. The paratroops, the heroes of Dien Bien Phu, were the center of attention when they marched down the Champs-Elysées in 1954. The government later used military reviews to demonstrate its resolve to maintain French rule in Algeria come what may, and the paratroops were the featured attraction. On the eve of Bastille Day of 1957, for example, *Paris-Presse* announced, "The paratroops will be the stars [*les vedettes*] of this review. In the eyes of metropolitan Frenchmen as in those of Algeria, these elite combatants incarnate the new army which is progressively adapting itself to its dual mission: to struggle against the rebellion and to construct, with the population, a new Algeria." And *Le Figaro* commented, "Blue berets, red berets, green berets, the 'paras' and their leaders received the welcome which was due them. There was, in the applause and the acclamations saluting their passage, both the admiration and the affectionate recognition that a people can express to youth and courage."[32]

Perhaps the politicians hoped some of the paras' glamour would rub off on them. Perhaps, as one observer suggested, governments of the Fourth Republic sought to compensate for the regime's mediocrity, its dullness and incoherence, with displays of military glory.[33] But by using these regiments as the symbol of a particular policy—the maintenance of a French Algeria—and not as the executants of any policy the government chose to undertake, the political leaders encouraged the paratroops in their belief that they were carrying out a special mission.

The crowds that lined the Champs-Elysées on Bastille Day regarded the paratroops as different from other participants in the parade—not only because of their reputation but because of their distinctive appearance. A paratrooper is a soldier trained to jump out of airplanes; an athletic skill, rather than military prowess, establishes membership in this particular elite. There is some irony in this. Few airborne operations in military history have been notable successes; many have been bloody failures.[34] But the direct utility of parachuting appears to have been beside the point. The rituals, superstitions, and taboos of jump school, the humiliations visited upon washouts, suggest that parachuting is mainly a test of manhood, a kind of rite of passage. As one paratrooper wrote, "Jump training [was the] secret dread and secret desire of every one of us."[35] What the journalist Ward Just wrote of American paratroops applies to the French as well: "Jumping out of airplanes, as a critic later put it, was romantic as hell but also dangerous and wasteful of lives; what it did was put a very high premium on bravery of a certain kind."[36]

When the paratroopers graduated from jump school, they put on uniforms that made them look different from everyone else. Indeed, the paras' camouflaged combat fatigues cast a spell that in retrospect seems extraordinary, and even faintly ridiculous. Alain Jacob, correspondent for *Le Monde,* called them the equivalent of the matador's suit of lights.[37] One paratrooper wrote in his memoirs that "a volunteer paratrooper is never at the start anything but a grown-up little boy . . . dreaming of . . . the glamorous uniform, red beret, jungle-green combat suit, and commando dagger slipped into the boot."[38] The mottled appearance of their fatigues caused the paras to be called the leopard men (also a reference to their supposedly feline gait); at least one "leopard," a regimental commander, is said to have worn his spots to an official reception at the Opera.[39]

The paras' uniform, along with their distinctive headgear —red berets for the colonial paratroops, green for the paratroops of the Foreign Legion, blue for the metropolitan paratroops—became as much a staple of political cartooning as the capitalist's top hat, and as symbolic of the cause of *Algérie française* as the rhythmic honking of automobile horns

—three short, two long—that sounded in the streets of Paris and Algiers in the last years of the war. For some of the diehard settlers, the leopard uniform became a sort of talisman; they dressed their children in it and took to wearing it themselves on occasions of high seriousness.[40]

The paratroops claimed to have the best officers in the army; certainly they were the best known. Most of them had established reputations in Indochina; a few were heroes of Dien Bien Phu. Marcel Bigeard, commander of the Third Regiment of Colonial Paratroops, was one of these. His outspokenness and flamboyance made him a favorite of newsmen. Bigeard's biography was highly appropriate for popular magazines: humble origins (his father was a railroad signalman); a Teddy-Rooseveltian transformation from sickly childhood to vigorous manhood; escape from the dreary existence of a bank clerk into a life of adventure; one narrow scrape after another in World War II; six years as a guerrilla fighter in Indochina; hero of Dien Bien Phu; prisoner of the Vietnamese; and now commander of a crack regiment in Algeria.[41] So well known a public figure did he become that in early 1958 Hubert Beuve-Méry, editor and publisher of *Le Monde,* wrote in an editorial of rumors that Bigeard would be called upon to form the next government.[42]

If the image of the paratrooper made him a man apart, he was also said to have a distinctive outlook on the world. To be sure, aspects of the *esprit para,* as it was called, were simply the commonplace sentiments of any crack military outfit. What elite military organization does not boast of its skill in combat? Even military critics of the paratroops conceded that they were good at their jobs.[43] But other dimensions of the *esprit para* were more disquieting. The paratroops' sense of independence from the rest of the army, their lack of respect for the traditional forms of discipline, their clannishness evoked memories of the *Freikorps,* the bands of German army veterans who roamed the countryside in the aftermath of the Great War, "drunk," Maurice Duverger wrote, "with the idea of compensating for the humiliation of their country with action and violence."[44]

The paratroop officers believed that they belonged to a "militant sect."[45] As one of them put it, "We like war and we are tooled up for it; we have our chaplains to bless us before the battle and to put us underground after it; our *toubibs* [doctors] to treat us, our quartermasters to feed us and our courts to judge us if we don't behave according to the laws in force among us."[46]

As befits a militant sect, the paratroops had their own patron saint—the Archangel Michael—and their own prayer, which went as follows:

> Give me, my God, that which you have
>   left over. Give me that for which you
>   are never asked
> I do not ask for wealth
> Nor for success, nor even for health
>   You are asked so often, my God, for
>   all that
> That you must not have any left
> Give me, my God, that which you have
>   left over
> Give me that which people refuse to take
>   from you
> I want insecurity and restlessness
> I want torment and brawling
>   And that you should give them to me,
>   my God,
> Once and for all
>   Let me be sure to have them always
> For I will not always have the courage
> To ask you for them.[47]

This prayer, nailed up in barracks throughout Algeria, enunciates several themes in the *esprit para:* the rejection of materialism, the exaltation of asceticism, violence, and risk, of action for action's sake.

Nowhere was the military romanticism of the *esprit para* better exemplified than in Jean Lartéguy's novel *The Centurions,* a best seller in 1960, and in the writings of Colonel Bigeard himself. Lartéguy follows the careers of paratroop officers—the central figure, Colonel Raspéguy, is modeled on Bigeard—from captivity in Indochina to the Battle of Algiers. Alienated from French society, strangers in their own country, where they have spent little time since 1940, contemptuous of civilian life, they despise intellectuals and politicians, whom they blame for the "mess" in France; they are at peace only when among themselves, only when in battle.[48] Bigeard wrote the text for a volume of photographs of paratroopers in action. His captions betray a fascination with death and sacrifice: "At each turn of the road, behind each dune, each rock, we had a rendezvous with our death." Of the sergeant dead in combat to whom he dedicated the book, Bigeard wrote: "Of us all he was the luckiest, for he made a success of his death after having led the tormented life which he had chosen."[49]

The photographs in Bigeard's book show the paras in their leopard uniforms, roaming the Sahara in search of an unseen adversary—an adversary their equal, one assumes, in military prowess. These images have a kind of purity in the shots of the desert, in the suggestion of a contest between equals, in the absence of civilians able to blunder into harm's way. They have an element of timelessness too. Save for the modern weaponry, Bigeard's paratroops might as well be Roman legionaries.

These photographs were a far cry from the usual realities of the Algerian war. As the main instruments of the government's policy of repression, the paratroops resembled less the warriors of antiquity than an especially nasty police force. By 1957 the regiments acclaimed on the Champs-Elysées had acquired a sinister reputation among opponents of the war.

*   *   *

The one military operation in the war in which the paratroops actually put to use their skill at jumping out of airplanes—and a spectacularly successful one, at that—was the
Suez expedition of November 1956.

The joint Anglo-French action against Gamal Abdel
Nasser has been seen as the event that signaled the end of the
capacity of France and England to act as world powers. It
has been portrayed in countless books, especially in books
written before the rise of the Organization of Petroleum
Exporting Countries, as a foolhardy and ruinous enterprise.[50]
And in many respects, especially in the calculation of the
organizers that the United States and the Soviet Union
would let them get away with it, perhaps it was.

Still, the reasoning that led the French leadership to undertake the strike against Suez had an alluring plausibility.
Civil and military leaders alike were convinced that Nasser
was the presiding genius of the Algerian revolution; in their
view, Suez was simply another theater of the same war.[51]
The French also saw Nasser as the Hitler of the Middle
East—a power-mad, expansion-minded dictator. The British leadership shared this Munich-haunted view. Acceding
to Nasser's nationalization of the Suez Canal, a move he
made in the summer of 1956, would have consequences as
catastrophic as those following the reoccupation of the
Rhineland. An expedition would also ensure that Middle
Eastern petroleum continued to flow through the canal. In
the thinking of the French, however, it was the Algerian
connection that was paramount, and that made it worth-
while to divert from central North Africa an entire division
of paratroops.[52]

The diverse aims of the British and French coincided with
the ambitions of the Israelis, who had persuaded themselves
of the need for a preventive war against Nasser. The French,
convinced they had a greater stake riding on a successful
outcome than the British, worked more closely with the

Israelis. Unbeknownst to the British government, they lent material support to the Israeli offensive against Egypt.

On the pretext of establishing a buffer between Egyptian and Israeli combatants, the Anglo-French offensive began in the early morning hours of October 31, 1956. On November 5, a simultaneous paratroop drop and amphibious assault against Port Saïd succeeded brilliantly. But success was short lived. At midnight on November 6, the British and French governments, bowing to pressures from the United States and the Soviet Union, called a halt to the operation.

Suez had a strikingly different impact on Britain than on France. For Anthony Eden's government and for Eden's career, Suez was calamitous—both were wrecked in the storm of criticism the expedition provoked. But in France, Suez enhanced Guy Mollet's popularity. Such protest as arose was directed against the meddling of the Americans, whose interference was perceived as having robbed France of a chance to put an end to the war in Algeria.

What if the Suez expedition had succeeded, or had been allowed to succeed? Had Nasser been toppled from power, the Algerian revolution would have lost the one sure friend it then possessed. Losing his aid and support would have been a devastating blow, but it is doubtful that such a turn of events would have deprived the revolutionary leadership of the will, or even the means, to continue the struggle. If Nasser supported the revolution, he was neither its instigator nor its driving force. Besides, as André Beaufre, a planner of the Suez expedition, has pointed out, Mollet would have needed to follow victory over Nasser with reforms in Algeria. Flushed with their success in Egypt, the French might have decided reforms in North Africa could be dispensed with. In this case, deposing Nasser would only have delayed the end of French rule; it would not have brought about a different outcome.[53]

Anthony Eden was one casualty of the Suez expedition; the French army—and especially the group of paratroops who landed at Port Saïd—believed itself to have been another. In knuckling under to Soviet-American demands, many soldiers felt, their own government had cheated them of the fruits of a success all the headier for its rarity. The outcome of Suez was added to the military's already lengthy list of grievances against the Fourth Republic.[54]

If the Suez affair left a bitter aftertaste, its popularity on the mainland temporarily strengthened the Mollet government. Nevertheless, as the historian Hugh Thomas has remarked, if the Suez expedition was popular, "so was Alcibiades's expedition to Sicily, before it left Athens."[55]

Equally popular was the capture, in the midst of the Suez crisis, of much of the external leadership of the FLN. On October 22, a DC-3 left Rabat for Tunis bearing, as guests of the Sultan of Morocco, Ahmed Ben Bella and three other organizers of the All Saints rising, Mohamed Boudiaf, Hocine Ait Ahmed, and Mohamed Khider. On orders of the French high command, the aircraft was diverted from its course and forced to land in Algiers. The FLN leaders were arrested and transported to France, where they remained imprisoned for the duration of the war.

FLN sympathizers regarded the incident as an act of piracy. Anti-French rioting broke out in Morocco at the news of this insult to the Sultan; Tunisia recalled its ambassador from France; Alain Savary, minister of state for Tunisian and Moroccan affairs, resigned from the French government. In Algeria, however, virtually nothing happened. Word of the arrests dismayed some members of the Mollet cabinet and delighted others. The prime minister was angered and embarrassed, but in the end he covered with his own authority the military's *fait accompli.*

Some of the actors in this episode—notably Ben Bella and Christian Pineau, the minister of foreign affairs—have seen the capture of the FLN leaders as an important turning point in the war, or rather as a turning point that failed to turn.

By means of unofficial emissaries, mainly Socialist party leaders, the Mollet government had made at least five contacts with the external leaders with a view to establishing official negotiations on the Algerian question. The leaders' arrest put an end to these secret meetings, thereby dashing, so it has been argued, any possibility of an early end to the war. Knuckling under to the army, Mollet helped prolong hostilities by nearly six years.

This judgment is hard to accept. In the first place, it is by no means certain that the FLN would have been willing to settle in 1956 for less than it received in 1962; and for a French government to have acceded to independence at such an early date would have been entirely out of the question. Moreover, by late 1956 important issues of military and political strategy sharply divided the FLN leadership. Those in charge of conducting the terrorist campaign in Algeria had grown increasingly suspicious and resentful of such leaders as Ben Bella, whose duties exempted them from the hard and dangerous life of the revolutionaries of the interior. The terrorists, who controlled the armed force of the liberation movement, would probably have repudiated any compromise agreement that the leaders of the exterior might have worked out on their behalf. Indeed, the interior leadership was far from displeased to learn of the arrest of men they had come to regard as their rivals. The capture of Ben Bella, in itself, did no more to prolong the war significantly than it did to "decapitate" the revolution, as supporters of the arrest action hoped.[56]

By early 1957 one of every three Europeans in Algeria wore a French army uniform. These soldiers made up the largest army France had ever sent overseas. Meeting this new Army of Africa's needs in goods and manpower depleted foreign-exchange reserves (France bought much of its military equipment abroad) and drove up prices on the mainland.[57] Calling up hundreds of thousands of conscripts made the war the intimate concern of as many French households. As a young reserve officer just back from North Africa wrote in *Le Monde* later in the year, "France today is the slave of her preoccupation with maintaining Algeria under her dependence. This preoccupation weighs heavily on the present and compromises the possibility of thinking about the future."[58]

It was the Socialist party, the party of Jean Jaurès, Léon Blum, and other enemies of colonialism and war, that controlled the government conducting the biggest and most expensive colonial war in France's history. The war divided the Socialists as the war in Indochina later divided Lyndon Johnson's Democrats in the United States. Many party members, from the parliamentary leadership down to local activists, managed to square the championing of repression overseas with social progress at home; others saw the party's role in the war as betraying everything it stood for.[59] Many wavered between supporting the party leadership and breaking with it. (Gaston Defferre was one such figure.) Some were torn by conflicts of conscience and ambition; others could not make up their minds on the subject of Algeria. As the journalist Jean Lacouture later put it, "Everything should have brought me to the taking of a clear position. And yet I politically stammered. Beginning from the moment I returned to *Le Monde* to concern myself above all with Algeria, in November 1957, I remained nearly a year in a perpetual internal debate. I made up my mind only at the end of 1958."[60]

As early as the spring of 1956, anti-Mollet, anti-Lacoste sentiment manifested itself within the Socialist party. Daniel Mayer, soon to be president of the League of the Rights of Man (the civil rights organization founded to defend Captain Dreyfus), former secretary-general of the party, and long-time antagonist of Guy Mollet, expressed at the Socialists' national congress his unhappiness with government policy in Algeria. Another member of the SFIO's right wing, André

Philip, published *Le Socialisme trahi* (Socialism Betrayed), its title an expression of his views on what responsibility for the war had done to the party.

For the most part, though, minority leaders opposed government policy by proposing antiwar motions in party meetings and making occasional public statements of dissent.[61] Rare were outright resignations from the government, such as that of Alain Savary, or from the party. For one thing, the SFIO was dominated by the parliamentary leadership, on whose good favor depended the prospects of political advancement. Not many members were willing to risk defying Mollet on questions of principle. Those who were, however —senior members of the party, for the most part—in January 1957 made formal their opposition to the Socialists' continuing responsibility for the war. They founded a Comité socialiste d'étude et d'action pour la paix en Algérie. Drawing members from both the left and right wings of the party, the committee was an example of how issues of the war smudged long-standing ideological lines. It succeeded in defying the party executive committee's order to dissolve, but it failed to attract more than a small minority of Socialist activists to its ranks. It did not mount a serious enough challenge to the parliamentary leadership to put party unity at risk.[62]

If Socialist dissidents decried their party's role in conducting the war, Communist dissidents deplored their party's timidity in opposing it. The Communist party's opposition to Algerian policy did not come close to matching the incendiary words and illegal deeds of their opposition to the war in Indochina. Mao Tse-tung is said to have remarked in 1957 that on the Algerian question the French party leadership had adopted a "national-chauvinist attitude."[63]

Several explanations for the party's caution, a charge the leadership always denied, have been put forward. The party's severest critics believe the cause to be a fear of offending the anti-Arab sensibilities of its working-class clientele. Michel

Crouzet suggested the Communists "had decided they would not compromise their political capital in the Algerian hornets' nest."[64] Especially, Crouzet and others have argued, the party leadership did not want to risk an irreparable break with the Socialists. Pursuit of the tactic of the *front unique,* according to this view, overrode all other considerations, including the war in Algeria.[65]

By the time the war broke out, the French Communist party had wandered in the wilderness nearly as many years as Moses. Since the party's founding in 1920, Communists had sat in a government for less than two years. For the rest of its existence, save for the extraordinary interval of the Resistance, the party had not just opposed the government of the day but had dwelt in deep isolation from the rest of the political system. Twice the Communists had escaped, both times on bridges built to the Socialists. In the mid-1930s, the Popular Front experiment had shown that all the bad blood between Socialists and Communists, all the doctrinal, organizational, and tactical differences, need not stand in the way of an alliance when both parties had compelling reasons for coming to terms. Owing to the unusual circumstances of wartime, the Communists had participated in the provisional government of General de Gaulle, until they were expelled in the postwar government of Paul Ramadier. Their winning a majority of seats in the National Assembly did not seem at all likely. They knew they could not count on any party but the Socialists to offer them a share in power, and strenuously opposing the war risked that relationship. Yet not opposing the war threatened to call into question the party's anticolonialism and its ties with the Third World. By making words seem to speak louder than actions, the party tried to avoid impaling itself on either horn of its dilemma. On the one hand, the Communists called for peace in Algeria; on the other hand, they went along with the Socialists on the Special Powers Law of 1956.

The Communist party's steady pursuit of the *front unique* did not alone account for its ambivalence on Algeria. Suspicious of the FLN's intense nationalism, the party did not call for Algeria's independence until fairly late in the day. Like their enemies on the extreme right, the Communists charged that an independent Algeria might fall into the clutches of the Americans. The party also had to contend with the force of nationalism at home. It hesitated to suggest that an army composed of so many working-class and peasant boys had been sent to North Africa on a futile adventure. It shied away from accusing such an army of criminal misdeeds. When the party did speak of misconduct, it was careful to lay blame on foreigners in the Foreign Legion.[66]

Despite all this, some antiwar activists never ceased hoping the Communists would cast aside their hesitations and their ambivalent pronouncements and bring their own rank and file into the streets at the head of a vast outpouring of popular protest.[67] But this never happened. If organizing such a campaign went beyond the means of antiwar activists, it ran counter to the inclinations of the two main parties of the organized left.

4 The Battle of Algiers

In 1956 the FLN faced as many troubles within its own ranks as it was capable of making for the French. Its spread over the countryside stretched the revolutionary movement beyond its means, leaving it short of money and arms, without central direction, torn by quarrels over tactics and personalities. More troops poured in daily from France, and the French army grew more adept at counterinsurgency warfare. These troubles threatened to extinguish the revolution if left unattended, and in August most of the internal leadership met in a secluded place in the valley of the Soummam in an effort to resolve them. The Soummam Congress laid down new aims and founded new institutions. It met—or at least patched over—the leadership crisis by establishing a five-member Comité de coordination et d'exécution (CCE). Ben Bella's arrest, shortly after Soummam, eliminated the CCE's main rival for leadership, and until September 1957 the committee led the revolution.[1]

The CCE decided to take the war for independence, hitherto confined to the countryside, into the city of Algiers. This urban offensive was to consist of a general strike and a terrorist campaign. By demonstrating its ability to keep Algerians off the job and out of the street, the FLN aimed to discredit French claims that the revolution had little popular support. Calling the strike for January 28, 1957, the opening day of United Nations debates on the Algerian question, it aimed at getting attention in New York as well as Paris. The revolutionaries may also have hoped a general strike would distract the French army from its efforts to cut off arms smuggling at the Tunisian frontier. French authorities claimed to see an insurrection afoot and later took credit for heading off an armed uprising. But the FLN insisted it never had anything but a strike in mind, and such evidence as is available tends to support this claim. Certainly, an uprising would have been a foolhardy undertaking.[2]

The terrorists of the FLN were undoubtedly seeking publicity for their cause. One bomb exploding in Algiers was far more newsworthy than countless skirmishes in the countryside. The FLN also subscribed to Lenin's dictum that the purpose of terrorism is to terrify. The terrorists meant to make the settlers fear that a trip to the market or a drink in a bar might end in violent death and to caution Algerians that mingling with Europeans might invite a knife between the shoulder blades or a bullet in the brain. Such fears were calculated to drive deeper the wedge of hostility and suspicion between Muslims and settlers. For who could tell whether a faithful servant by day was not a terrorist by night? And who could know whether a European friendly on the job was not after hours a vigilante? Finally, terrorism in Algiers, it has been widely suggested, was intended to provoke from the French authorities a response so savage as to drive previously uncommitted Algerians into the revolutionary camp.[3]

The FLN's stronghold in Algiers was the Casbah. Eighty thousand Algerians made it one of the most thickly populated slums in the world. The Casbah's narrow, twisting streets and alleys, its secret passageways and flat rooftops made it seem, like eighteenth-century Paris, "designed for escape, for hiding."[4] By 1956 the quarter that had once charmed tourists and movie fans frightened and repelled outsiders; Europeans sought their pleasures elsewhere. The withdrawal of European authority gave FLN organizers free run of the area.[5]

A neighborhood in which half the men were out of work and half the inhabitants were under twenty years old was a promising recruiting ground for troublemakers. Residents of the Casbah who did not work with the FLN were intimidated into giving money and keeping quiet. For gunmen, goons, and intelligence agents the FLN drew on the pimps, whores, drug pushers, and small-time crooks of the Algerian underworld. Police informers—spies for the French police—became spies *on* the police, passing on to the FLN news they gleaned from hanging around station houses.[6]

Five thousand is the generally agreed-upon estimate of the size of the membership of the FLN's Autonomous Zone of Algiers. On paper, the Autonomous Zone had three branches: political/financial, military, and intelligence. Realities were far less tidy. The intelligence section hardly existed; members of the political branch did its work. Besides collecting money, the political/financial branch ran mimeograph machines, distributed tracts, acted as couriers. But collecting money always came first. And the flow of money into the treasury became a fairly accurate gauge of the FLN's control of the population.[7]

Collecting money requires many persons, but a few can terrorize a city. At any one time, the military branch of the Autonomous Zone never had more than one hundred fifty members.[8] Most observers put its strength at about a hundred, the majority of whom were gunmen. The gunmen did not kill at random, but selected as targets prominent settlers, Algerians identified as collaborators, or agents suspected of betraying the cause.

For terrorizing the settler community, the FLN chose bombs. The bomb network had at most fifty members. A secret organization within a secret organization, it lived a life independent of the political/financial or military branches, answering directly to the head of the Autonomous Zone, Yacef Saadi.[9]

Residents of the Casbah regarded Yacef as a loafer, a

soccer enthusiast, a ladies' man. The French police knew his record as a political agitator—he had belonged to the short-lived Organisation Secrète—but they did not suspect he was the chief terrorist of Algiers.[10]

The bomb network divided its labor. Casing-makers set up welding shops in deserted garages and other hiding places around the city; artificers fashioned the innards of the bombs; transporters conveyed them to depots; planters left them at sites Yacef selected. Most of the planters were young women, university students who could pass as Europeans (one, Danielle Mine, *was* a European).[11]

The CCE did not approve launching a terrorist offensive in Algiers until the end of the Soummam Congress, in September 1956.[12] But the Autonomous Zone began making bombs at least as early as the spring of the same year.[13] Some of these weapons were exploded before September. Whether they were set off without provocation, as the settlers and their friends have claimed, or as reprisals against European vigilantism, as the FLN and some of its defenders maintained, has been argued ever since.

The FLN leadership may have thought twice about attacking settlers within the crowded city, for fear that reprisals against the Algerian population would lose them support. In June, however, the French authorities executed two FLN terrorists. On August 10, a small group of settlers blew up an apartment building in the Casbah, killing at least fifty Algerians. The FLN's bombing campaign has been seen as vengeance for such acts.[14]

Still, simple revenge hardly required setting up an elaborate terrorist network, or bombings, shootings, and stabbings in the number that marked the last months of 1956. On September 30, the bomb network planted three explosives. Toward five o'clock in the afternoon one was set off at the Milk-Bar, a popular European hangout on the corner of the Place d'Isly opposite French army headquarters, killing one and wounding thirty; the second detonated at La Caféteria, another European café on the rue Michelet, killing two and injuring sixteen; the third, planted at the Algiers airport, failed to fire.[15]

And so it went into October and through December 1956 (in November a bomb-maker accidentally blew up himself and a month's supply of explosives).[16] According to one estimate, terrorist attacks of all kinds—bombings, shootings, stabbings, and destruction of property—soared from 4 in January 1956 to 50 in July, 96 in September, and 122, or roughly 4 a day, in December.[17] Yacef Saadi's agents left their deadly bundles everywhere—in streetcars, shops, the hollow bases of streetlight poles, cafés, movie houses, soccer stadiums, dance halls.[18]

The rising incidence of terrorism bewildered the police and left them looking ineffectual. They were woefully shorthanded, even for the ordinary run of police work.[19] More security men might have made it harder for the terrorists to get around, but more information would have served the authorities better than greater numbers. As long as the FLN maintained the anonymity of its agents, it had an intelligence advantage over the French.

Toward the end of December Amedée Froger, mayor of Boufarik and a leading hard-line settler, was assassinated on his doorstep. Europeans assumed the FLN was to blame. Fearful for their own safety, exasperated by their sense of helplessness, settlers attending his funeral set upon Algerian passersby. Rampaging through the street, the mourners became a lynch mob.[20]

As 1956 drew to a close, the Mollet government's Algerian policy gave the odd impression of being both brutally repressive and hopelessly inept. Having spread across the country a military apparatus approaching a half-million men, the government found itself unable to maintain order within a few square miles of Algeria's capital city. Under the noses of the authorities, and the eyes of the press, the terrorists blew up settlers and gunned down Algerians in the streets. And if terrorism were not enough, a general strike loomed.

*   *   *

On January 7, 1957, Robert Lacoste ordered the Tenth Paratroop Division into Algiers. Lacoste called in the paratroops under authority of the Special Powers Law, which accorded him "the most extensive powers for undertaking any exceptional measure dictated by circumstances with a view to the reestablishment of order, the protection of persons and property and the safeguard of the territory."[21]

General Jacques Massu, the Tenth Division commander, in effect took over as police chief of Algiers. But the Special Powers Law made him a special kind of chief, independent not only of the municipal authorities, by virtue of his military status, but also of the military chain of command. A veteran of the prewar Army of Africa, of the Free French forces, of Indochina and Suez, a man whose rough-hewn looks and reputation as a warrior reminded observers of one of Napoleon's Imperial Guardsmen, Massu had the operational responsibility for conducting what quickly became known as the "Battle of Algiers." His division of eight thousand men was composed in large part of regiments shot to pieces in Indochina, then rebuilt and renamed. The paratroopers faced the task of restoring order in a hilly seaport roughly the size of San Francisco.

General Massu replied to the FLN's call for an eight-day strike by declaring his intention to act as a strikebreaker.[22] By threat, invitation, and coercion the paratroops induced Algerian workers to return to their jobs and Algerian children to their schools. They forcibly opened Algerian shops. The strike order was widely obeyed at the outset, but by midweek most workers had returned to their places of work. Both sides claimed success—the FLN for what it had done at the beginning of the week, the army for what it had accomplished by the weekend.[23] It may be true, as one paratrooper later remarked, that the FLN committed a tactical mistake in calling for a week-long strike; the army would scarcely have had time to react to a one-day stoppage.[24]

Rousting Muslim workers from their lodgings or breaking
in the storefronts of recalcitrant shopkeepers was one thing;
smashing the terrorist network was another. The European
half of the Algiers population had welcomed the paratroopers as deliverers. But the terrorists lived among the Algerian
half, whose loyalties to the established authorities were far
from certain. Patrolling the Casbah's narrow streets, the
paratroopers could not distinguish a member of the terrorist
network from a harmless old lady, a shoeshine boy from an
FLN courier. They found themselves in the position of the
Germans in occupied France, the British in colonial Boston,
the French in the Vendée, the Americans in Saigon. The
virtual sanctuary offered by the Casbah, the silence of the
Muslim population, the elaborate structure of the terrorist
network—withal, the paratroopers had scarcely the slightest
idea for whom they were looking.

Despite the peculiarities of the urban setting, the war in
Algiers closely resembled the war in the *bled* (countryside).
In both city and country, the FLN relied on terror as its main
weapon against settlers and Algerians alike. In Algiers, as in
the *bled,* the FLN used its intelligence advantage to keep a
step ahead of the French. Urban guerrillas ask the established authorities the same question their rural counterparts
ask: Are you willing to continue your rule at the price we are
exacting?[25]

But the cost to the authorities may come higher in the city
than in the country: the ratio of innocent bystanders to combatants is much higher in town. Pursuing a guerrilla band in
the desert makes less of an impression on public opinion than
conducting house-to-house searches in a thickly populated
slum. By sending in the elite of the professional army, the
government signaled its willingness to pay whatever price the
FLN demanded for the extirpation of terrorism in Algiers.

The paratroops liked to contrast the purity of fighting in
the countryside with the disagreeableness of their work in the
city. The desert chase, the mountain hunt conformed to their

idea of the soldier's vocation. Combing a city for persons unknown, they complained, was *un boulot de flic,* a cop's job.[26]

For all their likening of themselves to the police, the paratroops wanted no lessons from them. One police official noted that the army protested its own inexperience and then ignored the advice the police offered. Army officers complained that police officials did nothing but duck their own responsibilities and criticize the military's methods.[27]

The paratroopers laid out their intelligence-gathering apparatus with the greatest of care.[28] The checkpoints in the streets, the barbed-wire barriers and the armed patrols, one regimental commander recalled, were mainly displays meant to reassure the settlers.[29] The army did not expect the terrorists to fall into such traps. It expected to piece together thousands of bits of information to reveal the structure of the clandestine organization, the identities and intentions of its members.

The paratroopers cast their dragnet into every Muslim neighborhood in Algiers. Night and day, patrols moved from door to door, rounding up "suspects"—a word to which the loosest of definitions attached—bringing them in for interrogation.[30] Over and over, intelligence officers put to the smallest fry a single question: "Who in your district collects the organization's funds?" Disclosure of the collector's name swiftly brought his arrest and the question, "To whom do you turn in your money?"[31] And so it went—interrogations followed arrests followed interrogations. Presently the paras overcame the intelligence advantage of the FLN. When the terrorist network lost this edge, it had effectively lost the Battle of Algiers.

Some of the thousands questioned by the paratroops volunteered information; others were forced to talk. Torture was the army's response to terrorism. In a revolutionary war, it has been argued, the one follows the other as the night the day. The army's choice lay between putting an end to terrorism by the quickest and most efficient means at hand or abandoning Algiers to the terrorists and withdrawing from Algeria.[32] The government had decided to keep Algeria French; the soldiers who resorted to torture believed themselves to be meeting the requirements of the government's policy.

This is not to say that the military command ever received from the government explicit orders to resort to such methods. But the authority under which the Tenth Division acted, the Special Powers Law of March 16, 1956, permitted the prefect of Algiers to delegate to the military exceptional authority beyond ordinary police powers.[33] These powers, as exercised in the circumstances prevailing in Algiers in early 1957, opened the door to the practice of torture. It is not hard to see how this happened.

The laws of the Fourth Republic required a suspect to be brought before an examining magistrate *(juge d'instruction)* within twenty-four hours of his arrest. Such a procedure was one of the safeguards against frivolous arrests and illegal detentions. But in Algiers the paratroopers arrested and detained for questioning hundreds of men and women suspected of nothing more than possessing useful information. The key provision of the Special Powers Law, and in some respects the key to much of the controversy over the Battle of Algiers, was the authority to intern suspects, the right of *assignation à résidence.* In effect, a prefecture official's signature on an order of internment regularized arrests to which no judicial authority had given approval.[34]

Requests for orders of internment were to follow immediately on the arrests of suspected terrorists. And the paratroopers were supposed to hand over expeditiously for internment suspects for whom a case for detention had been made. But the Algerians who actually ended up in internment camps could consider themselves fortunate indeed. Those who aroused the army's interest ran the greatest risk when they were in the hands of its specialists in interrogation.[35] Many in the custody of the paratroops, subjected to endless interrogations, found their internment repeatedly delayed. Many never reached the internment camps at all, but disappeared.[36]

The army was far less interested in what eventually became of those it arrested—it cared little for putting people behind bars—than in the immediate exploitation of whatever information the detainees could be made to divulge. Beatings, water, fire, and electricity yielded to intelligence officers the answers they wanted.[37]

By such methods, the paratroops deprived the secret organization of its secrets. They forced the terrorists on the run, discovered their caches of bombs and guns, disrupted the flow of money and supplies, discouraged recruitment, reduced and then nearly eliminated the bombings, shootings, and stabbings that had brought them to the city. In mid-April the army command removed every regiment but one from Algiers.

This move failed to reckon with the regenerative powers of the Autonomous Zone.[38] In the middle of May, a recrudescence of terrorist activity brought the Tenth Division back into the city for a renewed counterterrorist offensive. By mid-September, Yacef Saadi had run out of hiding places. Cornered behind the false wall of an apartment in the Casbah, he gave himself up. A few days later Ali la Pointe, his second-in-command, similarly cornered, chose to be blown up, along with his companions, rather than surrender. By October, according to official figures, the incidence of terrorism amounted to only one action a month.[39]

The terrorist campaign worked as long as the terrorists faced an undermanned and poorly informed police force and benefited from the restraints that civil and criminal law put on the use of state power. The removal of these restraints robbed the terrorists of their anonymity, turned them into hunted men and women, made them informers against each other, stripped them of the protection of their neighbors' silence.

The Battle of Algiers strained the FLN to the limit of its capacities. The army forced the CCE to flee Algiers. The leadership of the revolution changed hands, names, and forms in ensuing years. Having repaired to Tunis, it did not return to Algeria for the duration of the war.[40] Between October 1957 and February 1961, when the settlers themselves turned to widespread terrorism, Algiers was nearly free of political violence.

Success may have cost the French as dearly as failure cost the FLN. The Battle of Algiers was an important step in the paras' identification with the cause of French Algeria. In general, and especially in rural areas, the relationship between the army and the settlers was not a happy one; European farmers tended to regard the army at best as a necessary nuisance and to resent the presence of soldiers in their fields. The soldiers, in turn, thought of the settlers as selfish ingrates. But the Europeans of Algiers regarded the paras as their saviors. The paras, after all, had eased the fear of being shot in the back on the sidewalk, or blown up while sipping an apéritif, and the settlers were not inclined to inquire too closely into how order had been restored. Massu became a special hero, and regimental officers socialized with the settler elite.[41]

In metropolitan France, champions of the hard-line policy echoed the sentiments of the settlers. Such right-wing publications as *Carrefour,* for example, liked to draw pointed contrasts between the efficiency of the paratroops and the ineptitude of the government.[42] The Gaullist *Courrier de la colère* lavished its hysterical brand of praise on the paras. The left-wing press, on the other hand, portrayed the leopard men as a reincarnation of the SS.[43]

The left's image of the paratroops was as farfetched as the right's. The *para démoniaque* and the *para angélique* were telling projections of attitudes toward the war, but neither was a very good representation of reality. And the para-trooper myth may have worked subtle distortions in perceptions of the issues, in ways that traders in the myth could not have intended or desired. The effect of the series of charges against the paratroops may have been to distort the question of responsibility for the conduct of the war: the paratroops were the executants of policy, not policy makers. It was the civilian government that sent the Tenth Division into Algiers with orders to put an end to terrorism by whatever means necessary.

The civilians did not take back the sweeping powers they had handed the soldiers, once the crisis passed. They did not think to close the lid of Pandora's box.

5 Against Torture

On February 9, 1957, at the height of the Battle of Algiers, paratroopers arrested a lawyer named Ali Boumendjel. On the morning of February 12, they found him in his room with his throat slashed. Perhaps Boumendjel had cut it himself; perhaps someone had cut it for him. In any event, he spent the next two or three weeks in the psychiatric ward of a military hospital and was then returned to the custody of the paratroops. Meanwhile, in a series of press conferences, paratroop officers announced that Boumendjel had confessed to furnishing guns and money to the FLN and to distributing propaganda leaflets on its behalf. Yet, despite having this confession in hand, the paratroops did not turn him over for arraignment. The *procureur général*'s (district attorney's) written inquiries as to his whereabouts went unanswered.

On March 23 Boumendjel fell to his death from the roof of the seven-story building in which he had been confined. The official announcement stated that Boumendjel had committed suicide. At the end of March, René Capitant, a well-known Gaullist and former cabinet minister, suspended his lectures in the Paris faculty of law in protest against the mysterious death of his former student.[1]

In the February of Boumendjel's arrest a pamphlet called *Le Dossier Jean Muller* was published in Paris. Muller, a Catholic boy-scout official, had been recalled to active duty in June 1956. In letters home to friends he expressed his dismay at the conduct of the war. He wrote of summary executions of prisoners, of the widespread use of torture, of the deep and unremitting enmity in which the Algerians held the French. Muller promised one of his correspondents that on his return he would devote his energies to "ending this bloody and useless struggle."[2] In October 1956 he was killed in action. But his friends saw to it that his letters got published.[3]

A few weeks after Muller's letters appeared, General Jacques Pâris de Bollardière asked to be relieved of his command. He was the first general officer, and the last, to protest publicly against the army's methods in Algeria.[4] The same month the Catholic Comité de Résistance spirituelle brought out *Des Rappelés témoignent,* a collection of reservists' letters and statements generally critical of the conduct of the war. In March, too, the distinguished critic and novelist Pierre-Henri Simon published his essay *Contre la torture.* In April, *Esprit* printed "La Paix des Nementchas," a reservist's firsthand account of excesses committed against FLN guerrillas by settlers and soldiers alike. In May *Les Temps modernes* issued "Les Jeunes Soldats devant les tortures," a collection of eyewitness accounts.[5]

The rivulet of allegations made since the outset of the war had thus swelled to a flood. "Algeria is ruining the spring," the Catholic editor Georges Suffert wrote. "This land of sun and earth has never been so near us. It invades our hearts and torments our minds."[6]

The charges that made their way into print were only a fraction of those circulating in manuscript. Simone de Beauvoir remembered that ten articles on torture came over the transom at *Les Temps modernes* for every one the journal published. Robert Bonnaud's "La Paix des Nementchas," the editors of *Esprit* pointed out, had been selected from among a great many similar pieces. The editors of *Des Rappelés témoignent* emphasized that their pamphlet contained only a portion of the evidence they had in hand.[7]

The literature on torture and other forms of misconduct

in Algeria was as repetitious as it was abundant. This was especially true of reservists' accounts; most of them consisted of variations on three main themes: the practice of torture, acts of reprisal, and accidents of war.

At length, reservists told what they had seen of the army's uses of the sun, of beatings, of water and deprivation of water, of splinters pushed under the nails of fingers and toes, of lighted cigarettes pressed to the flesh, of bottles rammed into vaginas, of bodies twisted and contorted by means of pulleys and ropes. But the appliance that evidently impressed the reservists most, perhaps because of its ubiquity, was the hand-cranked field generator, or "magneto." Torture by means of electric shock was simple and efficient. It required no elaborate equipment and left no telltale marks; it caused excruciating pain but rarely killed anyone.[8]

Reservists were as dismayed by the shooting of prisoners as by the whirring of the magneto. This practice was known as the *corvée de bois* (wood-gathering party), yet another expression carried over from the Indochina war.[9] French soldiers assigned to the *corvée de bois* took prisoners aside, executed them, and then reported them as having been "shot while trying to escape." Sometimes, one reservist wrote, such reports were made out before prisoners were shot.[10] Sometimes, another claimed, shootings were made to look as if they had been the work of the FLN.[11]

Shootings were occasionally carried out as cold-blooded acts of reprisal. Reservists also reported what they had seen of hot-blooded acts of vengeance. Robert Bonnaud recounted one such incident in "La Paix des Nementchas." At the close of a skirmish with the FLN, Bonnaud and his comrades watched transfixed as a group of settler militiamen moved among the wounded the guerrillas had left behind and emptied their automatic weapons into them at point-blank range.[12]

Reservists reported, too, the same kinds of trophy-hunting and accidents experienced in countless other wars. The practice of cutting off a dead enemy's ears came early to Algeria. Servan-Schreiber's *Lieutenant in Algeria* opens with a truck-load of Algerian miners being mistaken for a band of terror-ists and wiped out to the last man. An artillery barrage mistakenly laid down in the midst of a village; a family of shepherds strafed by a fighter plane; a child cut in two by machine-gun fire—Algeria had its share of the accidental horrors common to twentieth-century wars.[13]

Indignation is not an easy emotion to sustain, and the floodtide of protest against torture, once passed, never reached the same level again. Spring 1957 was the high-water mark. Allegations continued to be made, and the most com-mitted antiwar activists continued to agitate against the army's methods. But the same order of charges, endlessly repeated, lost their power to shock; they became monoto-nous. The American writer Paul Zweig, who lived among Parisian radicals at the time, remembered that around 1960 the "war had long since entered a period of stalemate. On both sides were only victims about whom less and less could be said. The result was a sort of moral numbness which made even death, torture, and humiliation seem boring."[14] Writing in her journal in the last full year of the war, Simone de Beauvoir remarked: "In this sinister month of December 1961, like many of my fellow men, I suppose, I suffer from a kind of tetanus of the imagination. . . . One gets used to it. But in 1957, the burns in the face, on the sexual organs, the nails torn out, the empalements, the shrieks, the convulsions, outraged me."[15]

In the news from North Africa French intellectuals heard the Dreyfus echo.[16] Once again, as at the turn of the century, the French army stood accused of violating human rights. But Alfred Dreyfus, the army's critics emphasized, had been a solitary victim. The Algerian drama counted Dreyfuses by the thousands.

Many Frenchmen heard in the news from Algeria an echo of events much nearer their own times than the Dreyfus Affair. Arrests in the dead of night; the forcible interrogation of prisoners; screams of pain from behind shuttered windows; mysterious deaths and disappearances; an army of occupation patrolling the streets—Frenchmen old enough to remember thought of the German Occupation of France. As early as January 1955, Claude Bourdet, editor of *France observateur,* asked, "Is there a Gestapo in Algeria?"[17] That single hideous word, along with the equally evocative "Nazi," resounded again and again in the writings of left-wing opponents of the war.

Nothing could have been better calculated to embitter the controversy over Algeria. For "Gestapo" and "Nazi" were not epithets to be used lightly. They abraded wounds that had not yet had time to heal. They revived an all-too-recent past, when Frenchmen had chosen sides against each other and sold each other out.[18] Officers who had fought against the Germans in the Second World War heard words for their erstwhile enemies turned on themselves. Men who had risked their lives in the Resistance found themselves compared to their former tormentors. It was, after all, the generation of the Resistance that made policy for the Algerian war, just as it was the Resistance generation that led the attack against it. Men such as Robert Lacoste and Claude Bourdet turned on each other the enmity they had both once borne the Germans and the contempt they had both reserved for the men of Vichy.

The campaign against torture drew on the same techniques and the same forms of expression as the campaign for Captain Dreyfus. Emile Zola, whose "J'Accuse" made the loudest explosion in a battle of the printed word, would have found himself at home in it. Algeria was not the "living-room war" that Vietnam later became.[19] Only in the 1960s did a television set become a fixture of practically every French household. In any event, it would have been extremely unlikely for a government-controlled television network to be allowed to become a vehicle of protest against the war.

The leaders of protest were men and women who lived in Paris and wrote for magazines of the political left. Theirs was a small world.[20] If it is not literally true that everyone in it knew everyone else, many were linked not only by political conviction but by friendship, blood, and marriage. Jean Muller's friends were also the friends of Georges Suffert, editor of *Témoignage chrétien.* The historian Pierre Vidal-Naquet took his friend Robert Bonnaud's manuscript to his friend Jean-Marie Domenach, who printed it in *Esprit.* General de Bollardière deliberately got himself in trouble with his military superiors by means of a public letter to Jean-Jacques Servan-Schreiber, who had served his tour of active duty under Bollardière's command.[21]

As a vehicle of protest, print had its limitations. In the same spirit in which Stalin is supposed to have inquired as to the number of divisions under the command of the Pope, a French police inspector might have asked about the circulation of the magazines of the left. The readership of such magazines tended to be persons who inhabited the Left Bank of Paris, in spirit if not in the flesh: writers, students, professors, journalists, members of the liberal professions, artists, and assorted hangers-on. Their world was remote from much of the rest of France. Nonetheless, an article written and printed in Paris circulated everywhere the mails reached. An important article passed from hand to hand, one copy consumed many times over, especially in the Catholic press. Print gave allegations on torture specificity. Print, giving historical permanence to outrage, endured as proof of the existence of opposition to the army's methods.

The Mollet government charged that "enemies of France"— a code phrase for the Communist party—were orchestrating the campaign against torture. Pierre-Henri Simon retorted that the outcry "expressed the spirit of a culture, not the aims of a party."[22]

This was not to say that protest had no political ramifications. Some protesters hoped the issue of torture might serve to unite the factions of the left, just as anticlericalism had done under the Third Republic. Opposition to the army's methods, they hoped, might serve to bridge profound differences over social and economic policy. But this was to overlook differences concerning the war itself. Some critics of torture contested the aims of government policy in Algeria; others opposed the army's methods and supported the government's aims. Some wanted to keep Algeria French; others favored Algerian independence; still others advocated some intermediate solution.

Of the leading magazines of protest, *L'Express* was nearest the political center. It also had the biggest circulation. Its reporting on the war, chiefly the work of Jean Daniel, who had grown up in Algeria, was extremely well informed. In his weekly column, François Mauriac made some of the earliest allegations on torture against the army and police.[23] But it was the views of Jean-Jacques Servan-Schreiber, the publisher and editor-in-chief, that represented for most of its readership *L'Express*'s position on the war.

Servan-Schreiber was recalled to active duty in June 1956, at about the same time as Jean Muller. Some of his friends believed that the ministry of defense put him in uniform in order to silence his editorial criticism of Algerian policy. At any rate, for six months he went off to war and kept quiet. On his return in early 1957, just as the storm over torture broke, he began publishing in weekly installments an account of his experiences.

Lieutenant en Algérie—half novel, half reportage—became the best known, and probably the most widely read, of all the memoirs on the war. In his own memoirs General Massu blamed *Lieutenant in Algeria* for instigating the campaign against torture.[24] Servan-Schreiber makes much of excesses committed by French troops; he begins with an account of a stupid and horrifying accident (described above) of a kind common to this or any other war. His portrait of the settlers is unflattering, and his assessment of French prospects in Algeria grim.

Nevertheless, he ends up romanticizing the officer corps and sympathizing with its plight. Few officers emerge as villains; it is the settlers who play that role. Despite its criticism of army and settlers and its discussion of some of the cruelties of the war, *Lieutenant in Algeria* does not question whether France ought to remain in North Africa. Servan-Schreiber shared with Germaine Tillion and other liberals the view that social and economic reforms might bring an end to the revolution and leave a place for France in Algeria. Pacification, its excesses removed, might still be made to work. Despite all this, such high-ranking soldiers as Massu insisted on reading *Lieutenant in Algeria* as a stinging attack on the army.[25]

At the opposite extreme from *L'Express* on the terrain of protest stood *Les Temps modernes.* Its clientele had no interest in making pacification work. In 1946, in its first editorial, Jean-Paul Sartre's journal stood with the colonized against the colonizers, for wars of liberation against French rule. No matter how often or how drastically the journal—meaning Sartre—changed its mind on other issues, it remained faithful to its militant anticolonialism.[26]

Sartre and his friends held reformism in contempt. "Colonialism," he declared in early 1956, "is in the process of destroying itself. . . . Our role is to help it die."[27] Nor did they share the liberals' squeamishness about violence. That repression begat terror begat repression was a fact of revolutionary life. Violence on the side of history was justified. As Sartre put it in one of the more bloodcurdling pronouncements to issue from his study:

The native cures himself of colonial neurosis by thrusting
out the settler through force of arms. . . . Once begun, it
is a war that gives no quarter. . . . When the peasant takes
a gun in his hands, the old myths grow dim and the
prohibitions are one by one forgotten. The rebel's weapon
is the proof of his manhood. For in the first days of the
revolt you must kill: to shoot down a European is to kill
two birds with one stone, to destroy an oppressor and the
man he oppresses at the same time.[28]

The French could not escape their role as oppressors
whether they resorted to torture or refrained from it; their
position in Algeria was doomed. The *Temps modernes* group
cared nothing for rescuing the army from lapses of conduct.
The more allegations the better, for in them lay opportunities
for discrediting the entire French enterprise in Algeria.

Despite their differences on the war in general and torture in
particular, *Les Temps modernes* and *L'Express* had something in common: the authors of the first allegations of torture to appear in either magazine were Catholics. Also Catholic was Jean Muller; so were General de Bollardière and
Pierre-Henri Simon. *Esprit* was a Catholic magazine almost
in spite of itself. The "Jeunes Soldats" of *Les Temps modernes* were predominantly Catholic reservists.

Never in modern times had French Catholics figured so
prominently in an essentially left-wing protest movement.
For most of the republican era (since the 1870s), Catholics
had played the role of right-wing outsiders. Enemies of a
republic they had regarded, since the Great Revolution, as
the enemy of the Church and of religion, yearning for the
monarchy they imagined to have been the steadfast defender
of the faith, Catholics had eagerly enlisted in every anti-
republican cause from Boulangism through the Vichy re-

gime. They had a weakness for men in uniform. For Catholics raised in this strong tradition, criticism of the army had been unthinkable. François Mauriac remembered that Catholic children of his generation had been taught to call their chamberpots "Zolas."[29]

The dominant tradition had long provoked controversy. But between the world wars, dissent gathered force—within the hierarchy, in the Catholic youth movement, in Christian democratic (and Socialist) politics, in new Catholic journals of opinion. The progressives sought to reconcile Catholicism with the modern world, to convert Catholics from enemies of the republic to actors in it, to convince them that making the right wing their exclusive political choice enclosed them in a prison, not a fortress.

The dissenters argued that demands for equality and social justice contained nothing incompatible with the teachings of the Church. They urged Catholics to live their faith not only at the altar rail but in the everyday world. These Catholics benefited from the papacy's efforts to reconcile the Church with modern society. To be sure, their interpretations of papal initiatives sometimes alarmed the French hierarchy and provoked its disapproval. And for all the excitement they stirred within the Church, the progressives continued to speak for a minority within the large body of Catholic opinion.[30]

In their youth, writers and journals prominent in the outcry against torture had given this minority its distinctive voice. No journal played a larger role in the intellectual renaissance of the 1930s than *Esprit.*[31] No "Catholic" journal was more vocal in opposition to the Algerian war. In the early thirties, *Esprit* published some essays of Pierre-Henri Simon. A quarter-century later the journal and the writer found themselves still struggling together against what Emmanuel Mounier, *Esprit*'s founder, had called "the established disorder."

More temperate than Zola's "J'Accuse," far surer of the

facts on which it rested, Simon's *Contre la torture* had the same purpose as the most famous utterance of the Dreyfus Affair. As Simon put it, "The knowledge of certain facts obsesses my conscience as a Frenchman; one who is not a writer for amusement or profit, in a spirit of commerce or vanity, but in the service of the mind, must raise above the chaos of events, over the bleatings of the herd, a cry that awakens men."[32]

Simon thought of himself as a patriot, hostile neither to the army he was proud to have served in nor to French rule in North Africa. He knew how profoundly the study differed from the battlefield; he understood how remote were the intellectuals from the soldier's predicament: "Those who are face to face with action are in general absorbed by it, compelled to respond incessantly to challenges which call for immediate decisions and do not allow time for reflecting."[33]

Simon dealt with the soldier's quandary in *Portrait d'un officier,* a long essay written in the form of a dialogue between himself and "Major Jean de Larsan." Published a year after his first essay on Algeria, it reveals a deeper understanding than *Contre la torture* of the moral dilemmas of the war in question.

Nothing in Larsan's long experience as a warrior has quite prepared him for Algeria, where gunmen strike from the shadows and melt away in the crowd. In Larsan's musings Simon posed the central dilemma of the Algerian war.

How to fight, and against whom? We lived surrounded by ghostly enemies. To respond with force, which meant striking blindly, burning a mechta where we thought a terrorist had taken shelter, taking hostages, shooting some at random—this wasn't pretty work, and it didn't solve anything; for the fires of hatred spread between us and the people whose friendship we had the mission of restoring. On the other hand, if we shouldered our arms, if we gave up being cruel for remaining just, our weakness encouraged the enemy and discouraged our friends, and terror

spread. It remained to strike a rough compromise, to com-
bine severity and benevolence, executions and hand-outs,
torture and hygiene; this is what the official style called
pacification and which was really the extension of the war,
in the form of a pitiless struggle between fanatical gang-
sters and soldier-cops.[34]

Taking command of a battalion, Larsan tries to impose his
own rules on the struggle. He outlaws the harsh treatment
of civilians. He forbids the use of torture. Larsan's superiors
assign him a new intelligence officer, Santelli, who abides by
Larsan's edict against torture. The more "interesting" suspects he passes on to divisional headquarters. Larsan goes
along with this subterfuge—at least he has preserved a space
free of torture.

But the war soon breaks in on Larsan's sanctuary. An
important guerrilla leader named Achour falls into the
hands of troops under Larsan's command. The latter
refuses to allow him to be tortured, though he would gladly
have had him shot for acts he is known to have committed
in Larsan's sector. He hands Achour over to Santelli only
on the order of division headquarters. "You can't," he is
told, "accept the principle [of a revolutionary war] and refuse its form. Either don't do it, or do it as is necessary."[35]
Repeatedly his attempts to fight a war he can square with
the demands of his own conscience put him in conflict with
his superiors, and he is at last summoned to headquarters
and told he must choose between the official war and his
own.

In his absence, guerrillas ambush Captain Astruc, Larsan's executive officer, and mutilate his body. In reprisal
Astruc's men shoot up the ambushers' village. Larsan is sped
to the scene of the massacre by his Algerian jeep driver,
Kadour Sahoun, son of a comrade killed in action near
Hanoi. Kadour had joined the French army mainly out of
respect for his father's memory. But he feels torn, as his
father had been, between old loyalties to the French and the

new promptings of Algerian nationalism. The massacre of
Algerians in reprisal for the killing of Captain Astruc drives
Kadour to a choice: ransacking the battalion's arsenal for an
assortment of automatic weapons, he steals a truck and de-
serts to the FLN.

Larsan must hunt down his old friend's son. Kadour is
cornered, but not before he has delivered the stolen arms to
the FLN. He refuses to disclose the whereabouts of the weapons; Larsan, faithful to his old convictions, will not make
him talk. But he turns Kadour over to a military tribunal.
He knows he cannot excuse his actions without betraying his
own sense of justice: "He [Kadour] had believed his duty
required the betrayal of France; from the point of view of his
humiliated and rebel race, he was right; and we were right
to shoot a man wearing our uniform who had turned over
arms to the enemy."[36]

The day he receives the news of Kadour's execution, Larsan resigns from the French army. On his way home from
Algeria he encounters a friend in the railway waiting room
in Marseilles. Once his fellow inmate in a German prisoner-
of-war camp, he listens to Larsan's story as the train carries
them deep into the French countryside.

In his first essay on the war, *Contre la torture,* Pierre-Henri
Simon took the position that in Algeria France had fallen
away from the behavior every citizen of a liberal-democratic
state had a right to expect and demand as a condition of his
own membership in it. France was historically the champion
of human rights, the liberator of oppressed peoples, the civil-
izer of less advanced societies. The use of torture in Algeria
betrayed this tradition and threatened the existence of liberal
democracy itself. For how could anyone be sure that state
agents, convinced such methods had paid in Algeria, would
not be tempted to try them out on the mainland—not only
on suspected revolutionaries but on anyone who happened to

fall into the hands of the police? Perhaps such agents might set out to subvert the political order itself.[37] Perhaps the military police state already established in Algeria might spread to France, where the relations prevailing between state and society in a liberal political system had so far been preserved.[38]

The defenders of liberal democracy not only thought that the use of torture in Algeria might bring irreversible political decay to France; they also feared that exposure to such practices might infect the youths serving in Algeria with a kind of virus deadly to public and private morality. Returning home, they would transmit this virus to the rest of French society. Some feared the Algerian experience might leave some young men so unhinged they would embark on a life of crime and violence.[39]

In *Contre la torture,* Simon held that if France returned to the straight and narrow, then not only would liberal democracy on the mainland be preserved but French rule in North Africa might be maintained. Abandoning the use of torture, France might conduct a humane and successful war. By the time he wrote *Portrait d'un officier,* Simon had changed his mind. He had come round to the position, common in radical circles, that the use of torture was a tactic buried deep in the logic of the war. On this ground, radicals, settlers, and some army officers met. But from their agreement they drew different conclusions.[40] Army officers regarded torture as a necessary means to the necessary end of preserving French rule. Radicals, and some liberals, held that a war that must be fought by such means should not be fought at all. At such a price, France had no business keeping Algeria French. The only alternative to torturing the Algerians was negotiating their independence.

If Jean de Larsan had a counterpart in real life, it was Jacques Pâris de Bollardière. Unlike Larsan, however, Bollardière did not resign his commission and quietly repair to his country estate. He tried to show in the sector under his command that Algeria could be pacified without resorting to torture. But the Battle of Algiers, and its methods, spilled over into his territory. Unable to acquiesce in the use of such methods, unable to extract from General Massu anything but a defense of them, he asked to be relieved of his command. He then sent a letter to *L'Express.* Ostensibly responding to Servan-Schreiber's request for his opinion of *Lieutenant in Algeria,* Bollardière wrote of "the frightful danger there would be for us to lose from sight, under the fallacious pretext of immediate effectiveness, the moral values that alone have up to now made for the greatness of our civilization and our army."[41]

The government could not dismiss Bollardière as one more left-wing intellectual eager to outdo his friends in displays of indignation at the treatment meted out to terrorists. The general had put in nearly two continuous decades as a combat soldier. He had served on the Narvik raid, the fall of France, the Resistance, the final push against Germany; he had done three tours in Indochina. He had been not only a paratrooper but a Foreign Legion officer.[42] He could not be charged with ignorance of the exigencies of war.

For such a soldier to add his voice to the chorus of allegations of misconduct threatened to validate them in circles deaf to the charges of Paris intellectuals. Ignoring Bollardière would have excused a breach of military discipline (by writing to *L'Express* he deliberately defied army regulations) and antagonized brother officers deeply resentful of the epithets hurled their way. Bollardière's letter forced the Mollet government to take action on the issue of torture. Denying the allegations, impugning the motives of those who made them, or suppressing the publications that printed them was no longer enough.

The Bollardière affair divided the cabinet. Maurice Bourgès-Maunoury, the minister of defense, and Max Lejeune, secretary of state for war, wanted the general cashiered. But Gaston Defferre took up for Bollardière and headed off his dismissal from the army. Conceding something had to be done about the general's breach of military regulations, Defferre went along with punishing him in exchange for Mollet's assurances that the allegations filling the left-wing press would be investigated.[43]

For his indiscretion Bollardière received sixty days fortress arrest. Mollet had to appease the army, as well as dovish cabinet ministers, and it is probably no coincidence that Bollardière's punishment equaled that of another general, Jacques Faure. In December 1956 the reckless and flamboyant Faure, known throughout the army as a champion skier and alpinist, had walked into the office of Paul-Henri Teitgen, secretary-general of the Algiers police, announced he was planning a coup d'état, and asked Teitgen whether he wanted to be in on it. Teitgen captured Faure's inquiry on tape and turned the recording over to higher authorities.[44]

Faure had a knack for getting mixed up in harebrained schemes, and his "coup" was probably one of them. Nevertheless, to give Bollardière the same punishment as Faure was to equate plotting to overthrow the republic with publishing an unauthorized letter in the press. Faure's views, of course, were widespread in the army, while Bollardière's were not.

Moreover, Bollardière had gone outside "the family." By publishing his letter in a magazine unfriendly to the military and critical of the government's Algerian policy, he left himself open to the charge of being a dupe. Well intentioned, perhaps, the naïve "Bollo" had been played for a sucker by the gang of unscrupulous reservists, Servan-Schreiber at the fore, who had served under his command in Algeria.[45] In any event, soldiers were left to draw one of two conclusions from comparing the Faure case with that of Bollardière: either sending an unauthorized letter to the press was as reprehensible as plotting against the republic, or plotting against the republic was no worse than writing unauthorized letters to the press.

Lacoste, Bourgès-Maunoury, and Lejeune strenuously op-

posed the inquiry Mollet promised Defferre in exchange for
his support of Bollardière's punishment. Mollet steered a
middle course between the two factions of his cabinet. Defferre got his investigation, but it had no teeth. A communiqué following the cabinet meeting of April 3, 1957, announced the creation of a Commission de sauvegarde des
droits et libertés individuels. Lest the army think the government meant to throw anyone to the wolves, however, the
communiqué assured it of "the nation's gratitude" and denounced a "campaign organized by the enemies of France
. . . who would want to present 700,000 reservists as so many
torturers."[46]

What Defferre had in mind was the naming of a panel of
distinguished jurists, a kind of collective special prosecutor,
to investigate the allegations of torture. But Mollet's commission turned out to be a feeble instrument indeed, appointed by and reporting to the prime minister and resident
minister (Lacoste, who opposed the whole idea), powerless
to subpoena documents or to hear sworn testimony. No one
who had raised the allegations found a place in the inquiry.
Except for the noted criminal lawyer Maurice Garçon, and
another attorney, Jean Moliérac, the commission was composed of high-ranking civil servants. François Mauriac and
Albert Camus refused appointment when they failed to receive sufficient guarantees of the inquiry's independence of
the government.[47]

Pressure from within his own cabinet left Guy Mollet with
no choice but to make at least a show of investigating allegations of torture. The government's more characteristic
response to such allegations was to suppress them.
Throughout the war it freely indulged in what *The Economist* called "squeezing the press."[48] For some editors, visits
from the police became as routine as visits from the mail-
man.

Freedom of the press suffers in wartime. In the early years of the Great War, French authorities virtually smothered under a thick blanket of censorship the legal guarantees of the press. For the most part, editors saw compliance as their patriotic duty. But the Algerian war did not raise the cry of *La patrie en danger!* No government tried to establish a formal apparatus of censorship. But each did its best to prevent the press from publishing certain kinds of information, especially allegations or revelations of the use of torture. Nothing was more likely to invite the attention of the authorities than charging the army with misconduct.

The police most carefully watched the weeklies and monthlies of the left. Save for *L'Humanité,* the Communist party's newspaper, seized twenty-eight times in the course of the war, most dailies either left the issue of torture alone or treated it too circumspectly to provoke the government. But between January and September 1957, the authorities in Algiers seized *France observateur* nearly every time it hit the newsstands. The police also zeroed in on *L'Express, Témoignage chrétien,* and *Esprit.*[49]

"Press seizure" evokes an image of police swooping down on editorial rooms, grabbing copy, and hustling reporters off to jail. The reality was more prosaic. *France observateur,* for instance, appeared on newsstands every Thursday. On Wednesday evening, a police officer picked up several copies of the forthcoming issue at the printer's and distributed them among the prefecture of police, the ministries of interior and defense, and the office of the prime minister. Officials perused them for offending articles. If they found something to which they objected, they asked the prefect of police to confiscate the issue. The prefect sent out officers to intercept *France observateur* before it reached the kiosks.[50]

The authorities seized publications as evidence of their "injuring the army's morale" or "inciting to disobedience," but rarely did they prosecute the journals' authors, editors, or publishers.[51] Putting reporters and editors behind bars interested the government less than harassing them into silence. Antiwar publishers believed the authorities aimed at intimidating them into self-censorship. Every time the government prevented a newspaper or magazine from appearing on newsstands, its publisher lost the chance of recovering the costs of printing. Such tactics served to deliver the warning that publishing articles on torture and other sensitive questions might frighten away advertisers and drive a publication out of business.[52]

The government had an easier time keeping an eye on book publishers than on the periodical press. Until late in the war, large French publishing houses shunned antiwar manuscripts. Perhaps they believed such books would not sell; perhaps they feared that issuing them might result in trouble with the government.

The one imprudent exception was Editions de minuit, which still maintained the adventurous spirit of its Resistance origins. The firm was virtually a one-man outfit. From his tiny office in an alleyway off the rue de Rennes, Jérôme Lindon, the publisher and editor-in-chief, alone decided what manuscripts to publish. After the war he had made Editions de minuit a leading publisher of the literary avant-garde—of Samuel Beckett, Nathalie Sarraute, and Alain Robbe-Grillet. He also kept a hand in politics.

In late 1957 the young historian Pierre Vidal-Naquet brought Lindon some documents he had collected on an incident that had taken place at the height of the Battle of Algiers. A mathematician named Maurice Audin had disappeared from the custody of French paratroops. Vidal-Naquet charged that Audin's captors had staged the "escape" themselves, to cover up their having killed him in the course of an interrogation on his connections with members of the Algerian Communist party.[53] As Audin's fate came to symbolize for antiwar activists the fate of thousands at the hands of the French army, the affair to which his disappearance gave rise bears mentioning in some detail.[54]

On the morning of June 16, 1957, five days after her husband's arrest, Madame Audin, released from virtual house arrest, began to make inquiries about her husband. Convinced she was not getting the truth from the authorities in Algeria, she turned to the mainland for help. In a letter published in *Le Monde* in mid-August, she set forth the circumstances of her husband's arrest, the report of his escape, and the rumors circulating in Algiers that he had been confined in a secret prison.

Despite its appearance in the midst of the annual *vacances,* when every Frenchman who can manage it is far from his usual haunts, Madame Audin's letter provoked a large correspondence. That many letters carried several signatures suggests that the case had provoked considerable discussion. The teachers' trade unions and the League of the Rights of Man demanded an investigation of Audin's disappearance. Jacques Duclos and Pierre Mendès France publicly charged that the paratroops had murdered Audin.

On December 2 more than a thousand persons, including a number of well-known writers and politicians, gathered at the Sorbonne to hear the defense *in absentia* of Audin's doctoral thesis in mathematics. The fact that only a handful were capable of following the discussion hardly mattered; the absence of the author was what counted. The university's display of solidarity with one of its members failed, however, to elicit much response. Jean-Jacques Mayoux, professor at the Sorbonne, lamented in *Le Monde* the public indifference to Audin's fate.

In mid-December *Le Monde* breached the wall of official silence around what had now become the Audin Affair.[55] Guy Mollet's Commission de sauvegarde had been on a tour of inspection in Algeria at the time of Audin's disappearance, and Madame Audin had appealed to it for help. In September the commission submitted to the government its findings on the Audin Affair and other cases. The government did not release this report, as it had promised, and this gave rise to suspicions of a coverup.

But a copy of the commission's report was leaked to *Le Monde*. Its contents do not explain the authorities' reluctance to release it. Zigzagging between condemnation of the FLN and censure of members of the French army, the report betrayed, in both tone and substance, the weakness of the commission's investigatory powers and the existence within it of deep differences of outlook and opinion. Indeed, before the findings were compiled, three of the commission's more liberal members had resigned in frustration at their powerlessness. In the matter of Audin, the report simply laid out the military version of what had happened.

The army's steadfast insistence that Audin had escaped, the government's unswerving support of the army's version of his fate, the leisurely pace of the judicial inquiry into his disappearance, the inconclusiveness of the Commission de sauvegarde's report—all made the prospects of discovering the truth about Maurice Audin's fate seem gloomy indeed.

Frustrated in their efforts to discover what had taken place in Algiers, Audin's friends settled in for the long haul. In late January 1958, some one hundred university and lycée professors, men and women who for the most part had followed the case from the beginning, founded the Comité Audin. They continued to press for an inquiry into his disappearance, but this became a battle of briefs and appeals, carried on behind closed doors and reported, if at all, in the back pages of the press. The energies of the greater share of the committee's members went into campaigning against the use of torture in Algeria. Indeed, insofar as protest had any organization, any structure establishing aims and coordinating the efforts of protesters, the Audin committee was it.

The committee in Paris set to work organizing branches in the provinces. These committees—charged with disseminating literature on the use of torture, organizing local meetings and demonstrations, and raising funds to support these activities—proliferated. But their rapid growth also betrayed their narrow social base. In the main the provincial groups, like the parent committee, were composed of professors and schoolteachers, persons who resembled Audin himself. They had no trouble raising crowds for antiwar rallies held in meeting halls near the universities, but these were exercises in preaching to the converted. The audiences of protest meetings tended to be the readership (and writership) of protest literature.

Indeed, the Audin committees, especially the parent committee in Paris, were more effective as publicists than as organizers of mass protest. The first important publication of the committee, Vidal-Naquet's *L'Affaire Audin,* was issued in May 1958, in the midst of the crisis that returned de Gaulle to power. In the summer of 1957, Vidal-Naquet had written to Madame Audin, volunteering his assistance as a trained historian in getting at the truth. He proposed to compile a small collection of documents setting forth the contradictions in the official thesis of Audin's escape.

Using the scanty evidence available in the fall, Vidal-Naquet wrote a four-page brochure; Jérôme Lindon saw to its printing. But Lindon also insisted that to be taken seriously the book must rest on a wide base of evidence. In early 1958 Madame Audin's lawyers acquired in Algiers a copy of the examining magistrate's dossier on Audin's disappearance, and this satisfied Lindon's demand for more documents.

In March 1958 Vidal-Naquet wrote a draft of *L'Affaire Audin* and showed it to Lindon, who contributed revisions so substantial as to make the book as much his as Vidal-Naquet's. But he declined to put his name on the cover. Most booksellers refused a wrapper promising the lowdown on "Massu and his accomplices," but were willing to accept the neutral-sounding "Massu and his men." Despite the distractions of the political crisis, *L'Affaire Audin* quickly sold around thirteen thousand copies.

L'Affaire Audin was only one of the books Editions de minuit published on the war. Others included Henri Alleg's *La Question,* an account of torture at the hands of the same paratroopers who arrested Audin that became a classic in the literature of protest. The police seized eleven of them, far more than they did from any other publisher.[56]

But the government could have squeezed the press much harder. It bolted no newspaper's doors, smashed no printing presses, left no writers rotting in jail. The authorities feared that the controversy over torture would not only diminish support for keeping Algeria French but further antagonize an already unhappy army. They may have wanted to take sterner measures against critics of the Algerian policy, but they resisted the temptation. The laws respecting freedom of the press were bent and strained but not trampled under.

Assessing the impact of political protest is one of the historian's harder tasks. The views of a handful of intellectuals no more represent those of a majority of the French than ripples on the surface of a pond signify agitation at its depths. But neither can the silence of the majority in the face of the outcry against torture be read as approval of the methods in question. None of the available evidence establishes a link between revelations on the conduct of the war and diminution of public support for keeping Algeria French. But that the controversy over torture stiffened the determination of the French to remain in North Africa would be an astonishing discovery indeed.

Many who raised their voices against torture later regarded their protest as futile. They spoke as if their writings had been messages in bottles, lost at sea unread.[57] It is true that the outcry of the spring of 1957 and later did nothing to shorten the war. Protest did not help bring down a government, as protest against the war in Vietnam helped discourage Lyndon Johnson from seeking reelection. Nor did it even have much effect on the conduct of military operations in Algeria. Torture went on after 1957. And if protest forced Mollet to establish a committee of inquiry into the charges against the army, his government showed that it was not eager to have the committee find out anything.

Despite all this, the protesters made too gloomy an assessment of their achievements. A substantial body of French opinion refused to countenance actions carried out in pursuit of the French government's Algerian policy. Protest against these actions stands as part of the historical record.

The campaign against torture, like the campaign for Dreyfus, was a symptom of the French parliamentary system's inability to resolve a national crisis. In each case, extraparliamentary forces tried to drive the government into taking action, each time with equivocal results. No matter how fervently politicians expressed in private their wish for an end to the war, parliament contained no force, or constellation of forces, capable of bringing about the end. The main antiwar power was a loose coalition cutting across party lines. But like the alliance that had made up the Resistance, the group against the war in Algeria offered no basis for putting together a stable parliamentary majority. What Pierre-Henri Simon regarded as a strength of the protest movement was also its chief weakness: "It expressed the spirit of a culture, not the aims of a party."

6 The Ides of May

The right-wing parties (chiefly the Independents) gave Guy Mollet everything he needed to keep Algeria French except higher taxes. When Mollet asked for a tax increase in May 1957, they refused their support, and the longest-lived government in the history of the Fourth Republic fell. The Socialists still controlled the National Assembly, however, and the new government turned out to be the Mollet ministry without Mollet. Maurice Bourgès-Maunoury became prime minister in a cabinet composed chiefly of Socialists and Radicals. As Mollet's former minister of defense, friend of the army, and scourge of civil libertarians, Bourgès reassured the right. Nevertheless, he squeaked through the vote of investiture by a narrow margin.[1]

Despite Bourgès's reputation for toughness, his Algerian policy departed in no significant way from his predecessor's. Indeed, repression, reform, and discreet "unofficial" talks with the FLN characterized the Algerian policy of every prime minister from Pierre Mendès France on. Mendès France sent troops to North Africa; Guy Mollet sent more troops. Jacques Soustelle drew up a plan for political, economic, and social reform; his successor, Robert Lacoste, declared similar aims. Bourgès maintained Mollet's "tryptich": cease-fire, elections, negotiations (a formula the FLN regarded as designed to exclude it from a role in Algeria's future); he also pursued Mollet's secret contacts with the FLN.

Running true to form, the assembly gave Bourgès-Maunoury the tax increase it had withheld from Mollet. But when he brought in a *loi-cadre* (a "framing," or fundamental, law) for Algeria, the right dug in against him. The government's bill contained nothing very bold or very new: a single electoral college, somewhat greater internal autonomy, a hint—but only a hint—of a move toward a federal relationship between Algeria and the mainland. But the single college, especially, was the settlers' bugaboo. They opposed any electoral system giving free play to the weight of numbers. The bill divided Bourgès's cabinet and forced him into endless discussions with representatives of the major political parties. These round-table conferences did no good; even by going hat in hand to the party leaders, the prime minister could not come up with an acceptable bill. On September 30, 1957, the assembly defeated the *loi-cadre* 279 to 253. Bourgès had not staked his government on the outcome of the vote, but he resigned anyway.[2]

It took five weeks to find a successor, but finally another Radical, Félix Gaillard, became prime minister, at thirty-eight one of the youngest men ever to hold the office. France had been without a government for 58 of the 169 days that had passed since the fall of Guy Mollet on May 21. Gaillard managed to get the approval for the *loi-cadre* that had eluded his predecessor, but only at the cost of cutting out its heart. Promises it made to Algerians were vitiated by guarantees made to settlers. In any event, partisans of *Algérie française* extracted from the government assurances that the *loi-cadre* would not go into effect until "calm" had been restored.[3]

In February 1956, a volley of tomatoes had persuaded Guy Mollet against pursuing his liberal inclinations with respect to Algeria. In November 1957, parliamentary lobbying prevented Félix Gaillard from carrying a strong Algeria reform bill. From the settlers' point of view, these were not so much victories as holding actions. Betrayal might still lie just around the corner.

The settlers were in the predicament another ascendant minority had faced since late in the nineteenth century. Prot-

estants in a Catholic land, the Orangemen of Ulster had
opposed home rule for Ireland as soon as Gladstone came
out for it in 1886. They succeeded in creating a profound
division in English politics, but they could never relax their
vigilance against a home rule bill, nor did they succeed in
keeping the Liberal government elected in 1905 from pressing
ahead with the realization of Gladstone's hopes. When they
won the support of the English officer corps, however, they
were able to bring to bear against home rule the threat of civil
war. In 1914 the Great War intervened, leaving forever suspended the question of whether the soldiers would have
obeyed the King or their consciences.[4]

The Europeans of Algeria needed no history lessons.
Every plotter in Algiers, down to the crackpots and barflies,
dreamed that in a showdown with the mainland, the army
would take their side.

Despite their common interest in keeping Algeria French,
the army and the settlers did not see eye to eye. The infatuation of European Algiers with the paratroops was misleading. An attempt in January 1957 to kill General Raoul Salan,
the commander in chief in Algeria, by means of a homemade
rocket launcher, was as characteristic of settler activism as
an affinity for the leopardmen (the so-called "Bazooka
Affair" remains to this day one of the murkier episodes of the
war).[5] True, the settlers were not all of one mind. In Jacques
Soustelle's integration scheme, for instance, the rich saw a
plan that threatened to strip them of the economic privileges
they enjoyed in mainland markets; the poor saw a counter-
weight to the Algerians' overwhelming numerical superiority.[6] But neither rich nor poor were eager to give up the old
ways.

The army's impatience with the settlers' obdurate resistance to change manifested itself in its commitment to reform
in the countryside. The Sections Administratives Spéciales

(SAS), a kind of military Peace Corps, was the army's main tool of reform. Specially trained junior officers were sent to live among the Algerians. They busied themselves with dispensing medical care, overseeing village construction and irrigation projects, offering advice on improving crop yields, keeping the village school.[7]

While the SAS officers looked after the needs of the population at large, combat units roamed the countryside, dismantling the FLN's political-administrative apparatus. At least, this is how the scheme was supposed to work. The SAS officer in his village and the para regiment in its helicopters were the quintessence of the theory of pacification. In reality, SAS officers and combat units found themselves at odds. In the wink of an eye, paratroops could destroy projects and sympathies that had taken months to build. In any case, it was always hard to tell whether sympathies were real or feigned, whether they expressed the peasants' gratitude for assistance or their fear of the armed men in their midst.

The soldiers did not intend to reform themselves out of Algeria. They envisaged for the army a long-term role as tutor of the Algerian masses and, perforce, protector of the settlers. A minority of them were bent on breaking no more promises, suffering no further humiliations, undergoing no more defeats, enduring no more betrayals, dying in no more lost causes.[8] Their resolve rivaled the settlers' determination to keep Algeria French. But if the settlers needed the army, the army did not need the settlers. Nothing fated them to join forces against the Fourth Republic. But that is how things turned out.

A third party equaled the military and settler activists in strength of will and ruthlessness. For years General de Gaulle's most zealous followers had been looking for a chance to return him to power. In the Algerian crisis they found it. But an important difference distinguished the partisans of *Algérie française* from most of the followers of General de Gaulle: for the Gaullists, *Algérie française* was not an end but a means. In the history of the war this difference came to be decisive.

In the early months of the war, especially, gunrunners slipped easily into Algeria from Tunisia. FLN guerrilla bands made forays across the border from camps in Tunisia. FLN gunners shot at French aircraft from the Tunisian side of the frontier (seldom, if ever, hitting any). As Douglas MacArthur had done in Korea, French generals raged against the enemy's privileged sanctuary and demanded the right of hot pursuit.[9]

On February 8, 1958, French air force planes bombed and strafed Sidi Sakiet Youssef, a Tunisian village known to be contributing to the troubles along the border. A Tunisian antiaircraft battery emplaced nearby had hit a French plane that had drifted across the frontier. Sakiet harbored FLN guerrillas, but on the day of the raid none was in the vicinity. The action killed at least sixty-three Tunisian civilians, including twenty-five schoolchildren. Not a single Algerian was among the casualties.[10]

General Salan, who had himself approved the attack, defended it as an act of reprisal for Tunisian complicity in FLN border raids.[11] Robert Lacoste backed him up. Habib Bourguiba, President of Tunisia, lodged a complaint against France with the United Nations Security Council. The anticolonialist faction of the U.N. General Assembly seized on the Sakiet raid as an example of the perfidy and cruelty of imperialists in general and of the French in particular. In Paris, friends of *Algérie française* hailed the raid as long overdue and called for expanding the war into Tunisia, in order to wipe out the FLN's sanctuary once and for all. Alarmed by such talk, fearful the French might set all of North Africa ablaze and endanger Western interests in the Mediterranean, the governments of the United States and

Great Britain offered their "good offices" in settling the dispute between France and Tunisia.[12]

Félix Gaillard accepted the Anglo-American proposal. The army took his acceptance as another example of politicians jerking the rug out from beneath its feet. British and American negotiators came up with a settlement agreeable to both the French and Tunisian governments. But partisans of *Algérie française* were suspicious of it. The agreement ceded to Tunisia four French air bases—bases the French government had already decided to abandon—but in this concession the settlers saw a humiliating capitulation to the FLN. What, and whom, they wondered, would the government serve up next? One hundred Independents, the most devoted parliamentary champions of *Algérie française,* regarded the agreement as an insult to national honor and a sellout, and withdrew their support of Gaillard. On April 16, 1958, by a vote of 321 to 255, the prime minister lost the battle over the air bases and resigned, thereby bringing on the final crisis in the life of the Fourth Republic.[13]

At first, the tactics of the friends of French Algeria appeared to have backfired. For in the weeks following Gaillard's fall, negotiating with the FLN threatened to become a respectable idea. The settlers discovered they no longer had the votes to ensure that the next prime minister would be a man they could count on.

The "Four Musketeers" of *Algérie française*—Jacques Soustelle, Georges Bidault, Robert Lacoste, and André Morice—were all denied the office. The major party leaders prevailed on President René Coty to exclude Soustelle from serious consideration. Bidault gave up trying to become prime minister when his own MRP party refused to back him. The Socialists announced they would support but not join a cabinet formed by René Pleven; this meant the end of Robert Lacoste's term as resident minister, for no politician could belong to a ministry his party failed to join. And

Pleven's attempt to form a government collapsed when the Radicals refused to back a cabinet that included as minister of defense Morice, whose unswerving devotion to the army had helped get him expelled from the party.[14]

Having shown that the friends of *Algérie française* had played out their hand, Coty called on Pierre Pflimlin, leader of the MRP, to form a government—Pflimlin, who said on April 23 that the time had come to sit down and talk with those against whom France had actually been fighting. To the settlers, this was bad enough. But the announced membership of Pflimlin's cabinet included other liquidators of the empire: Pleven, named foreign minister, had been minister of defense at the time of Dien Bien Phu; Edgar Faure, the new minister of finance, had arranged the Moroccan settlement. Pflimlin had not asked a single champion of French Algeria to join him.

On April 24, in the midst of the governmental crisis, the French command in Algiers announced the execution of three FLN terrorists. In reprisal the FLN shot three French prisoners of war. Word of their deaths reached Algiers on May 9. Activists seized on this as a pretext for demonstrations expressing the settlers' objection to a Pflimlin government. They called for a general strike and a ceremony honoring the three dead soldiers on May 13, the date set for the National Assembly's debate on Pflimlin's investiture.[15]

The Gaullists and the extremist settlers had more ambitious plans. Some army officers were Gaullists; others sided with the settlers; still others kept a foot in both camps. These rival conspirators aimed to confound not only the investiture of Pflimlin but each other.

Since November 1957, a handful of Gaullist agents in Algiers had been waiting for something to turn up. These revolutionary Micawbers had friends in high places. The Gaullist network included Gaillard's minister of defense, Jacques Chaban-Delmas, who provided the cover enabling agents to shuttle unnoticed between Algiers and Paris; Senator Michel

Debré, the most outspoken critic of the regime; and Jacques Soustelle, the most prominent and articulate champion of *Algérie française*. There were Gaullist sympathizers in the military high command, the upper reaches of the administration, and the Army of Africa. They had made important contacts in the settler establishment. Léon Delbecque, eyes and ears of the Gaullist "antenna" in Algiers, had taken into his confidence Alain de Sérigny, editor and publisher of *L'Echo d'Alger*. Delbecque, Sérigny, and others established a Vigilance Committee whose purpose it was to make the political crisis begun by Gaillard's fall the occasion of de Gaulle's return to power.

The Gaullist scenario called for turning popular agitation against Pflimlin into popular clamor for de Gaulle. Committees of Public Safety organized in Algeria would demand the establishment of a Government of Public Safety in Paris. A march on government headquarters in Algiers would end in Lacoste appealing to de Gaulle to accept the leadership of such a government. The army, seeing in de Gaulle's return a guarantee of its remaining in Algeria, could not help but lend its support.[16] And, in essence, this is how the drama unfolded—not, however, without many complications of plot and changes in the cast of supporting characters.

The extremist settlers had written a different finale. The ultras set up a "Committee of Seven," a self-appointed executive board of Algiers extremism. Insofar as fascism may be said to consist of "hard measures by a frightened middle class,"[17] their leanings were fascist. The committee included Robert Martel, the Catholic farmer-mystic; Dr. Bernard Lefevre, an admirer of Portuguese President Salazar and a half-baked corporate theorist; Pierre Lagaillarde, a histrionic ex-law student and reserve lieutenant of paratroops; and others rather less flamboyant. The Committee of Seven aimed to get to government headquarters in Algiers before the Vigilance Committee did, and once there to force the army to choose sides between the insurgent settlers and the established government. Its candidate for power was not General de Gaulle but the army itself.[18]

The events of May 13, 1958, in Algiers have been too well recounted in too many books to tarry over here.[19] At the end of a day-long general strike, a large and volatile crowd gathered at the War Memorial for the ceremony honoring the FLN's three young victims. Elements of the crowd, mainly high school and university students, broke away from the ceremony and headed for the government headquarters building, which lay up a broad stairway and across a huge square from the War Memorial. The riot police who tried to bar their way were withdrawn and replaced with paratroopers, who stood by and watched as the demonstrators battered down the iron gates and surged into the building. The authorities could have easily kept them out.[20]

Once inside government headquarters, the leaders of the crowd took over the resident minister's office. Lacoste, refusing to go along with Delbecque's scheme, had left for Paris days before. The Vigilance Committee turned to General Massu, hero of the Battle of Algiers, and asked him to put himself at the head of a Committee of Public Safety. Massu agreed, telling a press conference the next day he had done so only in order to keep hotheads from spilling blood. Amidst scenes of great confusion, the Committee of Seven managed to get the majority of places on the Committee of Public Safety. Delbecque was named vice-president, but the ultra settlers seemed on the verge of snatching his revolt right out from under his nose.[21]

When word of the takeover reached Paris, the Fourth Republic suddenly acquired new friends. It looked for the moment as if the partisans of *Algérie française* had compounded the mistake they had made in bringing down the Gaillard government—for instead of scaring off support for Pflimlin, the riot in Algiers increased it. By a vote of

274 to 129, the Communists abstaining, he was made prime minister.[22]

Pflimlin acted immediately to deal with Algiers' defiance of the mainland's authority. Orders went out to arrest several right-wing figures (the Fourth Republic was extremely well informed as to the identities of its enemies), to put Soustelle under police surveillance, to bring more military police into Paris. But the cabinet also decided to take at their word Massu's and Salan's assurances that they had agreed to the demand for a Committee of Public Safety only in order to keep things in hand.

The political scientist Philip Williams thinks the policy adopted in the early morning hours of May 14 contained a fatal contradiction. Publicly, Pflimlin upheld Gaillard's conferral on Salan of civil authority in the Department of Algiers; privately, some cabinet members indulged in menacing talk against the army command, and the police arrested two air force generals.[23]

Some accounts of May 13 see Massu as the crucial figure in Algiers; others name Salan. Each played a key role in the unfolding of events. On the evening of the 13th, Massu "jumped aboard a moving train," lending the army's approval to the creation of the Committee of Public Safety.[24] The more cautious Salan might not have made such a snap decision. But May 15, as decisive a day as May 13 had been, was his.

The commander in chief in Algeria found himself in an unenviable position. Algiers suspected him of being Paris's man; Paris thought he might be conniving with Algiers. Salan had certainly gone a fair way toward siding with the revolt, but Gaillard, and then Pflimlin, continued to express confidence in him.[25]

An intelligence officer with decades of experience in the Far East, Salan had made a career of keeping everyone guessing. His reputation as a man of inscrutable cunning, a reputation his poker face enhanced, made him known throughout

the service as "Le Mandarin" or "Le Chinois." The China-
man was said not only to think like an Oriental but to behave
like one. He smoked opium, it was whispered; he had more
confidence in what could be learned from burning incense
before a statue of Buddha, it was said, than from staff reports;
he caressed an ivory elephant on the eve of making important
decisions, it was rumored, and sought guidance from the
movements of white mice running in a maze.

Salan's oriental proclivities had not kept him from becoming the most decorated soldier in the French army, or from
acceding to positions of high responsibility: commander of
the expeditionary corps in Indochina, commander in chief in
Algeria. He had been a loyal servant of the regime—he was
known as the most republican of generals—and had the
bazooka shell that settler extremists fired at his office in
January 1957 found its mark, he would now be remembered
as a martyr of the Fourth Republic.[26]

Not quite trusted by anyone, Salan managed to give the
impression of being on everyone's side. Pflimlin he assured
of his fidelity to Paris, the settlers of his sympathy with their
plight, his military colleagues of his devotion to the army, the
Gaullists of his admiration for the general.[27] On the morning
of May 15, Salan harangued the settlers gathered in the
Forum, the huge square in front of government headquarters. Closing an unremarkable speech with the conventional
"Vive la France, vive l'Algérie française," Salan turned as if
to go. Delbecque stepped forward and whispered something
to him. Salan turned back and shouted, "Et vive de
Gaulle!"[28]

Taken aback by his own audacity, Salan almost immediately denied he had said any such thing. The official transcript of the speech contained no "vive de Gaulle."[29] But it
was too late to stuff the cat back into the bag. At six o'clock
the same day, de Gaulle issued his first public statement since
the beginning of the crisis: "I am ready," he said, "to assume
the powers of the republic."[30]

What if de Gaulle had not replied to Salan's appeal, or had

refused to get involved in the crisis? The movement of sedition, unable to find a capable and determined leader, might have collapsed, sending the fainthearted running for cover and the foolhardy to jail. Pflimlin might have gained heart from de Gaulle's refusal and maintained toward Algiers the hard line he took at the outset. Or events might have taken a less happy turn. Many activists, including those in the army, had no use for de Gaulle, anyway.[31] Some of the colonels might have cast the army leaders in Algiers aside and attacked the mainland, a committee of Francos subjecting France to direct military rule. As it was, the appeal to de Gaulle kept the movement from either collapsing or falling into the hands of military adventurers and their diehard civilian allies.

On May 17 Jacques Soustelle turned up in Algiers. He had given the slip to the police stakeout at his Paris apartment and had made his way to Geneva, whence a waiting plane whisked him to North Africa. Soustelle's arrival in Algiers had two important consequences. First, it forced Salan to choose between Paris and Algiers. Second, the arrival on the scene of the man who was both an ex-governor-general and a leading Gaullist politician helped strengthen the connection between keeping Algeria French and putting de Gaulle in power.[32]

On May 19 de Gaulle held his first press conference in years. He managed to tell Paris and Algiers, the civilian authorities, the army, and the settlers a little of what each wanted to hear and to leave each a trifle disappointed. He committed himself to nothing.[33] The Algiers diehards thought de Gaulle was trimming his sails in order to win acceptance from the hated "system." Their confidence in him was restored only when the Socialists denounced him for attempting to subvert the constitution.[34]

The Communist party declared a general strike on the day of de Gaulle's press conference. Even, however, at the huge Renault plant in Boulogne-Billancourt, stronghold of the Communist-dominated Confédération Générale du Travail (CGT), only 4 percent of the workers went out. In the provinces, most workers stayed on the job. That even party activists failed to bestir themselves on behalf of the republic, or against de Gaulle, showed which way the wind was blowing.[35]

Within less than a week after May 13, then, all the players in the drama had made their appearance on the stage. The settlers rose against the republic; the army sided with the settlers; de Gaulle declared himself ready to assume power; Soustelle turned up in Algiers; a general strike fizzled out; the government wavered between standing firm against Algiers and giving ground.

These circumstances provoked much talk of France's being "on the brink of civil war."[36] Citizens raised this dire prospect as the only alternative to the particular solution they preferred: fidelity to the republic or civil war; pledges to keep Algeria French or civil war; de Gaulle or civil war. Perhaps, as many have maintained, France in the spring of 1958 really did come close to such a conflict.[37] But it is hard to think of who might have taken up arms to defend the Fourth Republic.[38] More likely, the alternative to de Gaulle's coming to power legally was the army's seizing power illegally, or a bloodless coup d'état.

The army did its best to convince the republican leadership that it must choose between a de Gaulle elected by Parliament and a de Gaulle imposed by bayonet. In his press conference of May 19, the general spoke of the events in Algiers as offering the occasion for a "resurrection" of France. "Operation Resurrection" became the code word for the army's plan for an airborne landing on the mainland. Some observers think Operation Resurrection was a ruse, an elaborate stunt designed to panic the republican leadership into calling on de Gaulle. Others believe the planners of the operation meant business, and in the event of Parliament's spurning de Gaulle would have landed the paratroops in France. In any event, the republican leadership never called the army's bluff.[39]

The planning of Operation Resurrection, the work of a small group directed by Colonel Ducasse,* a member of General Salan's staff, began between May 19 and May 22, growing more elaborate as the days passed and the Pflimlin government clung to power "like a mussel to its rock."[40] The main burden of the operation fell to four regiments of paratroops, two from Algeria and two from the military region of Toulouse. Two trustworthy battalions of infantry, some companies of riot police (CRS), of gendarmes, and of *gardes républicaines* were to assist them in overpowering whatever resistance might arise. From its garrison at Rambouillet, the armored group of Colonel Gribius would secure Le Bourget airport, north of Paris, and the military airfield of Villacoublay, to the south. From these airfields the paratroops would converge on the capital and seize such strategic points as the police perfecture, the Hôtel de Ville, the telephone and telegraph exchanges, the Eiffel Tower (which housed the military communications system), the key bridges crossing the Seine, the main roads in and out of the city, and so on. The operation would presumably end in the "installation of a republican government of public safety under the presidency of General de Gaulle."[41]

On May 24, news reached the mainland that paratroops had seized Corsica. The small risk of taking the Mediterranean island was designed to relieve the army of the great risk of assaulting the French capital. The sympathies of most Corsicans lay with Algiers, where many had relatives. The garrison consisted of paratroops who had fought in North Africa. The mayor of Bastia, a Socialist named Jean Casalta, tried to resist the takeover, but he could rally to his side fewer than a hundred like-minded men and women. Everyone else—the army, the police, local officials, the gendarmerie, even the riot police that

---

*The first names of this and a few other French army officers have proved elusive, and these men are therefore identified only by their surnames.

Jules Moch, the minister of the interior, dispatched from Nice—went over to the activists.[42]

The Corsican seizure betrayed the Fourth Republic's helplessness in the face of challenges to its authority. Moch made plans to retake Bastia, but soon found the army would not go along with them. The navy found excuses for not ferrying troops to the island. Salan's press officer, asked what the activists would do if the government tried to retake Corsica by force, replied, "What force?"[43]

Realizing they had lost the capacity to steer the republic safely through the storm, political leaders began preparing for shipwreck.[44] Now the Gaullists seemed to beckon from a welcoming strand, to offer an alternative to breaking up on the rocks of army rule. Politicians who had sworn to keep de Gaulle out at all costs began to see him as a guarantee against bloodshed and military dictatorship.

Some have suggested that Pflimlin himself was to blame for his government's predicament. By pretending that the generals in Algiers continued to be loyal servants of the regime—the pretense Gaillard established—Pflimlin lost a chance to divide the army. Had he denounced Salan, Massu, and the rest as military usurpers, it has been argued, he might have encouraged other generals to present themselves as defenders of the republic. By dividing the army, he might have saved the regime.[45] But this is to suppose that such a tactic could have produced officers eager to resuscitate a republic nearly everyone had given up for dead. As it was, the army was the one institution that remained united, despite severe internal stress, throughout the May crisis.

The army's unity left Pflimlin little choice but to turn to de Gaulle. No other alternative to a military takeover existed, at least none that Pflimlin and his colleagues could swallow. There was some talk of a Popular Front, but it was mainly scare talk; if anything, it had the effect of enhancing de Gaulle's appeal (Gaullist agents were probably not averse to spreading rumors that the Communists were arming themselves).

On May 27, the pivotal day of the crisis, events swung decisively in favor of de Gaulle. In the small hours of the morning Pflimlin and de Gaulle met, at the latter's request, at a house on the grounds of the château of Saint Cloud. Guy Mollet had just sent de Gaulle a long letter expressing his reservations about the general's candidacy. Mollet was especially worried about de Gaulle's refusal to appear before the National Assembly and to state his aims, in the traditional manner of prime-ministers-designate. Both Pflimlin and Mollet, who declined an invitation to the midnight rendezvous, wanted from de Gaulle a disavowal of the Corsican adventure.

But de Gaulle refused to disavow the army (to do so, he claimed, would destroy his effectiveness as an arbiter, a man above all factions in the crisis), just as Pflimlin refused to disregard the constitutional scruples of his parliamentary colleagues. The prime minister was willing to arrange a meeting between the general and other party leaders, but he would not abandon his office except by proper legal means and the customary ceremonies. The two men concluded that they were talking past each other. De Gaulle did not want to make public how far apart they remained, for fear of arousing his more excitable supporters. At 5:00 a.m. the prime minister and the general parted, without setting a date for another meeting.[46]

At midday, de Gaulle's office released a communiqué. "I have begun the regular process of forming a republican government," it said, and called on the armed forces in Algeria to obey the orders of their commanders.[47] Pflimlin was thunderstruck. The communiqué made it seem that he had sold out his parliamentary colleagues, ignoring the conditions they had put on de Gaulle's coming to power. But he resisted what must have been a powerful urge publicly to call the general a liar.[48]

At least three explanations for de Gaulle's communiqué have been put forward. One is that he was stalling for time, seeking to head off a paratroop landing he knew to be imminent in order to be able to keep on talking with Pflimlin.[49] Another interpretation is that he meant to increase the pressure on Pflimlin by showing him that only de Gaulle stood between Paris and the paratroops.[50] A third view is that the general was fanning the flames with one hand and pouring water on them with the other. Just as he knew that the prospect of a military coup d'état might hasten his coming to power, so he hoped to use the prospect of his ascension to delay the triggering of a coup.[51]

How much de Gaulle knew about Operation Resurrection, when he found out whatever he knew, and what he did with his knowledge—the most important question of all—remains uncertain. Some of his admirers see him as rescuing republican institutions from a plot he knew virtually nothing about. Jacques Soustelle, an apostate Gaullist, claims that at least two of de Gaulle's agents, Olivier Guichard and Jacques Foccart, were privy to the planning of Operation Resurrection from the start and kept the general well briefed.[52] In his own memoirs, de Gaulle took such a lofty view of his return to power that the details as to just how the return was accomplished—and just what the army had to do with it— are lost from sight.[53]

The only direct testimony available is that of General André Dulac. On May 27, day of the bombshell communiqué, de Gaulle asked General Salan to provide him with an officer with whom he could review the political and military situation in Algeria and France. Salan sent Dulac, who arrived at de Gaulle's home in Colombey-les-Deux-Eglises the next day. According to Dulac, de Gaulle told him that parliamentary resistance to his accession to power had stiffened; the Socialists, especially, were making trouble. He asked for details on Operation Resurrection, commenting only that he did not think the plan called for enough paratroops. He gave a history lesson on the misfortunes that had dogged regimes illegally installed. The most famous French case was that of Napoleon III, whose resort to violence in the coup d'état of 1851 had crippled his reign from the outset. But if the political parties should continue to block his own return, de Gaulle told Dulac, "then do what's necessary." Dulac took this to mean: proceed with Operation Resurrection.[54]

Dulac's report of this conversation squares with views that Operation Resurrection was no bluff, that de Gaulle knew a great deal about it, and that he was encouraging the army, at least, to think he meant business: he counted on the paratroops sweeping the politicians aside if they did not give way. At the same time, however, he was offering himself to the politicians as a vastly preferable alternative; they could count on him to save the republic from the soldiers.

Whatever the truth in the matter of de Gaulle's complicity —or lack of it—with the army, two things about the crisis are beyond dispute. One is that the general never lifted a finger in defense of the Fourth Republic, a regime he despised. The other is that in the absence of a threat to the government as dire as that of a coup d'état, the republican politicians would never have resorted to de Gaulle. When they made him prime minister, they did so with a gun at their heads. De Gaulle owed his office to soldiers whom he later denounced as "military usurpers."[55] He overlooked what they learned about usurpation in the May 13 crisis.

The issuance of his communiqué of May 27 appeared momentarily to be de Gaulle's first blunder. For if it reassured an army grown increasingly restive over the delays attending the transfer of power to the general, the communiqué stiffened parliamentary resistance. The afternoon of the 27th, the American journalist Edmund Taylor reported, a kind of spontaneous Popular Front—a coalition of deputies of the Communist, Socialist, and Radical parties, the ghost of the grand alliance of 1936—formed on the floor of the National

Assembly.[56] The Socialist deputies and their party executive disapproved nearly to a man of Mollet's dialogue with de Gaulle and voted 112 to 3 never to accept the general's leadership. Pflimlin's party, the MRP, strongly supported his continuance in office. Even the Radicals, despite their reputation for voting in the direction of the wind, wanted Pflimlin to stay on.[57]

On the 28th the old Popular Front might truly have seemed to have risen from the dead. Communist, Socialist, and Radical demonstrators marched from the Place de la Nation to the Place de la République, parade ground of the left, just as in the heroic days before 1936. But their demonstration was a gesture, not a genuine act of solidarity in defense of the Fourth Republic. "Without any illusions," wrote Jean-Marie Domenach in notes made the day of the demonstration, "I shall march behind the leaders of the party of Budapest [the Communists] and the leaders of the party of Suez and Algiers [the Socialists]. . . . They will have brought me out, along with thousands of others, to participate in this dismal parody."[58]

Domenach thought the game was up. In the early morning hours of May 28, long before the demonstrators gathered at their places, Pflimlin found the flimsiest of excuses for resigning. What René Pleven said the night the paratroops seized Corsica remained true four days later: "We are the legal government, but what do we govern? The Minister for Algeria cannot enter Algeria. The Minister for the Sahara cannot go to the Sahara. The Minister of Information can only censor the press. The Minister of the Interior has no control over the police. The Minister of Defense is not obeyed by the army."[59]

"Sirius"—Hubert Beuve-Méry, publisher and editor-in-chief of Le Monde—summed up the views of Pflimlin and a good portion of the republican establishment when he wrote: "Today, right now, whatever reservations one could have about the present, and still more for the future, General de Gaulle would appear the lesser evil, the least poor risk."[60]

President Coty had reached the same conclusion three weeks earlier, when he had discreetly sounded out de Gaulle on his conditions for returning to power. Pflimlin's resignation passed the responsibility for resolving the crisis to Coty, and he took up where the disappointing exchange of May 5–8 had broken off. The president searched for a way of breaking the deadlock between de Gaulle's refusal to appear before the National Assembly and the Socialist party's refusal to make him prime minister under any other terms. A midnight talk between de Gaulle and the presidents of the two houses of parliament was unavailing. On May 29, convinced that Operation Resurrection was no bluff, Coty sent the National Assembly a formal message stating his view that de Gaulle was the only alternative to civil war. If the deputies refused to see things his way, he would resign.[61]

Coty's message stiffened the Socialists' resistance, but the intercession of Vincent Auriol, the party's Grand Old Man and ex-President of the Republic, brought them around. By showing them de Gaulle's conciliatory reply to Auriol's query as to his aims, he managed to convince his colleagues that the general had no intention of establishing a dictatorship. On the afternoon of the 29th, the Socialist deputies met and canceled a resolution barely twenty-four hours old declaring that under no circumstances would the party support de Gaulle's candidacy for office. That evening, de Gaulle went to the Elysée Palace and agreed to form a government.[62]

The crisis was not yet over. Activists in Algiers and on the mainland, fearful that de Gaulle was on the verge of conceding too much to the hated system, itched to go ahead with Operation Resurrection. Diehards in Toulouse urged General Roger Miquel, commander of the military region, to shoot the prefect, the mayor, and the leading newspaper publisher as prelude to putting the plan into effect.[63] General

Rancourt, commander of military air transport, sent a squadron of aircraft from Orléans to Pau to collect the paratroops meant for the landing in Paris; only when the planes were in the air was the order canceled.[64]

De Gaulle emerged from the Elysée Palace without having agreed to appear before the National Assembly. But in the next two days, in the course of meetings in Colombey and Paris with the leaders of all parties save the Communists, he at last yielded on this point. He agreed to present himself and his program to the deputies as had all the prime ministers before him, even as undertaker of the Fourth Republic. The Gaullists kept General Salan on the alert, just in case something went wrong at the last minute. At 3:00 p.m. on Saturday, June 1, de Gaulle entered the assembly he had sworn never to set foot in again. Many Socialists, and many other deputies who had declared not long before that de Gaulle would become prime minister only over their dead bodies, voted for him. By 329 to 224, the Socialists splitting 42 for, 49 against, he was elected.[65]

On May 31, Simone de Beauvoir noted in her diary the remark of a taxi driver: "It's not going to be worse than what we had before."[66] Beauvoir was perhaps too eager to hear the Voice of the People in the voice of the taxi driver, but in this case she may have been right. Not many French were sorry about the demise of the Fourth Republic. So indifferent were they to the fate of the regime that their memories played tricks on them. Barely six months later, more than 50 percent of the respondents in a public-opinion poll believed that the republic had died of natural causes.

As for General de Gaulle, in power once again after a dozen years in the wilderness, not once during the long crisis had he uttered any promises about keeping Algeria French.

7 Self-Determination

An aging politician called on to master a national crisis years after his enemies had written him off: Charles de Gaulle played in 1958 the role Winston Churchill had played in 1940. A more piquant parallel existed in the French past. An old army officer, hero of a previous war, called on as a savior in a time of national emergency and voted full powers by a parliament once dominated by a coalition of the left: Philippe Pétain performed the same role in 1940.[1]

De Gaulle had been Pétain's protégé. The irony of coming to power in circumstances so similar to those that had made his former patron his bitter antagonist surely did not escape so keen a student of history.[2] As if to mitigate the wartime conduct of his erstwhile regimental commander, de Gaulle had written: "Old age is a shipwreck."[3] At the age of forty-nine, he had called on his countrymen to continue the struggle Pétain had abandoned. By 1958 he was sixty-seven, and he confronted the perils of shipwreck himself. He faced a crisis that had destroyed a regime and worn out much younger men.

What he planned to do about Algeria and what he actually did have provoked endless arguments. De Gaulle's bitterest enemies—the army activists, the settlers and their mainland friends—regarded him as a master of duplicity and deceit, bent on a sellout from the moment he assumed power.[4] Pierre Mendès France, former ally, grudging admirer, and relentless critic, thought de Gaulle never had a plan of any kind, but zigzagged from one set of views to another like a butterfly negotiating a flowerbed; in the end, he reached a settlement he could have achieved in his first months in office.[5] The ideologues of the French Communist party saw de Gaulle as the tool of monopoly capitalism, especially of that advanced sector which found direct political control of overseas territory a clumsy, expensive, and embarrassing means of maintaining access to markets.[6] His admirers insist that no one else could have extricated France from Algeria without provoking civil war.[7]

Before turning to the question of what de Gaulle did about Algeria, something needs to be said about what made him the man to whom the French turned in 1958.

Simone de Beauvoir noted in her diary that de Gaulle's "comeback" (she used the English expression, as if she were characterizing a washed-up movie star) had not been greeted with much enthusiasm.[8] The general himself commented on the popular indifference to his return to power. If the French considered de Gaulle a providential man, they did not perceive him as a messiah. Léo Hamon, one of his more analytical followers, has suggested that de Gaulle meant more to more groups in French society, as both symbol of the past and guarantor of the future, than anyone else.[9] He was not quite all things to all men and women—he was no political chameleon—but he managed to reconcile in his person political attitudes that in others would have seemed incompatible.

De Gaulle was first of all the living symbol of France's last great victory. If he spoke of the Algerian crisis as offering France the chance of resurrection, no one needed to be reminded who had led the last resurrection. Anyone who remembered the war years could recall that de Gaulle had brought the nation back from an hour far darker than anything the Algerian problem seemed to portend.

Many army activists regarded the resort to de Gaulle as a sellout to the system; they would have preferred military rule, or the rule of a civilian politician more obviously sympathetic to the cause of *Algérie française*. But in 1958 the officer corps as a whole was probably less determined to keep Algeria French than to avoid another defeat. And de Gaulle was the man who had refused to accept the most disastrous defeat in the country's history. This went far toward over-coming the soldiers' lack of sympathy for him.

Other politicians might have won a following among army and settlers. But only de Gaulle, Hamon maintains, could have gained their support without losing the endorsement of republicans. The general was, as he had boasted, the man who had restored the republic to France. The left, which had no candidate of its own—the Communists were not trusted, the Socialists had discredited themselves—would have ac-cepted no one else with the backing of the troublemakers in Algiers. De Gaulle's immense prestige as the Liberator; his reputation as the man who refused to accept defeat; his acceptability to soldiers, settlers, and republicans alike; his stance above the parties; his freedom from association with discredited policies—all made him the one man who could "immolate a regime without killing Frenchmen."[10]

In *Le Renouveau,* the first (and, as it turned out, the last) volume of his second set of memoirs, de Gaulle published his own version of his intentions, actions, and accomplishments with respect to Algeria. He did not endow himself with the prescience hagiographers accord him, but he did claim to have in mind a plan of action, and this is more than his critics and his more skeptical biographers are willing to concede him.[11]

In speeches of the war years and his time in the political wilderness, de Gaulle repeatedly raised the need for social and economic reforms in the overseas territories and for change in their political relationship with France. But he just as steadfastly insisted on maintaining French sovereignty over them. His famous address at the Brazzaville conference of 1944 contained this double-edged quality. It is true that he spoke of reforms. But it is also true, as Xavier Yacono has pointed out, "the ideal still remained that a French African would one day become an African Frenchman."[12]

The reforms de Gaulle undertook in the empire as head of the provisional government drew on the old compensatory theory: despite France's weakened and dependent status in Europe, the nation still had sufficient gravitational force to keep colonial possessions orbiting around it. The empire both proved and guaranteed France's status as a great power.[13]

When these possessions sought to end their status as moons of the French planet, de Gaulle had a hand in trying to stop them. In March 1945 he offered the Vietnamese a vaguely defined political and economic autonomy within a federal framework, choosing to ignore the fact that the Japanese had just broken France's hold on Indochina. In September French emissaries conceded to the Vietnamese nationalists much less than they had already taken for themselves. Three years later, with Indochina deep in war and de Gaulle out of office, he announced in a press conference: "We must take our time. We must stick it out. Why should we be in such a hurry?"[14] In February 1949 he issued a communiqué blaming the deteriorating military situation in the Far East on the government's "demagogical abandonments."[15] That fall, asked in yet another press conference for his position on the war, de Gaulle replied, "France must stay in Indochina. She must stay there for the sake of Indochina, for without the presence and assistance of France, the independence, security and development of Indochina would be compromised."[16]

Still, what French settlers elsewhere might have done well to notice was not how stubbornly de Gaulle insisted on France's remaining in Indochina but how suddenly he stopped insisting. Unlike some of his followers, he believed in abandoning lost causes, not in promoting them. In a press conference held in the early spring of 1954, a month before the fall of Dien Bien Phu, de Gaulle remarked, "In the interest of international détente, and in view of the losses and destruction inflicted on the French Union, especially in Indochina, France must attempt to end the war."[17]

Of course, ending the war in Indochina was a matter of cutting losses to the French Union, amputating a limb in the interests of saving a life. De Gaulle consented to yielding French rule in Southeast Asia for the sake of maintaining it elsewhere. He gave no sign in 1954 of doubting what he had said in Bordeaux in the spring of 1947: "For us, in the world such as it is and as it is going, to lose the French Union would amount to a decline that could cost us our independence. To keep it and to make it live, is to remain great and, consequently, to remain free."[18]

And of all the lands of the French Union, none was more essential to the safety and well-being of France than Algeria. De Gaulle subscribed to the Lockean notion of such nineteenth-century liberal exponents of empire as Prévost-Paradol that the French had "created" modern Algeria by the sweat of their brows. Hence the land was rightfully French. In August 1947, commenting on the statute then before the National Assembly, he insisted that "France, whatever happens, will not abandon Algeria. . . . Despite the intrigues of those who don't play her game, or the spirit of abandonment of a few illusionists, France, of which Algeria is an integral part, is at bottom resolved to assure herself the progress of all her children, while remaining mistress of her own house."[19] On the eve of the municipal elections of October 1947, de Gaulle warned Algerian nationalists—"separatists," he called them—against agitating for independence. "Any policy," he said, "which . . . would have the effect of reducing here the rights and duties of France, or else of discouraging inhabitants of metropolitan origins, who were and who remain the yeast of Algeria, or, finally, of giving Muslim Frenchmen to understand that it would be permissible to separate their destiny from that of France, would in truth only open the door to decadence."[20]

No wonder so many settlers assumed de Gaulle was their man, although once the general withdrew to Colombey in 1953, he had little to say about Algeria. But some of the most ardent partisans of *Algérie française* were taken to be his close associates: Jacques Soustelle and Michel Debré for two. From the rostrum of the Council of the Republic (Senate), in the pages of his rabble-rousing weekly, *Le Courrier de la colère,* Debré pushed in a shrill, self-righteous, and divisive voice Soustelle's themes. In the years before coming to power, the general did nothing to dispel the assumption that Debré spoke for him.

But neither did de Gaulle try very hard to scotch rumors that he had taken a more liberal position on Algeria than that of any of the Gaullists. For years, visitors to Colombey or the general's Paris office on the rue Solférino went away thinking they had heard him express doubts as to the wisdom, necessity, or possibility of keeping Algeria French. When Edmond Michelet, an early Resister and later a cabinet minister of the Fifth Republic, saw de Gaulle in February 1955, he recalled that the general had said to him: "Algeria? Lost. Finished." Mohammed Masmoudi, Tunisian ambassador to France, believed that when he visited de Gaulle in 1956, he had already made up his mind on the main outlines of the Algerian policy he later carried out. In October 1957 de Gaulle confided to Christian Pineau, foreign minister in Mollet's cabinet, that he regarded the independence of Algeria as "ineluctable." The journalist and historian J.-R. Tournoux reported that in a conversation of January 1958, de Gaulle said, "Algeria has a destiny, she has a calling. If the Algerians vote, they'll all vote in favor of independence. I don't know a single Algerian who thinks the future of Algeria lies with France." In April 1958 he told the Austrian journalist Arthur Rosenberg, "Certainly, Algeria will be independent."[21]

In the 1940s de Gaulle insisted on the need to keep the tricolor flying: yes to reforming the overseas territories; no to surrendering French sovereignty. In the 1950s he hinted to a long succession of visitors that he had changed his mind. Roger Stéphane was no doubt close to the mark when he suggested: "General de Gaulle wants to present himself as a new man, free, a prisoner of nothing, not even of what he said before."[22]

A new man, a prisoner of nothing, had the best chance of attracting wide support within the French political establishment; Mendès France taught that lesson in 1954. Many who were willing to accept de Gaulle's leadership on Algeria wanted to have nothing to do with each other. Most of the Gaullist faithful may have been pro-*Algérie française*.[23] But a prominent study group of liberal politicians, high civil servants, and trade-union officials looked to de Gaulle to intervene in favor of a policy of decolonization.[24] Caught in the middle of this tug of war, de Gaulle could lean neither to one side nor to the other without toppling a row of potentially useful allies. Only when he had power could he afford to alienate the faithful and the opportunistic alike.

De Gaulle seldom dissembled for dissembling's sake. He never concealed his aims in returning to power. In countless speeches, press conferences, and interviews he reiterated, between 1946 and 1958, the same handful of themes, which he recapitulated in the famous statement of May 15, 1958, when he announced his readiness to assume the powers of the republic: "The decline of the state infallibly brings about the alienation of associated peoples, discord in the army in combat, national dislocation, the loss of independence. For a dozen years France, at grips with problems too formidable for the regime of parties, has been engaged in this disastrous process."[25] All the calamities that had befallen France could be laid to the decline of the state.[26]

By "state" de Gaulle meant not only the apparatus of public administration but the ensemble of public institutions —the executive, the legislature, the judiciary, the armed forces. Under the Third and Fourth republics, Parliament had assumed both executive and legislative functions, leaving the president to name prime ministers, open flower shows, and mind his own business. De Gaulle wanted a president who not only reigned but governed.

His government, he told the National Assembly on June 1, 1958, would need full powers for six months to set things in order; then such extraordinary procedures could be dispensed with.[27] But only constitutional reform could get at the heart of the difficulties. Reforming the state was a means to the end of "une rénovation profonde." For years in public, in private conversations, in his war memoirs he had addressed himself to this theme. It was widely anticipated that on returning to power de Gaulle would demand a constitutional reform strengthening the executive power. He was bent on restoring France's independence, prestige, and prosperity. "Let us take the century as it is," he said at Bayeux in 1946.[28] Let us not fly in the face of realities, he meant. Let us recognize the requirements of the times, and tailor our national ambitions and policies accordingly.

Insofar as his words and deeds offer clues to the direction of his Algerian policy, they reside in the priorities he established in the relations he saw between one set of questions and another. In his declaration of May 15, he said nothing of Algeria. Opening his press conference of May 19, he named Algeria as one among several problems the "régime des partis" had shown its incapacity to resolve. Closing the conference, he answered a question no one had asked, turning again to the theme of renewal, the theme of Bayeux, and dozens of other speeches. France faced a grave crisis in a dangerous world. But the nation also had good reasons for optimism about the future—a high birthrate, a growing economy, advances in technology, the discovery of oil in the Sahara. "These facts in our case can tomorrow permit a real French renewal, a great French prosperity."[29]

De Gaulle's chief purpose in returning to power was to

endow France with institutions strong enough and durable enough to enable the nation to meet the challenges of modern times. Every problem of the moment had to be seen in light of this long-range goal. If some means of maintaining the ties between France and North Africa could be worked out, well and good. If Algeria became an insurmountable obstacle to achieving his overriding aim, some other solution would have to be worked out.

In the early days of his rule, de Gaulle had over his predecessors the distinct advantage of not having the Gaullists in opposition. Michel Debré no longer hectored the government from his bench in the Senate or attacked the republic from the pages of *Le Courrier de la colère;* he was helping to write the constitution of the new republic, and soon he became its first prime minister. Jacques Soustelle, deliberately excluded from any ministerial post having to do with Algerian policy, maintained a discreet and watchful silence. The National Assembly was prorogued until the end of 1958. Even so, deputies who had given way to de Gaulle because they despaired of resolving the Algerian crisis would probably not have made trouble for him had Parliament stayed in session. Polls showed that de Gaulle enjoyed much greater public support than any of his Fourth Republic predecessors.[30]

Despite these advantages, de Gaulle's hands were full; some of the circumstances that had left the Fourth Republic defenseless could have been his own undoing, had he not attended to them.

First of all, he could not allow the army to remain a state within a state. Everything in his temperament and in his experience as a career soldier warned him against leaving the army the enormous powers that had fallen (and been pushed) into its hands. De Gaulle watchers of the late 1950s might have profited from reading the de Gaulle of the early 1920s.

As a prisoner of the Germans in the last two years of the Great War, the young lieutenant passed his time reading the German press and collecting notes for his first book, *La Discorde chez l'ennemi* (1924). He blamed the German defeat and the collapse of the German empire on the wartime encroachment of military on civilian authority.

It was one thing to believe in the principle of civilian supremacy over the military; it was another to enforce the principle in circumstances that had swung so far the other way. Many senior officers showed no sign of desiring to relinquish the powers and responsibilities they had assumed in Algeria. Nor were the younger officers—the majors, captains, and lieutenants—eager to give up the freedom of action such measures as the Special Powers Law had bestowed on them. But de Gaulle moved at once to retrieve from the soldiers their de facto rule of Algeria.

First, he carried out a reorganization of the upper reaches of the Algerian administration and of its relationship to the mainland government. He wanted no more Lacostes siding with Algiers against Paris. The new government reduced the proconsular "resident minister" to the noncabinet status of delegate-general. Henceforth Algerian policy would be made in the Elysée Palace. And to the office de Gaulle appointed not a politician but a career civil servant, a financial expert named Paul Delouvrier.[31]

Among the new delegate-general's duties was cutting the army down to size by restoring to civilians the administrative responsibilities that had fallen to army officers. Whenever possible, the civilians chosen were Algerians. De Gaulle's men scoured the country for Algerians qualified to undertake high civil-service posts. Algerian army officers, a fairly rare commodity even in 1958, were prevailed upon to resign their commissions and take on civilian administrative jobs.

The new regime resorted to an old remedy in dealing with military troublemakers. After the events of May 13, army officers by the hundreds found themselves reassigned to garrisons on the mainland and in Germany, or to duty as "technical advisers" elsewhere in Africa. In such posts, it was thought, hotheads would cool off, or at least keep out of mischief, and avoid the more drastic disciplinary measures that could leave careers in ruins. Many officers had joined the extralegal Committees of Public Safety that had proliferated in Algeria in the wake of May 13. In October 1958 de Gaulle ordered them to resign from the committees. His conception of duty required an officer to have only one set of loyalties.[32]

No soldier in Algeria was more powerful than Raoul Salan, and after May 13, his loyalties became suspect. Having hesitated so long between Paris and Algiers, he had finally chosen Algiers. Perhaps the acclamations of the settlers had turned his head. At any rate, his choice began to show in his questioning of directives sent from Paris. In December 1958 de Gaulle eased him out, naming Maurice Challe commander in Algeria and Salan military governor of Paris, a post full of honor and empty of duties.[33]

Challe, at fifty-three a youngish air force general, had a reputation as a gifted and energetic tactician as well as an able administrator. But from the beginning he and de Gaulle seem to have misunderstood each other. Challe assumed de Gaulle wanted a military victory over the FLN for the purpose of keeping Algeria French.[34] De Gaulle probably had the more limited aim of making sure the FLN could not inflict on the French a military reversal significant enough to impinge on diplomatic negotiations.[35]

After all the talk of *guerre révolutionnaire,* all the articles on winning hearts and minds, all the insistence on putting aside outmoded conceptions of warfare, the Challe offensive used tactics that Père Bugeaud, the nineteenth-century conqueror of Algeria, would have recognized. True, helicopters gave small-group operations a mobility surpassing anything seen in previous wars. But helicopters aside, Challe's offensive resembled the campaigns of the 1840s against Abd El Kader. The troops of the *quadrillage* kept up their guard and patrol duty, blanketing the countryside with their numbers and discouraging large-scale enemy attacks. In the meantime, the troops of the "General Reserve"—chiefly the paras of the 10th and 25th divisions and other elite units—conducted sweeps the length and breadth of Algeria. "Operation Steamroller," code name for one such sweep, conveyed the French intention.[36]

Indeed, such operations did the ALN serious damage. After 1959 guerrilla bands did not appear in the countryside in units larger than company size, or roughly eighty men.[37] This was a far cry from the experience of the Vietminh, who sent divisions—thousands of men at a time—against the French.

The success of the Challe offensive encouraged de Gaulle's critics to charge that he wasted a grand opportunity. A little more patience, they contended, and the army would have destroyed the FLN's capacity for continuing the war.[38] But demonstrating that the FLN could not put units of more than eighty men in the field is not the same thing as proving it was close to giving up. By reverting to hit-and-run terrorism the FLN could have continued making life miserable for French and Algerians alike, despite its lack of organized military forces.[39]

The Gaullists have never liked to recognize continuities in the Algerian policies of the Fourth Republic and the Fifth, but many existed. Military repression plus social and economic reform—the policy known as pacification—had been supported by every prime minister of the Fourth Republic save Pflimlin, who scarcely had time to announce a policy. The policy remained de Gaulle's during his first fifteen months in office.

The Challe offensive amounted to the war's most ambitious strategy of repression. The "Constantine Plan," announced in that city on October 3, 1958, represented a more

sweeping program of social and economic reform than anything de Gaulle's predecessors had undertaken. Nevertheless, the plan subscribed, just like the Soustelle Plan, to Germaine Tillion's notion that the Algerian problem was
essentially a problem of economic underdevelopment, a mil-
lennial poverty worsened by the long French presence.[40]

The plan was the work of technocrats filled with enthusiasm for the science of developmental economics. Some may
even have believed that furnishing Algerians plowshares and
pruning hooks would be enough to force the FLN into dropping the sword. It was envisaged that by 1964 a plentiful
energy supply—oil and gas from the Sahara—would fuel the
heavy industry that Algeria had always lacked. In five years
the state would erect housing for one million people. The
plan provided for a vast program of road building, port
dredging, and rural electrification. Algerians of both sexes
would at last be sent to school in large numbers. The agricultural sector would be propelled from the fourteenth century
into the twentieth.[41]

Sometimes de Gaulle talked as if he shared the technocrats' faith in the miracle-working powers of the Constantine
Plan. Three weeks after the Constantine speech, on the eve
of elections to the new National Assembly, he held his first
press conference since coming to power. "Insofar as the
economy develops," he suggested, "political solutions [will]
take shape."[42] But later he made it plain that political and
military questions overrode everything else. For in this press
conference of October 23, 1958, de Gaulle chose to direct his
first overture to the FLN.

The FLN's struggle, he said (without mentioning the organization by name), had become pointless. Little by little, the
French army was getting the upper hand. The time had come
for a "peace of the brave." In the old days warriors had used
a white flag to signify their willingness to lay aside their arms
and explore the possibilities for a truce. De Gaulle assured
the internal leadership that such a gesture would be well

received. If the external leaders wanted to talk, they had only to get in touch with the French embassies in Tunis or Rabat, and de Gaulle would assure them a safe conduct from North Africa to Paris and back.[43]

The "Peace of the Brave" declaration made de Gaulle the first French leader since the insurrection had broken out to describe the FLN as something more than a gang of cutthroats and assassins. But the revolutionaries did not respond to his respectful treatment. They chose to interpret de Gaulle's white flag as a flag of surrender, not of negotiation. After a few days of silence the FLN announced that de Gaulle had given it only the chance to abandon its aims. Nearly another year passed before the general sent another signal to the FLN, or to the Gouvernement provisoire de la République algérienne (GPRA), as the leadership henceforth called itself.

The change of initials was meant to signify the transformation of a revolutionary movement into a government-in-readiness. The change was accompanied by a shuffling of the leadership. Ferhat Abbas, having aligned with the FLN in 1956, brought his prestige and his reputation for reasonableness to the presidency of the GPRA. The rest of the leadership agreed on little else but making Abbas president, and this lack of cohesion complicated French attempts to reach a settlement. The leaders' disagreements may have caused their rejection of de Gaulle's invitation to come to Paris for talks; some were as suspicious of each other as they were of the French.[44]

As 1959 wore on, de Gaulle held to the course he had plotted in the Constantine speech and in the appointment of General Challe. He reiterated the need for France to transform Algeria economically as vigorously as it prosecuted the war. But he did not say where he thought all this effort should, or would, end. His actions in the early months of 1959 confirmed the historian Charles Morazé's view that de Gaulle's only maxim was not to promise too much and not to commit himself to anything.[45]

De Gaulle himself described 1959 as a year "spent in gaining ground."[46] During these months of intense military and administrative activity, nothing much happened politically, which encouraged widespread speculation. Raymond Aron, whose hunches were often sound, supposed that de Gaulle hoped to find some kind of formula midway between the integration dear to the army and the independence dear to the GPRA.[47] "Association," to which Edmond Michelet also thought de Gaulle to be partial, had the advantage of being a protean concept; it could be molded into many shapes and structures, from the close embrace envisaged at Brazzaville to the loosest of formal ties.[48] Elements of the left harbored dark fears and suspicions. They suspected de Gaulle of looking for some way to hang on in Algeria; they feared he might lose in a showdown with the army.[49]

If de Gaulle's public comments on Algeria were utterances of Delphic ambiguity or generalizations of unfathomable meaning, his remarks to close associates—but not all close associates—were plainspoken. The recollections of Bernard Tricot are invaluable for the light they cast on the evolution of the general's intentions with respect to Algeria. A career civil servant and specialist in North African affairs, Tricot was appointed in June 1958 to the newly established general secretariat for Algerian affairs. In this capacity he became de Gaulle's chief adviser on Algeria. Tricot does not claim to know de Gaulle's innermost thoughts; he notes only what he saw and heard and the impressions he formed on the basis of his frequent contacts with him.

By August 1958, Tricot was convinced that de Gaulle was as unsympathetic to the idea of integration as he was. In March 1959 the general told Tricot and a military aide that Soustelle's scheme would not work.[50] The same month he publicly reduced the formula dear to army and settlers to just another slogan: "I doubt anyone really thinks that peace and prosperity can suddenly reign on an anguished Algeria, that it really suffices . . . to shout some slogan against some other slogan in order for all interior and exterior grounds for the war to disappear as if by magic."[51]

In August 1959, de Gaulle repaired to Colombey for his first vacation since taking office. The communiqué following the cabinet meeting of August 12, on the eve of his leaving Paris, disclosed that the president had taken part in a discussion dealing with "the Algerian problem as a whole," a signal alerting public opinion to expect an important announcement.[52] In this month of contemplation and decision, de Gaulle asked his ministers for their written opinions on the Algerian problem. Tricot and the other Algerian experts prepared a lengthy memorandum and submitted it to de Gaulle before the cabinet meeting of August 26. The memorandum addressed itself to the question of a cease-fire. An army study envisaged the surrender of a thoroughly beaten enemy. But were the FLN to suffer the military collapse the army meant to provoke, the question of a cease-fire would be beside the point: the guerrillas in the field, demoralized and beaten, would lay down their weapons and seek to work out with the French commanders the best deal they could.

Suppose the FLN kept its forces in being, Tricot's group asked, and fought the French army to a draw—unable to achieve victory but undefeatable, and still capable of keeping up a low level of terrorism. As the GPRA was not the government of a state in being (whatever its claims), it had none of a state's traditional preoccupations or responsibilities with respect to territory or population. Fear of losing lives or property at an unacceptable rate would not press it to ask for a cease-fire. France must recognize, the memorandum concluded, that the revolutionaries had nothing to lose. Only if the GPRA believed it had a fair chance of winning politically what it could not win by violence would it find a cease-fire attractive. Whatever impression this memorandum made on de Gaulle, he soon moved to establish circumstances that would either tempt the FLN to negotiate or leave it out in the cold.[53]

At the end of August 1959, de Gaulle visited Algeria for

the first time since he had become president. The ostensible purpose of the trip was to check on the progress of the Challe offensive, but everywhere he went he took his own soundings of Algerian opinion, and nearly everyone able to speak frankly spoke of the desire for independence.[54]

On September 16, de Gaulle delivered his self-determination address. The speech was artfully contrived to create the impression that each step he had taken thus far led to the steps he now proposed to take. The Challe offensive was well on the way toward reestablishing order. The creation of a *collège unique* and the extension of voting rights to all adult Algerians had established the conditions of political equality. The Constantine Plan had already produced encouraging results.

Now the time had come for Algerians to decide on their own future. De Gaulle offered them three alternatives. The first was independence, or what he chose to call "secession." "Secession," he said, "would lead to a dreadful poverty, a frightful political chaos, generalized murder, and soon, the political dictatorship of the Communists." Furthermore, in this case France would be obliged to retain the oil of the Sahara for itself. The second choice was "Frenchification." The ugliness of the neologism betrayed de Gaulle's distaste for this alternative. Frenchification meant the same thing as integration: the Mediterranean would become a watery divide between the two halves of a greater France stretching from "Dunkirk to Tamanrasset."

Third, Algerians might decide to remain associated with France. Such a choice would mean the "government of Algerians by Algerians." France would take a hand in economic development, defense, and the conduct of foreign relations. Internal relations would rest on a federal structure designed to enable the diverse communities of Algeria to get along together.[55]

The number of alternatives de Gaulle offered the Algerians mattered far less than his offering them a choice at all. By embracing the principle of self-determination, he committed

France to a new course. In the nearly five years that had elapsed since the outbreak of the insurrection, no one in a position of authority in France had said the Algerians should decide their own future. Declaring that "the political future of the Algerians depends on the Algerians" conceded what no French political leader before him had been willing—or thought himself able—to concede: established by the force of arms, French rule in Algeria might be disestablished by the weight of numbers.

8 Barricades and Manifestos

The day after Christmas 1959, General de Gaulle composed a handwritten memorandum on the Algerian question. He reviewed the advantages the French held over the revolutionaries: crushing material superiority; officers and noncommissioned officers "incomparably better trained than the illiterates of the insurrection"; a much lower casualty rate; a vastly superior propaganda apparatus; an influence in world politics beyond comparison with that of the FLN. "It is perfectly true," he went on, "that our crushing military superiority is putting an end to the greater part of the [guerrilla] bands. But, morally and politically, it is less than ever toward us that Algerian Muslims are turning. To claim they are French, or that they want to be, is a dreadful mockery. To delude oneself with the idea that the political solution is integration or Frenchification, which is and can only be our domination by force—what the people in Algiers and a number of soldiers call *l'Algérie française*—is a lamentable stupidity. . . . It is simply mad to believe that our forced domination has any future whatsoever." De Gaulle sent a copy of this memorandum to a senior army officer with whom he had just clashed over Algerian policy.[1]

What would have happened if he had said the same thing in public in his New Year's address just a few days later? Would the army have immediately revolted against him, risen in fury against this "betrayal"? Or would it have been grateful to be told, after years of weak and vacillating leader-

ship, precisely what it must do in the service of an unambigu-
ous policy? Some critics think de Gaulle squandered the
army's eagerness to be led and the French people's desire to
have done with the war in a time-consuming and ultimately
futile search for a better deal.[2]

Between 1959 and 1962, de Gaulle's Algerian policy enjoyed the support of never fewer than two out of three mainland Fre ̣ ̣h. This figure scarcely varied from one sounding
of opinion to the next, no matter what the circumstances of
the moment. The turbulence of events in these years and the
purposeful ambiguity of many of the general's public statements suggest that supporting de Gaulle's Algerian policy
really meant trusting de Gaulle to work out a satisfactory
solution. Weary of the struggle, two-thirds of the French
were willing to follow wherever de Gaulle led them, so long
as he continued in the direction of ending the war. If con-
cluding a war were simply a matter of holding a referendum,
the conflict in Algeria could have been ended immediately on
de Gaulle's appealing to the electorate.[3]

But important minorities did not trust de Gaulle to work
out a satisfactory solution. The most desperate and distrust-
ful of his opponents were the settlers; the most dangerous
were the army activists. Equally suspicious of his intentions
was the antiwar left. If the minorities at the extremes of the
Algerian question hated each other, they also had some
things in common. Most important, both were willing to
break the law. Between 1960 and 1962, Frenchmen shot or
blew up other Frenchmen; a good many more defied the state
on what seemed to them legitimate grounds. De Gaulle faced
a kind of low-intensity civil war at the same time he confronted the problem of disengaging France from Algeria.
This war among the French impinged on the war between
the French and the Algerians enough to affect the negotiation of a settlement.

In retrospect, 1959 looks like a year left to de Gaulle. The
next year saw a recrudescence of activity on the part of both

extremes. One side sought to keep de Gaulle from making good on his commitment to self-determination. The other tried to push him farther and faster in the direction of a settlement than he was willing to go. Members of both factions crossed the line into territory that made them fugitives from justice. As Robert Buron noted in his diary of the war: "What a curious country ours is in which mystical young Christians zealously transport intelligence, money, and even arms destined to terrorists who massacre their co-religionaries in Algeria, nay Paris, while the bourgeois who demonstrated two and a half years ago against the Fourth Republic now curse de Gaulle and plot with the soldiers in the hope of making him give up power."[4]

Compared with previous outbursts over initiatives from Paris, the self-determination speech provoked from Algiers surprisingly little response. But trouble was in the offing. And when it came, at the end of January 1960, Hubert Beuve-Méry, writing as "Sirius" in *Le Monde,* remarked that it had been obvious for months that a showdown between Paris and Algiers could not be avoided.[5] Algiers harbored men waiting for a pretext to move against de Gaulle as they had moved against the political and military leadership of the Fourth Republic. Most of the ultra leadership—the veterans of February 6, the Bazooka Affair, May 13, and of many vigilante raids into Algerian neighborhoods—remained intact.[6]

On January 18, the Munich newspaper *Süddeutsche Zeitung* carried an interview that General Massu had granted Hans Kempski, an ex-paratrooper turned journalist. Kempski quoted Massu as saying that the army no longer understood General de Gaulle's Algerian policy. Of May 13 he remarked, "De Gaulle was the only man at our disposition. Maybe the army made a mistake." Massu protested that he had been misquoted, but he was summoned to Paris forthwith, excluded from an important meeting on Algerian policy the Elysée Palace had scheduled for January 22, and informed that he would not be returning to his command.[7] General Jean Crépin took his place.

Massu's recall gave the ultras the pretext they were looking for. De Gaulle's depriving them of their champion, they told their followers, only foreshadowed his abandoning them altogether.

In the predawn hours of Sunday, January 24, barricades went up in the heart of European Algiers. If they were of no use against well-armed troops, barricades remained powerful symbols of defiance: knock this down, a barricade said to the authorities, and you will regret it. Once again Pierre Lagaillarde donned his leopard fatigues and rode out in defense of *Algérie française*. His men occupied the Faculty of Algiers. Joseph Ortiz, saloonkeeper on the rue Michelet, commanded the other center of defiance from a large apartment on the rue Charles Péguy, near the War Memorial.[8]

Ortiz and Lagaillarde both had the same old scheme in mind: to force the army to choose between Algiers and Paris. The ultras' unswerving dedication to this tactic perhaps betrayed a certain lack of imagination. But it also confirmed Beuve-Méry's observation that, despite the apparent complexity of daily events, "the fundamental givens of the tragedy remain rather simple."[9] The ultras had hitherto tried their tactics only against the decrepit Fourth Republic. Now they wagered that the army would defy de Gaulle as it had defied Pflimlin. Despite his sympathy for them, the Foreign Legion captain Pierre Sergent thought throwing up barricades betrayed the settlers' poor political judgment.[10]

Lagaillarde's group was short of experience and guns. Ortiz's men were better armed but even more disorganized. An early show of force might have sent the barricade builders packing. Instead, the authorities waited. And their temporizing allowed Ortiz and Lagaillarde to arm and organize the barricaders and to take courage from the ridiculous ease with which they were able to defy Paris.[11]

Certainly, the local authorities dragged their feet because they sympathized with the barricade builders. This was especially true of key military officers, from Challe on down. And as the day wore on, it became obvious that some of the soldiers not only sympathized with the insurgents but were in cahoots with them. Colonel Jean Gardes, head of the psychological warfare branch, was seen in the company of Ortiz, and Challe sent Ortiz emissaries. General Jean Gracieux, commander of the Tenth Paratroop Division, paid him a visit. Officers of lesser rank kept appearing at one command post or the other.[12]

But the chief go-between—and mastermind—of the "Week of the Barricades" was Colonel Antoine Argoud, Massu's chief of staff. A graduate of "X"—the Ecole polytechnique—and not of Saint Cyr, whence came the majority of line officers, Argoud was the youngest colonel in the French army. A specialist in mechanized warfare, he had been in charge of assembling the most modern and mobile armored brigade in NATO. Then he threw himself into the war in Algeria, where such outfits were nearly useless. Commanding a sector at Arba, he became a fanatic of *guerre révolutionnaire.* Argoud spurned the use of torture; his method of dealing with suspected FLN agents was summary execution, a procedure he did not hesitate to recommend to whoever would listen. A latecomer to Algeria and to political activism, a never-was in Indochina (the chief disability some observers thought he was trying to overcome), he seemed bent on proving himself the army's most devoted champion of *Algérie française.* Everyone who met Argoud was struck by his intelligence, his volubility, his small stature, and his piercing dark eyes. Many saw in him a future chief of staff of the army. He was certainly among the ablest of the army activists.[13]

A few officers wanted to dismantle forcibly the insurgents' homemade fortifications. But Challe and his advisers drew up a plan calling for military units to converge on the center of the city from three directions, in the hope that such a show of force would be enough to send the barricaders scattering for home. The task of clearing out the throng, barricaders and onlookers alike, fell to fifteen squads of gendarmes, or *gardes mobiles,* under the command of Lieutenant Colonel Jean Dubrosse; the First Regiment of Foreign Legion Paratroops, under Colonel Henri Dufour; the First Regiment of Light Infantry Paratroops, led by Colonel Joseph Broizat. Challe gave these units orders to fire only if fired upon.[14]

The defenders of the barricades had been busy collecting weapons. By six in the evening, the hour set for the clearing operation, they were not only well armed but trigger-happy. The gendarmes arrived on the scene first, moving down the broad stairs running from the Forum toward Ortiz's headquarters at the corner of the rue Charles Péguy and the Boulevard Laferrière. Using a portable loud-speaker, Dubrosse gave the crowd the formal summons to disperse. A shot rang out, then a burst of machine-gun fire. The civilian bystanders ran for cover. The gendarmes, strung out along the steps, came under a crossfire from the upper stories of adjacent buildings. A woman in a dressing gown was seen emptying a pistol into them from the window of her apartment, reloading and firing again. The shooting went on for several minutes. Finally Dubrosse's men retreated up the steps, dragging their dead and wounded with them. The gendarmes had 14 killed and 123 wounded.[15] On the ultras' side of the barricade, the casualties were 6 dead, 26 wounded.

In the meantime, the two regiments of paratroops were nowhere to be seen. Dufour and Broizat, within earshot of the gunfire, stood talking with Lagaillarde's men.

Witnesses to the shooting of January 24 allowed their hearts to color what they saw and heard. To the partisans of *Algérie française* and their friends, the gendarmes' advance down the stairs was a menacing gesture, a "veritable charge," as one of them put it. To the gendarmes and their defenders, the same advance was an appropriate riot-control maneuver. Who started the shooting the ultras found an unfathomable mystery. The gendarmes put the blame for opening fire squarely on Ortiz's camp. The paratroopers claim they did not come to the assistance of the gendarmes because they did not realize help was needed; anyway, the gendarmes acted precipitately, moving from the Forum earlier than the paras had expected. The gendarmes charged that the paras as good as set them up for an ambush; the paras' failure to advance at the first sound of gunfire was proof of their collusion with the ultras.[16]

If the army had not moved to dismantle the barricades, it had not rallied behind them, either. But the ultras could interpret this standoff as a victory of sorts. Without the army's complicity they could not have gotten away with defying Paris. Still, complicity was a wasting asset. Each passing day diminished the likelihood of the army's going over to the settlers.

On January 28, some movement in the stalemate finally took place. Challe and Delouvrier left Algiers for Reghaia, a short distance from the capital. Challe thereby escaped the colonels who wanted him at the head of the revolt against de Gaulle; Delouvrier broke off his efforts at talking the ultras out from behind their barricades. The activist leaders could no longer hide behind Challe or claim to be acting in his name. They could not put off followers demanding to know when the army was coming over to their side. The withdrawal of Challe and Delouvrier left the city to the barricaders and colonels, free to act as they dared. After all the week's talk, nothing happened.[17]

The next evening, de Gaulle went on radio and television, dressed in his brigadier-general's uniform (he had resisted his advisers' pleas to advance his address to an earlier date). He delivered one of the most moving and effective speeches of his career: "Ah well, my old and dear country, here we are together again once more, facing a

grave test." He emphasized that nothing would deflect him
from the course he had announced the previous fall. "Self-
determination," he said, "is the only policy worthy of
France. It is the only possible outcome." To the settlers he
offered reassurances and admonitions. France would not
have poured so many men, so much money, so much time
and energy into Algeria if it meant to abandon them. The
barricaders risked making France lose the struggle, just at
the moment the insurrection showed signs of faltering. To
the army de Gaulle offered admonitions and exhortations.
"Your mission," he declared, "allows for neither equivocation nor interpretation." This being the case, "no soldier
must, under penalty of a serious offense, associate himself,
even passively, with the insurrection."[18]

De Gaulle's speech took the starch out of the barricaders.
The army activists who egged them on at the beginning of
the week spent the weekend arranging a dignified surrender.
Ortiz, however, wanted no part of a dignified surrender—or
a murder rap. Under cover of night he slipped away from his
command post and made good a getaway that eventually
took him to Spain.[19] Looking for the touch that would invest
the end of his "Alcazár" with a sense of tragic drama, Lagaillarde succeeded only in making himself and his bedraggled
followers look pathetic.[20] While one leader hid out in the
countryside and the others were carted off to jail, the remnant of the rank and file, roughly five hundred men, was
transported to Zéralda, the Foreign Legion base west of
Algiers, to be signed up in a special commando group for
duty against the FLN. A month later the unit was disbanded,
having never left Zéralda.

The Week of the Barricades left most of the ultra leadership on the run, under arrest, or lying low. The colonels'
failure to deliver the rest of the army put their relationship
with the settlers under a severe strain. Dismantling the barricades appeared to have swept away the last obstacle thwarting de Gaulle's course toward self-determination. But to

jump to such a conclusion was to underestimate the fight left in army activists and settlers, and the lengths to which they were prepared to go in defense of *Algérie française.*

In any event, de Gaulle lost no time exploiting his short-run victory. There was another round of military transfers and reassignments. From Massu on down, officers who in some way compromised themselves in their dealings with the settlers were given new posts on the mainland and elsewhere in Africa. Challe's overly solicitous attention to the views of the barricaders earned him command of NATO forces in central Europe; he was replaced by General Vézinet. Delouvrier's reputation as an able administrator did not compensate for his shortcomings as a crisis manager; in November he, too, was called home, with Jean Morin succeeding him.

Pierre Guillaumat, minister of armies, torn between his loyalty to de Gaulle and his sympathy for the soldiers, resigned. Pierre Messmer was recalled from a tour of active duty as a reserve officer to take his place. By far the most important resignation was Jacques Soustelle's. He had been kept at a considerable distance from the shaping of Algerian policy; his open sympathies for the insurgents put him totally at odds with de Gaulle and most of the rest of the cabinet, and the crisis brought an open break.[21] Bernard Cornut-Gentille, minister of posts and telecommunications, followed Soustelle out of the government.

The barricaders' challenge tempted de Gaulle to avail himself of the sweeping emergency powers contained in Article 16 of the constitution, but Bernard Tricot talked him out of this drastic step. He recommended instead asking Parliament to grant the president the power to legislate by decree. Eager to hand de Gaulle all the authority he required for dealing with the Algerian problem, the National Assembly readily assented. Establishing at the Elysée Palace a Committee on Algerian Affairs also gave de Gaulle a better purchase on events. The committee included ex-officio the president, the prime minister, the principal members of the cabinet, the secretary-general for Algerian affairs, the delegate-general, the commander in chief. In consultation with the president and the prime minister, Tricot drew up the agenda (an indication of how influential in the making of policy he had become). Tricot maintains that the committee did not usurp the functions of the cabinet, but complemented them. On the face of things, this is hard to believe. In any event, the administrative reorganization that followed the Week of the Barricades enabled de Gaulle to gather the reins of policy much tighter in his own hands. Henceforth, nearly every major policy decision on Algeria was first aired in the Committee on Algerian Affairs.[22]

The defeat of the barricaders aroused hopes for a quick end to the war. De Gaulle himself soon dashed them. In early March 1960, the general made another trip to Algeria, this time for the purpose of inspecting the army. In every mess hall he stressed the need for pressing the offensive against the FLN; he emphasized how long the struggle might last; he insisted on the importance of France's staying on. As reports of his talks with the soldiers reached France, they were interpreted as a retreat from the policy of self-determination.[23]

Where de Gaulle's critics perceived a zigzag, associates saw a straight line. In the spring of 1960, Tricot insisted that de Gaulle's policy remained one of "putting the Algerians in a position freely to choose their future, and toward this end, reestablishing order and peace."[24] The *tournée des popotes* ("mess-hall tour") did not mark a reversion to a policy of pacification, Fourth Republic style, but an attempt to educate the army to the military requirements of the policy of self-determination. Dropping in at mess tents from the Tunisian frontier to the Moroccan border, from the sea to the Sahara, de Gaulle carried to the officer corps the same message he had sent to Delouvrier in a memorandum written toward the end of February 1960: ". . . the success of operations under way or envisaged is the condition of everything."[25]

If de Gaulle's pedagogical purpose was as plain as this, why was he so badly misunderstood? Why did he think he had explained the relationship between the end of self-determination and its military means, only to have his listeners hear something else? People dead set against the policy took heart from what they heard of the mess-hall talks; those who wished the policy well were puzzled and dismayed; those who thought de Gaulle had been feigning a commitment to self-determination believed themselves vindicated. Most observers agreed that the line de Gaulle took on the *tournée des popotes* marked a departure from the line he had laid down in September 1959.[26]

The government had only itself to blame for much of the confusion. Only one reporter, Jean Mauriac, of the government news service Agence France Presse, was allowed to accompany de Gaulle. Denied the opportunity of seeing and hearing for themselves, journalists left behind in Algiers fell back on filing stories based on rumor and speculation. Much of the news dispatched to the mainland had been filtered through the distorting lens of the settler press. De Gaulle chose to speak extemporaneously on a subject on which he almost never uttered an unguarded word. Hearing de Gaulle speak of "victory," many officers may not have paid attention when he explained victory's purposes.[27]

In the aftermath of the barricades, de Gaulle may have gone to Algeria to tell the officer corps what he knew it wanted to hear, lulling the soldiers into his confidence with talk of achieving military victory and maintaining the French presence. But the *tournée des popotes* does not appear to have been an instance of Gaullist dissembling. Taken aback by reactions reported from the mainland, the general issued a communiqué warning against misleading interpretations of the trip's purposes.

On the return to France a statement issued by Louis Terrenoire, the minister of information, sounded a new and important note, reminding the army that Algeria was not the be-all and end-all of its existence: "The General has called the officers' attention to the fact that the Algerian problem, as important as it is, is only one of those that present themselves to France internally and externally, and whose scope is going to be increasing since our country has once again become a world power in a dangerous universe. Therefore the army must, while accomplishing its present task in Algeria, also have its mind fixed on missions that could fall to it elsewhere. It is this comprehensive duty, and not only to a local and momentary phase, to which the French army must adapt itself and morally and materially prepare itself."[28]

The statement broadcast a signal loud and clear. De Gaulle had never so plainly warned the army that it must get ready for the day Algeria no longer absorbed all its energies. But the signal went forth in an atmosphere filled with static and jammed with other messages.[29] Perhaps it encountered too much interference. Perhaps de Gaulle failed to realize that many citizens were not as good at recognizing clues as he was at giving them.

On February 24, the Paris police arrested nearly a score of persons on charges of "endangering the external security of the state." A handful of actors and their wives, a few high school teachers, an electronics-plant worker, a ceramicist, a nurse, and a medical student—all were suspected of belonging to an underground network devoted to supporting the FLN. None was a known political activist. Francis Jeanson, the organizer and leader of the network, eluded capture. A warrant was put out for his arrest.[30]

Jeanson himself was well known in left-wing circles. Thirty-eight years old when he became a fugitive from justice, Jeanson had made his reputation as a disciple, interpreter, and associate of Jean-Paul Sartre. For a time he managed *Les Temps modernes.* But he fell out with Sartre when the latter broke with the Communists over the repression of the Hungarian revolution.[31] Algeria ruined Jeanson's own relations with the Communists, for his support of the insurrection was far more enthusiastic than theirs ever became. With his wife, Colette, Jeanson wrote *L'Algérie hors la loi* (1955), the first important left-wing statement on the Algerian question to appear after the outbreak of the war.

The Jeansons soon decided that championing the Algerian revolution in print was not enough. Deeds, not words, were proof of commitment. By mid-July 1957, Francis Jeanson had contrived to put together a network of support for the FLN.

From the outset of the insurrection the FLN had worked to capture from Messali Hadj, erstwhile leader of radical nationalism, the loyalties of the four hundred thousand Algerian workers resident in France. The numbers of Algerians who turned up dead on the streets and sidewalks of Paris, victims of the revolutionary equivalents of gangland slayings, indicated the ferocity of the struggle between the FLN and Messali's Mouvement national algérien (MNA). By the same mixture of terrorism and persuasion as it practiced on the other side of the Mediterranean, the FLN succeeded in implanting among mainland workers the Fédération de France. The federation's membership dues, extorted or freely contributed, became an important source of funds for the Algerian revolution.

This is where the Jeanson network came in. Algerians traveling in France on suspicious errands invited the curiosity of the police; a European with a suitcase was unlikely to attract attention. He might be a salesman, he might be paying a weekend visit to his mother—he might be transporting thousands of francs in FLN dues.

Members of the Jeanson network not only acted as couriers of FLN funds but furnished automobiles and drivers to FLN agents, provided them with hideouts and meeting places, invented false names, concocted phony identification papers, and contrived means of slipping Algerians in and out of France. At the outset Jeanson recruited roughly forty friends for this work; on the eve of the police crackdown, the network may have had as many as three thousand members. Such figures are impossible to verify. As happened during the Resistance, some of the French may have confused knowing a member of a secret network with being one.[32]

In mid-April 1960, two months after the police had descended upon his associates, Jeanson surfaced briefly in Paris. He held a clandestine "press conference" in a friend's apartment. Georges Arnaud, a free-lance reporter of left-wing views, sold his piece on Jeanson's remarks to the mass-circulation daily *Paris-Presse*. This front-page article deeply embarrassed the authorities. That such right-wing diehards as Jo Ortiz were free left them open to suspicions of complicity; that such figures as Jeanson eluded capture left them open to charges of incompetence. At least when Ortiz went underground, he stayed underground; Jeanson kept surfacing.[33] In the summer of 1960 Editions de minuit published *Notre guerre,* Jeanson's defense of the course he had taken since 1957.

Jeanson wrote his longish essay in haste, on the run, without benefit of documents (lost when he fled the police). He and his friends had made the Algerian revolution *notre guerre,* he explained, in an attempt to flush the traditional left from its hiding place in a thicket of words. Everyone who had written against the war instead of taking action came under fire. An unadmitted racism and anticommunism, Jeanson claimed, accounted for the left's caution. Racism discounted the Algerians' political capacities; anticommunism prevented putting together an effective antiwar coalition.

Jeanson denied ever having said that legal action against the war was pointless, only that legal action was not enough, and needed to be supplemented with clandestine activity. Nor did such activity amount to "treason." The real betrayal, Jeanson insisted, belonged to liberal critics who had read him and his friends out of a nonexistent community. For the "community" of liberal-capitalist theory was only a formalistic structure, behind whose false front the worst forms of lawlessness went unpunished.

In Algeria, said Jeanson, this so-called community was conducting a genocidal war. As long as the French did not take the side of the oppressed, they belonged, like it or not, to the camp of the oppressor. Assisting the FLN did not mean participating in the killing of French soldiers. The revolutionaries did not need the money he and his friends collected for making arms purchases. Better to be an active accomplice of a just cause, Jeanson maintained, than the passive accomplice of genocide.[34]

Disillusioned with the revolutionaries at home, Jeanson and his followers idealized the revolutionaries in Algeria (and elsewhere). For things did not appear to be working out as Marx had predicted. Instead of growing increasingly impoverished, increasingly conscious of its exploitation, increasingly radical, the European working class appeared to be well on its way toward *embourgeoisement.* But if the industrial working class had forsaken its role as a revolutionary force, the poor and exploited of the non-Western and nonindustrialized areas of the world stood ready to take its place. In this neo-Marxist schema, the Third World took the place of the proletariat. Peoples assumed the role of classes. Revolution would come to the more developed countries by way of the less developed. Declaring their solidarity with the Third World reassured intellectuals of the left that they had not lost their revolutionary purity.[35]

Most of the French left was not prepared to go to such lengths. None of the organized parties embraced Jeanson's theories or his tactics. In the left press, only *Les Temps modernes* allied itself with the Jeanson network. Algeria repaired the breach Hungary had driven between Sartre and Jeanson.

If some dissenters from the war took to helping the other side, others made a separate peace, by deserting the army or resisting the draft. How many young Frenchmen were involved in such acts is uncertain. The French government has not published official figures, but the number most often cited is three thousand.[36] If this estimate comes close to being accurate, it is an astonishingly low figure.* It seems especially low when compared with the incidence of desertions from the United States armed forces during the Vietnam war, even though the United States had many more men under arms. In 1971 alone, 79,027 men deserted from the United States Army, of whom 48,568 were "returned to military control."[37] Forty thousand Americans are estimated to have chosen exile, most of them in Canada and Sweden, over military service.[38]

That the Algerian conflict was not, on the French side, a very dangerous war may partly explain the low rate of desertion. Except for those who volunteered for such elite units as the paratroops, conscripts seldom were involved in any shooting. The chances of being killed in Algeria would have needed to be greater than they were to make the risk of being caught and tried as a deserter seem preferable to serving out one's time.[39]

Military deserters risked not only the stockade but social ostracism; they could bring shame on themselves and dishonor on their families. In France, military service was part of a left-wing tradition that went back to the Great Revolution. The idea of the nation in arms, of an army composed of citizen soldiers, had long been most compelling precisely in the sector of opinion that was opposed to the Algerian war.[40] Military service, as Francis Jeanson put, "is the only

*Pierre Vidal-Naquet regards even three thousand as "an enormously exaggerated figure." Letter to the author, July 16, 1979. The French army is likely to have kept the most accurate records on deserters; publication of its figures may end guesswork as to their numbers.

lived test that is common to all citizens, so that the one who evades it seems to lose every concrete attachment with the national collectivity."[41] The prospect of cutting himself off from the community would have made any young man think twice about going over the wall.[42]

France had no law respecting conscientious objection to military service until the 1970s. Instead, the government played cat-and-mouse with conscientious objectors, putting them in jail for failing to respond to a draft call, releasing them when their sentences expired, calling them up again, jailing them again. No such thing as alternative service existed, although late in the war COs were permitted to become unarmed medical corpsmen in paratrooper units. The military authorities evidently believed that such dangerous assignments tested genuineness of conviction.[43]

An early deserter was Noël Favrelière. In 1955, having already done his military service, he was recalled to active duty and assigned as a sergeant to the Eighth Regiment of Colonial Paratroops. An artist working as a fabric designer, Favrelière had never been much interested in politics, but he had already decided that independence was the only tolerable solution to the Algerian problem. He was convinced that had he been an Algerian he would have been a guerrilla fighter. His father agreed, and this may have made his decision to desert easier.

On the train that took him to Marseilles, the port of embarkation for Algeria, he recalled his boyhood under the Occupation. The first dead man he had seen was a German soldier shot by members of the Resistance. Now he found himself cast in the role of that soldier. Not two months into his Algerian tour of duty, on August 27, 1956, Favrelière deserted, taking with him an Algerian prisoner of war and such weapons as he could carry. He made his way eastward, encountering a band of guerrillas in whose company he spent several weeks before crossing the Tunisian frontier. In Tunis the U.S. consulate grudgingly awarded him a visa. He eventually found his way to Ljubljana, Yugoslavia, and remained in contact with Algerians and antiwar Frenchmen.

When Favrelière left his camp and sought refuge with the Algerians, his only thought was to cease being a combatant on the French side. He meant not to set an example but to square his deeds with his conscience. Not until four years later did he publish a book on the experience. The government seized *Le Desert à l'aube* as soon as it appeared.[44]

Maurice Maschino's intentions better suited the strategy of Jeanson and like-minded radicals than did Favrelière's. He evaded the draft in the hope that other young men would follow him. Like Jeanson, Maschino had no confidence that the traditional left, Communist or non-Communist, would mount an effective opposition to the war. The non-Communist left, transfixed by its own nationalist and Jacobin sentiments, could not bring itself to advocate illegal actions against the army that embodied such feelings.

All the left activists who went off to Algeria, thinking they could act against the war from inside the war machine, were only fooling themselves. Their numbers were too few, their opportunities for effective action too slight. It would have been far better not to go in the first place, or having gone, to flee, than to undergo the demoralizing effects of military service.

Called up in 1958, Maschino failed to report. He conceded that in the early years of the war, not many young leftists had taken the course he recommended—most resisters went to jail. But however admirable and courageous the willingness to live behind bars might be, it was a poor means of proselytizing. Only a man free to move about was likely to attract converts to the cause.

By 1960 the scattered resisters and deserters had organized themselves into a movement. Jeune Résistance had as shadowy an existence as the Jeanson network. It is hard to say how many persons belonged—Maschino claimed a membership of three thousand—the same mixture of left Christians and trade unionists, pacifists, dissident Communists, and Socialists as assisted Jeanson. Jeune Résistance and the Jeanson network had similar aims. Deserting the army and evading the draft, like assisting the FLN, were intended to jolt the traditional left into recognizing the futility of its long campaign of words against the war. Maschino echoed Jeanson when he wrote, "The deserters have broken the silence, they have forced the Left to recognize its miserable prudence, they have unmasked the hypocrites [*tartuffes*]." Maschino thought the left was beyond regeneration: "It's an old Left, dying and senile, on which the living forces of the country —youth—don't count."[45] Like Jeanson, he expected the refusal to participate in the war against the Algerians to be the beginning of a withdrawal of support from all the institutions of existing society.

For every Favrelière and Maschino who made a separate peace, however, hundreds, perhaps thousands, of young men of the left went off to Algeria and put in their twenty-seven months, despite their opposition to the war.[46] They followed the example of their grandfathers, who endured four years of slaughter in the Great War, and under much severer stress rose up only once in defiance of the military hierarchy.[47]

On September 5, 1960, nineteen members of the Jeanson network went on trial in the same courtroom where Dreyfus had been convicted sixty-six years earlier. That day, 121 artists and writers issued a Manifesto supporting "The Right of Draft Resistance [*insoumission*] in the Algerian War." "The Algerian war," the declaration charged, "has little by little become an action peculiar to the army and to a caste which refuse to yield before an uprising of which even the civil power, taking into account the general collapse of colonial empires, seems ready to recognize the significance."[48] As the war had ceased being a national war, traditional obligations of citizens toward the state no longer applied. Indeed, in some cases, as victims of Nazism hardly needed reminding, refusing to go along with actions represented as state policy was a moral duty.

As the war posed a threat to French society and the political system—a threat the traditional left had shown itself incapable of meeting—drastic measures of opposition were required. "We respect and consider justified," the Manifesto concluded, "the refusal to take arms against the Algerian people. We respect and deem justified the conduct of Frenchmen who consider it their duty to give aid and protection to Algerians oppressed in the name of the French people. The cause of the Algerian people, which is contributing in a decisive way to ruining the colonial system, is the cause of all free men."[49]

Among the 121 signers were names police agents expected to find on antiwar petitions: Sartre and Beauvoir, Mandouze and Vidal-Naquet. But many were artists and writers who rarely, if ever, put their names to a political statement of any kind: the composer and conductor Pierre Boulez; the filmmakers Alain Resnais, François Truffaut, and Marguerite Duras; the novelists Alain Robbe-Grillet and Nathalie Sarraute; some actors, and a handful of radio and television reporters. Not a single member of the French Communist party was a signatory.[50]

The Manifesto was a self-conscious effort on the part of French intellectuals to live up to the tradition of protest they associated with the Dreyfus Affair, to assume a responsibility for speaking out for the "values they [intellectuals] defend, the principles on which they have founded their lives, even for the right of thinking."[51] Two of Maurice Nadeau's associates on the staff of *Les Lettres nouvelles,* Dionys Mascolo and Maurice Blanchot, drafted the Manifesto. Sartre made emendations. In the summer of 1960, the authors collected signatures. To Jérôme Lindon, as always, fell the task of finding a printer, and for this delicate job he resorted to a different shop from the one his firm usually employed. Despite such precautions, the police got wind of the project. As soon as the Manifesto appeared, the authorities moved swiftly against its authors and signers. They had an especially easy time of it. Many of the signers, amateurs in affairs of this kind, instantly told the police exactly what they wanted to know.[52]

The Manifesto of the 121 put the government in a dilemma. To round up the signers and throw them in jail, to press charges and hold trials would have bestowed martyrdom on them; to have let them go scot-free would have angered the friends of *Algérie française,* especially the army. The government took a middle way, ignoring some, singling others out for punishment. The Manifesto itself never appeared in any mass-circulation newspaper. *Le Monde* did not print it. *Vérité-Liberté* published the Manifesto in its September-October issue and was promptly seized.

The arrests of signers of the Manifesto got more attention than the statement itself. The police took in for questioning those whom they believed to be the ringleaders. Agents searched the premises of *Les Temps modernes, Vérité-Liberté,* and *Esprit* (the last-named despite its hostility both to desertion and to the Jeanson network). The government seized issues of *L'Express, France observateur,* and *Les Temps modernes.* Actors who had signed the Manifesto were banned from state-run radio and television stations and theaters; writers were denied performance of their works. The ministry of information announced a plan to withhold state aid from any film in which signers of the Manifesto appeared. Any civil servant who had signed the statement was liable to suspension with loss of pay, a measure aimed at the professors among the signers. Laurent Schwartz, a leading mathematician, an antiwar activist of long standing, Maurice Audin's thesis adviser, and, it so happened, Michel Debré's cousin, was dismissed from his professorship at the Ecole polytechnique.[53] Claude Bourdet, editor of *France observateur,* believed the last thing the government wanted was to give the signers of the Manifesto a forum in a court of law. Hence the press seizures—the old technique of intimidation —and the administrative punishments were a way of getting at signers without bringing them to trial.[54]

The friends of *Algérie française* organized demonstrations against the Manifesto of the 121. On October 4, ten thousand to fifteen thousand members of veterans' organizations marched to the Arc de Triomphe against those who had signed the Manifesto. Marshal Alphonse Juin, de Gaulle's classmate and his critic on Algerian policy, and six other members of the Académie française, including Henri Massis and Jules Romains, had their own group of 185 writers, artists, professors, journalists, doctors, and lawyers to match the signers of the Manifesto.[55]

In the meantime, the Jeanson network's trial went forward. The accused struggled to raise a series of general charges against the war. The prosecution fought to limit the proceedings to a hearing of the stated charges against the defendants. In the end, however, the presiding judges allowed the defense considerable latitude in the calling and questioning of witnesses. Paul-Henri Teitgen testified to his knowledge of the use of torture in the Battle of Algiers. Jean-Paul Sartre, absent on a trip to Brazil, signed a letter (actually written by Marcel Péju) declaring his "total solidarity" with the accused and recapitulating all the themes enunciated since their arrest in February. "If Jeanson had asked me to carry suitcases or shelter Algerian activists, and I could have done so without risks for them," he said, "I would have done it without hesitation."[56]

For all the efforts of defense witnesses to make the Jeanson trial an indictment of everything done in the name of keeping Algeria French, the military tribunal ruled only on the facts of the case in question. Those who freely admitted lending assistance to the FLN and to being aware of the implications of what they did were convicted. Those who claimed to have thought they were involved in some sort of Red Cross work were acquitted.[57]

After the flurry of threats, seizures, and sanctions that greeted the appearance of the Manifesto of the 121, the government showed signs of wishing the issue would go away. Despite talk of pressing charges against all the signers for "incitement to desertion," or "incitement of military personnel to disobedience," few indictments were brought and no signer ever stood trial.

In mid-October, when excitement over the Manifesto and the Jeanson network still ran high, a curious thing happened, or failed to happen. The novelist and playwright Jules Roy —veteran of Indochina, retired air force colonel, son of *pieds noirs,* close friend of Albert Camus—published a short book called *La Guerre d'Algérie.* Roy's was not the sort of book a *pied noir* soldier might have been expected to write. His main conclusion, as Janet Flanner wrote in her column in *The New Yorker,* "is that simple 'social injustice'—the white men's contempt, tyranny, psychological cruelty, and greed— opened the road to the Algerians' rebellion."[58] As for the way out, Roy declared, "The only way to stop this war is to negotiate, on condition that each of the adversaries abandon part of his pretensions."[59] On the way to this conclusion Roy described a ruined countryside, wasted villages, homeless Algerians, settlers ready to pull their houses down around their ears rather than give an inch.

Toward the end he recounted a night-long dialogue with a French captain on watch at the barrier along the Tunisian frontier: "Frankly, Captain, hasn't our army murdered twelve hundred men in the commune of Toudja alone? . . . Hasn't it tortured here, as it did in Indochina? Is it not directed by our officers? And is it to defend the West that these crimes have been committed? Then let the West fall, and all the captains who won't make peace, and I myself who denounce them. With them perishes the army of martyrs tortured by the Nazis, and all the men who fought in exile or in their own countries for the freedom to sit around their own tables with their families and friends! On your side, Captain, we must prepare for another Hundred Years War. . . ."[60]

La Guerre d'Algérie would have been a prime candidate for seizure under the Fourth Republic—or in the early days of the Fifth, for that matter. But in the same weeks that the police were laying hold of *France observateur, Les Temps modernes,* and *Vérité-Liberté,* Roy's book became a best seller. The government's failure to remove it from circulation may have been an oversight. The police may have left *La Guerre d'Algérie* alone, though, because Roy wrote what de Gaulle thought. To announce that France had nothing to gain from continuing the struggle in Algeria was to state views de Gaulle had already offered. Perhaps a best seller accustomed opinion to ideas unthinkable six years earlier. Perhaps its success showed that these ideas were already popular.

Roy's book suggests that at issue between de Gaulle and much of the left was less opposition to the war than the manner of expressing it. By the autumn of 1960, it was no longer daring to call for Algerian independence, no longer shocking to write of the army's use of torture, no longer unpatriotic to welcome the end of empire. But the French government's intolerance of appeals to desertion and draft evasion would have persisted, no matter what. For no army based on conscription can function unless young men report for the draft and answer at roll call. The authorities could come to regard the Algerian problem as a passing nightmare, but they could never bring themselves to consider the need for a disciplined citizen-soldiery as anything but permanent.

Jeanson and his friends saw themselves as an avant-garde who would shock the traditional left into action, shake the leadership of the organized parties and trade unions from their lethargy, pry the intellectuals away from their attachment to legal methods of opposition, awaken the rank and file. The left was shocked, but not with the effects the Jeanson network intended. Far from uniting the antiwar forces on a common ground of opposition to the war, Jeanson's tactics provided them with one more source of division.

The Socialists promptly denounced aiding the FLN and encouraging draft evasion as a "tragic aberration" more likely to prolong the fighting than to help end it.[61] The Communists reacted more equivocally to the Jeanson Affair, seeking to approve the motives of deserters, draft resisters, and members of the network without approving their actions. The Communists could see that draft resisters had good intentions. Nevertheless, as representatives of the masses, they could not lend their support to "individual gestures of despair." Lenin's position on the duty of the proletarian soldier was as valid in 1960 as it had been nearly a half-century before. As Maurice Thorez put it a few days before the opening of his party's Fifteenth Congress: "The Communist soldier leaves for every war, even a reactionary war, in order to pursue the struggle against war. He works where he is put."[62]

Critics took Thorez's invocation of Lenin as a noble excuse for lying low. Algeria was hardly the Russian front in 1917, when soldiers had laid down their rifles and walked away from the Great War. Indeed, Maurice Maschino asked, where in North Africa were the protests of the army rank and file that Lenin had advocated? He doubted if preparations for such actions were being made. This being the case, "the Communist soldier serves, as do all his comrades, the established order, and he is reduced, as they are, to the most total impotence."[63]

The Communists interpreted the Jeanson thesis as a thinly disguised attack on them. The organized left, a member of the central committee protested, was not the "decomposing body" that Sartre and others seemed to think. Nor was it mainly interested, as others alleged, in staying in de Gaulle's good graces. As the Communists had insisted at every turn in the war, from the early days of the insurrection, through the troop buildup, the voting of the Special Powers Law, the Battle of Algiers, May 13, so they insisted in the autumn of 1960 that the most urgent political task was reconstituting the unity of the left.[64] Through thick and thin the Communists relied on the long-range strategy of rebuilding the alliance with the Socialists. Such single-issue tactics as aiding the FLN or deserting the armed forces did not fit in with such a strategy.

The liberals were less indirect about the tactics of Jeanson and his friends. The group around *L'Express*—such figures as Jean-Jacques Servan-Schreiber, the economist Alfred Sauvy, the political scientist Maurice Duverger—found themselves unable to fathom Jeanson's motives or to countenance his actions.[65] Left-Catholic intellectuals had a more nuanced reaction to the Jeanson Affair. Jean-Marie Domenach, editor of *Esprit,* conceded that such tactics as Jeanson's might have some value in shocking others into facing up to their own complicity in the conduct of the war, but in the main he found them ill suited to the circumstances. Desertion might have powerful effects in revolutionary times and in an army on the point of disintegrating, but France in 1960 hardly fitted this description.[66]

Pierre-Henri Simon took a sterner line. He regarded the appeals for desertion, draft evasion, and assisting the FLN as failings typical of the radical intelligentsia. Such appeals were based on reason alone. They ignored the emotional side of patriotism, the nearly instinctive adherence of French men and women to the community and its institutions. Of these institutions, none conveyed a more powerful sense of the national community than the army. In Simon's view only the gravest circumstances could justify such a renunciation, and he did not think these circumstances applied to the war in Algeria.[67]

The philosopher Paul Ricoeur contributed one of the most thoughtful discussions of the issues the Jeanson Affair raised. Ricoeur sympathized with draft resisters, but he could not bring himself to advise anyone to desert the army or evade the draft. Breaking with the state, challenging its right to require citizens to do its bidding, was an extreme measure that only the most extreme circumstances called for. One such circumstance would be the state's loss of moral legitimacy, as had been the case in Germany under the Nazis. Whatever claims could be made regarding the illegitimacy of France's war against the Algerians, the French state retained a legal basis, a constitutional form, the support of opinion and, most important, avenues of legal action that had yet to be exhausted. The French were still far from being in the position of the Germans who concluded in July 1944 that they had no other recourse against Hitler except killing him. Ricoeur did not rule out the possibility of draft resistance provoking mass action, but he had his doubts. He thought it far more likely that such tactics would push settlers and army into an even closer embrace, that the very sound of the words *désertion* and *insoumission* would serve only to alienate those whom opponents of the war were trying to reach.[68]

A few hundred intellectuals were willing to declare that they "respected" and considered "justifiable" the actions of the Jeanson network and of the young men who refused military service. These carefully chosen words enabled the signers of the Manifesto to approve of assisting the FLN, deserting, and resisting the draft, but not to advocate such actions or to make it appear they had taken a hand in them. Such a remote expression of solidarity was no doubt the price that had to be paid for collecting many signatures. In the end only the *Temps modernes* group declared itself ready, as Sartre put it, to carry suitcases for the FLN.[69] Within the camp of protest, many signed a petition; few carried a suitcase. Or to use Albert Hirschman's terms, many resorted to "voice"; few had recourse to "exit."[70]

"No matter how well a society's basic institutions are

devised," Hirschman points out, "failures of some actors to live up to the behavior which is expected of them are bound to occur, if only for all kinds of accidental reasons."[71] But if failures go unattended, they are apt to multiply, to proliferate throughout the system, and the danger of an irreversible decline sets in. To keep this from happening, every society generates within itself "recuperation mechanisms," behavior designed to make actors live up to the norms from which they are perceived to have lapsed. One such mechanism is voice, "any attempt at all to change, rather than to escape from, an objectionable state of affairs";[72] another is exit, in which escape is preferred to change.

The outcry against torture was an expression of voice. Protesters used the institutions of liberal democracy, especially free speech and a free press, to call attention to the army's methods in Algeria. An awakened public opinion, they hoped, would at least force the government to call a halt to the practice of torture; perhaps revulsion against such methods would even lead to a negotiated settlement.

Assisting the FLN, desertion, and draft resistance were the actions of persons who no longer expected anything from the exercise of voice (or never had). They were expressions of exit—flights from an objectionable state of affairs—in this case the conduct of the war and the withholding of Algerian independence. Those who took this option aimed, in Ricoeur's phrase, to break the chain of complicity binding Frenchmen to the actions of the French government.

What held their numbers down, despite the hopes of Jeanson and his friends, were the workings of the mechanism of loyalty. For loyalty "holds exit at bay."[73] When members of an organization feel a special attachment to it, they are likely to persist in the use of voice far longer than they would in the absence of such feelings. In the marketplace, for instance, where loyalty is feeble, exit is easy and prompt. When loyalty is present, exit changes character: "the applauded rational behavior of the alert consumer shifting to a better buy becomes disgraceful defection, desertion and treason.''[74]

Loyalty's workings are especially powerful when the organization in question is the nation-state. For none is better equipped with loyalty-promoting institutions and devices: the family and the community, the school and the army, landscape and memory, language and culture, and countless other tangible and intangible things; few organizations are able to extract as high a price for exit. The higher the price, the less attractive the option of exit becomes, and the fewer the persons likely to make their way toward it. In the end, the intellectuals who declared their solidarity with those who had chosen exit did so by means of the Manifesto of the 121, an exercise characteristic of voice.

A year after the Manifesto appeared, the antiwar activist Robert Bonnaud looked back on the accomplishments of the movement against the war. Bonnaud, a lycée professor and ex-member of the Communist party, had himself been jailed for antiwar activities in Marseilles. He was a disappointed and disillusioned man. In a letter to *Vérité-Liberté,* he asked what progress the left had made in the year since the stir over the Jeanson Affair. "The clandestine grouplets have remained grouplets," he replied, "and the resisters not very numerous: a few hundred, the majority of them abroad. . . . No, youth has not disavowed its elders, nor the masses their organizations, nor the organizations their leaderships.''[75] Bonnaud did not need to add that a war seven years old had not yet ended.

9 The Putsch

In the summer of 1960, in his addresses to the nation and on his tours of the French countryside, Charles de Gaulle began talking publicly of an *Algérie algérienne*. "Algerian Algeria is in motion," he declared in a press conference on September 5. Under his leadership, he said in an address on November 4, France had been traveling a road leading to "an Algerian Algeria . . . an Algeria which . . . will have its government, its institutions and its laws." On December 20 he reiterated that "The Algeria of tomorrow will be Algerian." In his New Year's greeting to his countrymen, de Gaulle once again spoke of an Algerian Algeria.[1]

Army activists read the phrase as a death sentence pronounced on their hopes and ambitions. Rumors of military plots against the regime abounded, and finally, in April 1961, the army revolted. This "putsch" was a fiasco.[2] Some of the soldiers went underground, joining the settlers in the last and most desperate incarnation of Algiers activism, the Organisation armée secrète (OAS). But the French army's resistance to an *Algérie algérienne* was broken. And without the army's support, this ill-disciplined gang of renegade soldiers and settlers turned terrorists was doomed. Its campaign of bombing, shooting, and burning made it a murderous nuisance, not an effective counterrevolutionary force. The desperadoes of the OAS, if anything, hastened the outcome they were bent on preventing. Their actions made it well-nigh impossible for the French to remain in Algeria when Algeria ceased being French.

Thus did the coalition of May 13, fragile from the start, break apart. General Salan, who had once shouted "Vive de Gaulle" from the balcony overlooking the Forum, wound up joining the putsch and leading the OAS. The paratroop officers who dreamed up Operation Resurrection turned their plan for forcing de Gaulle on the country into a scheme for forcing him out. Settlers who formerly had regarded the general as the answer to their prayers now plotted to kill him. De Gaulle himself continued on his way, prowling a long and twisted corridor in search of an exit from the Algerian obsession.

The army might have revolted earlier, under different leadership: a coup was in the works for December 1960. But it is by no means certain that the soldiers would have followed this adventure's planners, who called it off. Most of them, save for the ineffable General Faure, were not known or respected by the officer corps.[3] Only in April 1961 did Maurice Challe agree to put himself at the head of a military insurrection that had already been in the making for months. Some observers think the conspiracy would have fizzled out had Challe refused the leadership. For no one else, they believe, would so many officers have put their lives and careers on the line.[4] In this view, understanding the putsch comes down to understanding Challe. Certainly, some of the putschists had far more ambitious aims than he, and different ideas about tactics.

Why did he agree to lead this doomed adventure? Challe had little in common with the army's numerous Don Quixotes. He was no embittered veteran of Dien Bien Phu, no son of settlers, no fanatical exponent of *guerre révolutionnaire,* no enemy of the republic, no antagonist of de Gaulle. Challe was an extremely bright and dedicated air force officer, a loyal servant of republican regimes, mildly socialist in his political opinions, a self-effacing and practical man whom de Gaulle himself chose to press the offensive against the ALN.[5] He did exactly as he thought he had been told. He reorganized French forces in Algeria. He devised a new strategy of counterguerrilla warfare. By all accounts, he was the most successful of the commanders in chief who occupied the headquarters of the Tenth Military Region. Everyone agrees Challe's plan put the internal forces of the Algerian revolution on the defensive, to the extent that at least one *wilaya* commander, as will be seen, discussed with the French the possibility of a separate peace. Cut off from the supply of men and arms that once flowed freely over the Moroccan and Tunisian borders, the forces of the ALN were flushed from their mountain sanctuaries and harried from pillar to post.

Challe was in some respects an innovator, in some respects a modifier of arrangements laid down by his predecessors. His plan consisted of making more efficient use of the enormous force the French command had at its disposal. The barriers along the Moroccan and Tunisian frontiers, for instance, were already in place when Challe took over from Salan. He made them more elaborate and effective. Running 750 kilometers and 460 kilometers along the borders with Morocco and Tunisia, respectively, the barriers were turned into no-man's-lands several kilometers deep. Infested with mines, barbed wire, and booby traps, ringed with radar-guided artillery and searchlights, kept under constant surveillance by aerial and terrestrial patrols, the barriers offered a profound discouragement to gunrunners and reinforcements seeking to make their way into Algeria. Reducing such traffic by as much as 90 percent, the French reached in North Africa the goal that eluded them—and their American successors—in Indochina. Cutting off infiltrators bringing help from outside, they threw the ALN back on its own resources, and as the offensive against it stepped up, these grew ever more meager.

By depriving the ALN of sanctuary, the barriers established a kind of closed hunting preserve. From the forces at his command Challe drew more hunters than had previously been available. The *quadrillage,* the configuration in which troops had been deployed since the beginning of the buildup, was maintained. But Challe wanted to reduce the ratio of soldiers guarding lives and property to soldiers pursuing guerrillas. To this end he set up *commandos de chasse,* company-sized units composed of both French and Algerians. It was a commando's duty to pursue relentlessly its ALN counterpart, the *katiba,* wherever it went—clear across Algeria, if necessary, until it could be cornered and destroyed.

Reducing the number of troops employed in the sedentary occupations of *quadrillage* enabled Challe to increase the size of the so-called Réserve générale, from which were drawn the troops engaged in large-scale operations against ALN strongholds. Just as he denied the guerrillas their sanctuaries beyond the Algerian frontiers, so Challe deprived them of their hideouts in the mountainous Algerian interior. There was nothing subtle about these operations. They contained little from the manual of *guerre révolutionnaire* and much from the combined air/infantry/artillery maneuvers of the Second World War. This aspect of the Challe Plan called for hammering away with firepower and large numbers of troops at one objective after another. The one new twist—a major one, to be sure —was the use of helicopters, which gave the French a mobility hitherto unseen in war.[6]

Reducing the ALN was not enough; Challe agreed that controlling the population was the key to winning the war. He redoubled efforts to root out the political-administrative structure that enabled the FLN to raise money, recruits, and antagonism to the French. The Challe Plan went to great lengths—too great, in the eyes of many critics—to put rural Algerians out of the reach of their revolutionary compatriots. Partly with a view to creating in guerrilla areas the equivalent of "free-fire zones" (which came to be interpreted as a license for shooting everything that moved), partly with the aim of depriving FLN agents of their clientele, the French indulged in wholesale resettlements of population. Often gathered up hastily, roughly, and against their will, Algerian peasants found themselves in unfamiliar and un- friendly surroundings. Every resettlement whose inhabitants were adequately fed, housed, and kept busy had as counter- parts miserable encampments whose inmates lived in idle squalor.[7]

Defenders of the resettlement program argued that it was a temporary expedient, to be borne only for as long as it took to master the insurgency. In 1959 and 1960, the army be- lieved, it went a long way toward achieving mastery. These were the years of the big sweeps that made up the heart of the Challe Plan. From the Oranais to the Constantinois (or from the thinnest to the thickest concentrations of revolu- tionary forces), the army relentlessly hunted down guerrillas who had gone through the war nearly unmolested.

The offensive was a statistical success. Or at least the evidence with which the army and its champions claimed success was mainly statistical. The statistics describe a kind of seesaw effect. The number of weapons lost to the ALN, the number of Algerians deserting to the ALN, the number of attacks on people and property committed by the ALN— all declined. The number of weapons captured from the ALN, the number of guerrillas killed or taken prisoner, the number of Algerians signing up with the French army—all rose. Such figures as Challe and other experienced soldiers read in intelligence bulletins, and other promptings of their hearts and minds, convinced them that victory over the ALN —over the revolution, for that matter—was only a question of time.[8]

The results of the Challe offensive may have been more equivocal than the commander and his like-minded col- leagues wanted to admit. The conclusions to be drawn from

Georges Buis's novel, *La Grotte (The Cave)*, are sharply at odds with the impressions the Challists drew from intelligence reports and talking with each other. Colonel Buis, a combat soldier of long experience and distinguished accomplishment—a seasoned warrior, despite his scholarly mien—in 1959 commanded a sector in the Hodna, whose wild and rugged terrain made it the ideal repair of guerrillas. *La Grotte* is an account of a military operation that might have taken place there.

The cave in question is the headquarters of a *wilaya* commander and his retinue, a battalion-sized force of ALN regulars. For months a squadron of hussars commanded by Major Enrico, a veteran cavalry officer, has been seeking to corner this quarry in its mountain hideout. The mountain is a *gruyère* of caves, and the hussars have poked into one after another without finding anything. Army corps headquarters, blanketing the mountainside with troops, has had no better luck. Finally, falling for a ruse of Enrico's devising, the guerrillas emerge from cover; and their redoubt is discovered. The cave is laid under siege, and for seventeen days the fighting rages on.

La Grotte is as vivid a description of military operations as exists in the literature of the war. Major Enrico's reduction of the cave is a virtuoso performance. He is everywhere at once, coordinating artillery barrages and air strikes, helicopter-borne para assaults and the ground movements of his company commanders. Enrico is also a dissenter from the prevailing military interpretation of official policy. In the course of the battle, in soliloquies and in dialogues with his colleagues, especially his executive officer, Captain Valère, he reveals his profound disagreement with army leadership.

Enrico believes that the policy of pacification rests on false assumptions. In the first place, the policy makers have taken the Algerian peasants for a mass of political illiterates whom terror and gullibility have put at the disposition of the revolutionaries. Enrico believes that if the peasants are not politicized, they nonetheless have a keen political sense; it is not fear alone that makes them complicit with their revolutionary brothers. He plays along with their assurances that they are ignorant of the insurrection, knowing they are in it up to their ears. He has made himself an ethnographer of the mountainside, and he detects signs of their complicity that not only give the villagers away but help lead him to the discovery of the cave.

Enrico is a traditionalist in the techniques of warfare. He deplores the army's infatuation with the theories of *guerre révolutionnaire*. A revolutionary war remains first of all a war: "We must fight, first, like dogs, and not play at being missionaries and nannies."[9] He is as disturbed by the impact of the fashionable doctrines on the officer corps itself as he is contemptuous of their effectiveness in the field. Valère, Enrico's executive officer, is tired of fighting and losing; he wants something to believe in, and he finds seductive the notions his chief rejects. "One isn't obliged to believe completely in what he's doing," Enrico warns, "in order to do it thoroughly."[10] By likening their roles as combatants/pacifiers to those of missionaries or worker-priests, the army activists were asking for trouble: "Because, as in the case of any [*juste*] engaged in action, they don't give a damn whether you're embittered or not, humiliated or not. You understand: 'they' don't give a damn. 'They,' in our case is the hierarchy, the administration, the state. And you, Valère, a captain, you don't even have the right, which others have, to show your displeasure. For you bear arms that the state has put in your hands with your promise always to be of its opinion, that is, satisfied with its policy. Or else you must lay them down."[11]

As the siege advances, Enrico identifies and arrests the members of the local administrative and political organization (OPA). Such actions let the villagers know that he is on to their double game, and their respect for him increases. He realizes he holds the upper hand over the *katiba*. Retreating toward the back of their cave, they will eventually run out of room, and their hiding place will become their tomb. Now is the time, the army command insists, to "regroup" the population, establishing around it a military quarantine capable of preventing the reintroduction of the revolutionary contagion.

A colonel comes out from headquarters to see why Enrico has not complied with the dictates of the official orthodoxy. There can be no such thing as Algerians who are 60 or 70 percent friends, this true believer exclaims. They must be either "for" or "against." And if they know the French insist on this categorization, they will be "for." In order to keep them on the French side, they must be physically cut off from contact with the revolutionaries. Enrico knows it is useless to argue, but he is convinced the policy of resettlement is self-defeating. Nothing could be better calculated to make the peasants vow eventually to reestablish contact with their revolutionary brothers than throwing up barbed-wire barriers between them.

In Enrico's military performance the command has nothing to complain about. But to the extent that his aims differ from the army's, Enrico is fighting his own war. He is committed not to coercing Algerians who have been more or less the accomplices of the revolutionaries into becoming accomplices of the French, but to enabling them to choose their own future, free of coercion from either side. To the village elders who profess their loyalty to him when they see he has the upper hand over the guerrillas, Enrico replies: "Listen carefully to me! My answer is: no. No to rallying. No to submission. Rallyings to me or to the force that I represent, I don't know what that means and I don't want to know. I didn't come to fight on this mountain to impose my law on you but so that you could get a start toward your own. I've done what you couldn't do. Now, if you wish, you can be free men. In the future it will be your turn to protect me when I come among you."[12]

For seventeen days the subterranean battle rages on. The

defenders of the cave, knowing they are trapped, turn on each other for control of their dwindling supplies of food and water. They throw up a wall between themselves and the advancing French. A squad of engineers blows up the wall, but the explosion accidentally brings down a rockslide, dooming the remnants of the *katiba* to die of hunger and thirst.

Enrico has achieved the kind of statistical success by means of which both the French government and its army have measured progress against the revolution. His squadron has killed 319 "rebels." It has captured 230 arms, including 11 automatic rifles and 5 machine guns. But Enrico is uncertain of what has been accomplished. At best, he thinks he has given the mountainside six months free of the ALN. What is more, neither Rostom Moustache, the leader of the *katiba,* nor Tahar Marseillaise, his ruthless second, has been identified among the dead. Enrico has the disquieting hunch that both have escaped. If such able leaders remain at large, he fears, the French will have their job to do all over again.

Returning to headquarters (presumably in Constantine) from his "victory" on the wild mountainside, Enrico learns he is to be reassigned. At fifty-three, soon to reach the age limit for his rank, he faces mandatory retirement. He is informed that he will complete his thirty-five years in the army as a riding instructor at the cavalry school at Saumur. He sees in this assignment, which his fellow officers are sure to regard as an insult or a punishment, the hand of the headquarters colonel who had exhorted him to regroup the population. He has the satisfaction of knowing that the colonel is ignorant of his eagerness to have done with the war.

One morning shortly before he is to return to France, Enrico is out exercising his horse Gama, the sole luxury he has allowed himself during his tour of duty in Algeria. The horse resists negotiating a tree-covered stretch of path, but Enrico coaxes it forward. A burst of automatic-weapons fire shatters the silence, instantly killing Enrico. Tahar Marseillaise, the missing guerrilla leader, emerges from his hiding place in the woods: "With his left hand thrust into its long silver hair he pulled back the drooping head. With his right hand, out of habit, for the edification of patrols and simply for pleasure, he slit its throat from one ear to the other."[13]

With Tahar Marseillaise administering *le grand sourire* to Enrico, Colonel Buis ended his novel dissenting from the military leadership's optimistic assessment of the army's accomplishments in Algeria. In his battle against the cave, Buis's fictional major came up with just the kind of statistics that, in the aggregate, enabled Challe and many of his aides and commanders to see victory over the ALN near at hand. What these wishful thinkers ignored, *La Grotte* maintained, were realities that lay beyond the reach of quantitative measurements of success. They mistook pledges of allegiance made under duress for pledges freely given. They mistook peasants keenly aware of their own self-interest for credulous country bumpkins. They mistook killing off the revolutionary rank and file for crippling the revolutionary leadership. They mistook promises made against the future as adequate compensation for injuries done in the past. They underestimated the difference between coercion at the hands of foreigners and coercion at the hands of neighbors and relatives; they underestimated how long it might take ever to come to an end of the rebellion.

Nothing better confirmed the army leadership, and especially Maurice Challe, in the belief that de Gaulle was cheating the army of its victory than the Si Salah affair. Knowledge of this strange and shadowy episode rests on the accounts of less than a handful of Frenchmen who were involved in it; the Algerian participants are all dead. All reports pretty much agree on the facts of the matter; they are wildly at odds as to their significance. General de Gaulle was its leading actor, but he kept his own views on the affair to himself; his memoirs breathe not a word of it.

Si Salah was the commander of Wilaya IV, which covered most of central Algeria—Algiers, its environs, and some back country beyond. In late 1959 French army intelligence intercepted messages indicating the existence of a deep rift between the leadership of Wilayas III and IV and the GPRA. The internal leaders accused the external leaders of pursuing a hopeless war for the sake of furthering their personal ambitions. The internal leadership's resentment of what it took to be the external leadership's safe and cushy existence in Tunis was nothing new. The despairing tone of the accusations, though, seemed to confirm that the Challe offensive had put the ALN—in Wilaya IV, at any rate—at the end of its rope.

In March 1960 two emissaries of Si Salah found an Algerian *cadi* (justice of the peace) willing to take a message to the French. Mistrustful of the French army, the Algerians wanted to talk directly with the political leadership in Paris. Through the *cadi* they conveyed to Edmond Michelet, the minister of justice, their willingness to discuss the possibility of a cease-fire. Michelet passed the word to the Elysée Palace, which chose to take seriously this rather startling offer.

Those who make the most of the Si Salah affair believe that much more was behind this approach to the French than the defeatist mood of a beleaguered *wilaya* commander. Not only were Si Salah and his subordinates willing to lay down their arms; they were ready to bring Wilayas III, V, and VI with them. The initiative seemed to promise a return to peace across the middle of Algeria, from Tiaret to Tizi-Ouzou—the richest, and strategically the most important, section of the country. The end of armed resistance in the Algerian midsection would at the least have isolated and discouraged the guerrillas at the wings; at the most it would have deprived the GPRA of its revolution. Such, at least, was the thinking of Challe and his close advisers.[14]

Challe left his Algerian command soon after talks began between the Wilaya IV leaders and the French, but

Colonel Jacquin, head of the intelligence bureau in Algiers, took part in them for the army. Bernard Tricot, by now de Gaulle's chief adviser for Algerian affairs, represented the Elysée Palace.

In March 1960 Tricot and a colonel on Michel Debré's staff opened secret talks at the prefecture in Médea with Lakhdar, communications officer for Wilaya IV, and Abdelhatif, the local ALN leader. Tricot was convinced that the men across the table from him wanted an end to the war. He was much less certain of what they expected from the future. Here, of course, is where differences as to the significance of the Si Salah affair arise. The technicalities of a cease-fire were quickly dispatched. The *wilaya* leaders agreed that all combatants under their command would turn in their weapons at the nearest gendarmerie and would be free to return to their homes. These were terms in which observers friendly to the army have seen nothing less than a surrender. The *wilaya* leaders repeatedly insisted on seeing the imprisoned Ahmed Ben Bella, a request the French repeatedly refused. But when they asked for time to go back and consult with their comrades in the bush, the French agreed.[15]

Talks resumed at the end of May. The *wilaya* representatives insisted they had found widespread approval of their efforts among their colleagues, but they still wanted to see Ben Bella. Unsure of themselves, uncertain of the good faith of the French, they needed something to show for the enormous risks they were taking. Unwilling to arrange a meeting between the revolutionaries and their imprisoned leader, for fear the rest of the FLN leadership might learn of it and sabotage the negotiations, the French representatives offered instead a conference with a high French official. Tricot takes credit for this idea. He thinks the Algerians probably guessed that the official in question was to be de Gaulle himself.[16]

For a meeting with the head of state, only the three principal leaders of Wilaya IV would do. On June 10 or 11, 1960, Si Salah, Lakhdar, the political officer who had been in on the talks from the beginning, and Si Mohamed, the military commander, who was known to have his doubts about the peace initiative, entered a side door of the Elysée Palace. The exchange with de Gaulle was the only face-to-face encounter that ever took place between a French head of state and Algerian revolutionaries.[17]

According to Tricot, who attended the meeting, the three *wilaya* leaders explained to de Gaulle that they did not want to appear to be selling out the revolution. They asked to be allowed to make contact not only with the adjacent Wilaya III but also with the GPRA in Tunis, for the purpose of convincing the external leadership that a cease-fire offered the best chance of salvaging something from the wreckage of their hopes. De Gaulle agreed to the contact with Wilaya III, but not the conference in Tunis, consenting only to convey a message from the *wilaya* leaders to the GPRA. De Gaulle concluded the exchange by disclosing that he intended to make one last public appeal to the GPRA for negotiations.[18]

Indeed, on June 14, toward the end of a televised address, de Gaulle declared: "Once more I turn, in the name of France, toward the leaders of the insurrection. I declare to them that we await them here in order to find with them an honorable end to the fighting which still drags on, to settle the disposition of arms, and to assure the lot of combatants."[19]

At this point, accounts of the Si Salah affair sharply diverge. According to Challe, Colonel Jacquin, and others sympathetic to the army, de Gaulle's disclosure consternated the *wilaya* leaders. Jacquin had understood Si Salah to say he would go to Paris only on the understanding that de Gaulle would not resume his dealings with the external leadership.[20] Tricot's account has Si Salah and his colleagues taking both de Gaulle's disclosure and his remarks of June 14 in stride.[21] It is true, in any event, that Si Salah went ahead as if nothing untoward had happened to rally support for a cease-fire among the internal leadership.

The GPRA accepted de Gaulle's invitation. Talks convened at Melun on June 25, only to break off inconclusively four days later. But a corner had been turned. Henceforth, the decisive events of the war took place at conference tables in Europe, not in the cities and countryside of Algeria.

What did Si Salah's peace initiative have to do with getting the GPRA to the table? Would the external leadership have gone to Melun in the absence of the *wilaya* leader's dealings with the French, or did news of his efforts toward a separate peace force its hand? It is impossible to say.

In any event, Si Salah's venture cost him his life. Despite the Melun talks, at the beginning of July he went to see Mohand ou el Hadj, the Wilaya III commander. In his absence, Si Mohamed, who had never been enthusiastic about the peace initiative, swung behind the GPRA. He ordered Lakhdar put to death, Si Salah arrested, and numerous subordinates liquidated. Seeing that de Gaulle meant to deal with the external leadership, French army intelligence theorized, Mohamed scrambled back in line. Dragged around Algeria as Si Mohamed's prisoner, Si Salah was soon killed in a French army ambush. Si Mohamed met a similar fate. Some army officers believed that the Elysée Palace was behind the deaths of the only Algerian witnesses to the face-to-face meeting with de Gaulle.[22]

The one clear thing about this murky episode is that it deepened the misunderstanding between the army leadership and de Gaulle. Challe, and such officers as were either privy to the affair or got wind of it, saw Si Salah's initiative as virtually offering the surrender of a substantial portion of the interior forces of the revolution. Consummating such a separate peace, they believed, would have left the GPRA high and dry in Tunis, and France in control of Algeria. Shunning this bird in the hand for two in the bush, de Gaulle sold out Si Salah and his colleagues.

In hindsight, at least, Bernard Tricot did not believe that the Si Salah affair amounted to as much as the army leadership made of it. He considered the *wilaya* leaders' initiative a most ambiguous gesture. He did not think his Algerian interlocutors were ready to put aside their hopes of independence. He did not believe they were ready to break with the GPRA and throw in with the French, or that they expected de Gaulle to cease dealing with the external leadership once he had opened discussions with them. Instead, Tricot saw an enterprise flawed from the beginning by the *wilaya* leaders' conviction that they could put an end to the fighting without abandoning their colleagues in Tunis. Their anxiety not to be regarded as betrayers of the revolution kept them from making the break with the GPRA that a separate peace would have required.[23]

Nevertheless, de Gaulle may have talked with Si Salah and his comrades only as a means of forcing the GPRA to the conference table. Once the men in Tunis agreed to talk, de Gaulle lost interest in the *wilaya* leaders. Whether the general abandoned, or double-crossed, Si Salah in the interest of peace in Algeria is a question to which such memoirs as Tricot's do not address themselves.

The army activists were readier to accept defeat than the consequences they perceived as stemming from defeat. As they made clear when they went on trial, most of the officers who threw away their careers in the April gamble against de Gaulle equated the loss of Algeria with the loss of honor. Honor was the most military of virtues, an anvil against which even oaths of obedience could be broken. Between dishonor and disobedience, how could any soldier fail to choose disobedience?

Such, at least, was the choice most of the rebels claimed they faced. A para, a legionnaire, a veteran of Indochina, a company commander in the crack 1er REP *(Régiment étranger des parachutistes),* Captain Estoup was an officer who took himself to be typical of those who joined the putsch. He had no political motive for joining, he explained to the military tribunal that tried him for his role in the rebellion. From 1955 to 1961 he had simply carried out government policy, regardless of its vicissitudes: colonialist to 1957, paternalist in 1957–58, fraternalist in 1958–59, opportunist after 1959. He had fulfilled missions for which nothing in his military education or his previous army career had prepared him. No one at Saint Cyr had taught him how to provision a city the size of Algiers; or how to lay out a police dragnet; or how to act as prefect of police over a population of around thirty thousand; or how to run an election; or how to set up a new municipality, complete with schools and markets; or how to disperse a crowd of rioters without resorting to deadly force. But in Algeria he had received orders to carry out all these tasks.

He and his comrades claimed no monopoly on patriotism, Estoup went on. For the civilian, however, patriotism was a special costume pulled from the closet only on the day of a general mobilization, whereas for the professional soldier it was his everyday work suit. Estoup and his colleagues were deeply resentful of seeing some of their countrymen laugh at this garb and others describe it as the clothing of fascist butchers.

Then Estoup got to the heart of the matter. "The army," he told the court, "had made a solemn pledge to preserve Algeria as French territory and not to abandon its population to the FLN." Like so many of his fellow officers, he had witnessed the fall of Indochina. In charge of a prisoner exchange, he had seen what became of Vietnamese villagers who had cast their lot with the French; he had watched as Vietnamese families swimming to departing French ships had been swallowed up by the tide. "When one has been implicated once in such a tragedy, one swears never to be an accomplice in it again."

Sensing that the tragedy was near to repeating itself in Algeria, Estoup had almost resigned from the army.[24] But he had taken heart when Challe, the exemplary leader, had put himself at the head of the attempt to keep the army's word. Here the paratroop captain's principal justification for joining the putsch—and that of most of his colleagues who wound up in the prisoner's dock—met the commander in chief's principal justification for leading it. The scales fell from his eyes, Challe wrote in his memoirs, when he realized that "we engaged at our sides hundreds of thousands of Muslims knowing perfectly well they would pay with their lives for their confidence in France, in the word of France."[25] It is hard to see what motive less high-minded than the salvation of honor could have led a commander as able, sensible, and well regarded as Challe to throw in with such a desperate and ill-fated enterprise.

The government was well aware of the army's profound discontent with its Algerian policy. If the military's complicity with Jo Ortiz and his friends in the Week of the Barricades was not enough of a warning, generals questioned the policy in the pages of *Le Monde;* such senior officers as General Salan and Marshal Juin denounced, from the relative impunity of retirement, the commitment to self-determination; in Paris rumors of plot circulated thick and fast as traffic around the Arc de Triomphe. Military security operatives kept some officers under surveillance. The inveterately conspiratorial General Faure, for instance, practically invited attention to himself.[26]

Since its inception, the Fifth Republic had worked to cure the army of its obsession with Algeria. Time and again, in public speeches and private remarks, de Gaulle warned the officer corps against the perils of disobedience. "Your mission," he reminded it in the aftermath of the Barricades, "admits of neither equivocation nor interpretation. What would the French army become, if not an anarchic and derisory collection of military feudalities, if it came to pass that some elements put conditions on their loyalty? Now, I have, as you are aware, the supreme responsibility. It is I who bear the destiny of the country. I must therefore be obeyed by all French soldiers. . . ."[27]

De Gaulle offered the officer corps not only admonitions but distractions. In the early years of the war, especially, the army had deliberately antiquated itself, casting aside its mechanized equipment as impedimenta useless to the task of hunting down guerrillas. The doctrine of *guerre révolutionnaire* had codified this ad hoc response to conditions in Algeria, made fashionable a hostility to military modernism. De Gaulle resumed with a will a program of modernization the emergency in North Africa had disrupted. Military modernization neatly fitted the quintessentially Gaullist plan of marrying France to the century. But it also, or perhaps especially, served to remind the army that it had other worlds than Algeria to defend. Modernization put the officer corps on notice that the day of the *baroudeur,* the quasi-feudal warlord in the manner of Bigeard, was past. The most spectacular, and controversial, expression of the new defense policy was the *force de frappe,* the nuclear striking force. However credible the theories of deterrence spun out to justify such a force may have been, creating it helped break the spell that archaic warfare had long held over the officer corps. Unlike *guerre révolutionnaire,* less esoteric than some of its theorists tried to make it, nuclear warfare put a premium on technical expertise. Strategic purposes aside, the *force de frappe* served to give the army's technicians the upper hand over its politicians.[28]

Reshaping of the army's mission did not proceed fast enough to allay its discontent over Algeria. In the main, the Fifth Republic continued to rely on the old-fashioned remedy of transferring potential military troublemakers to assignments in which they would find it hard to make trouble. Instead of hauling seditious officers before courts-martial, the government reassigned, decorated, and promoted them.

By avoiding direct confrontations with the activists, it avoided making martyrs to *Algérie française*. Sending an officer to central Africa or central Europe kept him under military discipline and out of the newspapers. By dispersing the disaffected, the government aimed to keep them from generating an explosion.

The referendum of January 8, 1961, made plain just how out of touch the army activists were with the rest of the country. In his speech of November 4, 1960, the same in which he referred to "the Algerian republic that will exist one day," de Gaulle hinted that he planned to put his Algerian policy to the test of public approval. In the face of agitation from the extremes of right and left—what he called "two enemy packs, one of sterile immobilism, the other of vulgar abandonment"[29]—and of Parliament's restiveness at the marginal role to which it had been relegated in the conduct of national affairs, de Gaulle probably wanted to show he still had most of the country behind him. A referendum was the most dramatic means available of giving voice to this silent majority.

A communiqué following the meeting of the council of ministers of November 16 proclaimed the decision: "General de Gaulle has announced his intention to submit to the country, by way of referendum, at the opportune moment, a bill relative to the organization of the public authority in Algeria, while awaiting self-determination."[30] The master of ambiguity must have composed this terse announcement himself. Either he intended to show the FLN, the army, and the settlers that he had the overwhelming support of the mainland, that the revolutionaries had better come to terms with him, and the others recognize that it was hopeless to resist his will; or he meant to signal, by referring to "the organization of the public authority in Algeria," that the FLN would be excluded from a settlement, in which case he could expect to win back at least some of the conservative support he had lost.

The text of the referendum did little to resolve the question of just what the country was being asked to vote for. Voters were to respond yes or no to the query: "Do you approve the bill submitted to the French people by the President of the Republic both 'concerning the self-determination of the Algerian populations and the organization of public authority in Algeria before self-determination'?"[31] The text conflated two distinct questions. Voters who approved of self-determination but disapproved of organizing a government for Algeria, however provisional, prior to the vote on self-determination—the position of many on the left—had no way of expressing this yes/no opinion. Parties who interpreted the referendum as an attempt to cut the FLN out of a settlement and thereby to prolong the war, as the Communists did, put out the order for a no vote; so did partisans of *Algérie française,* who wanted no Algerian Algeria—with the FLN or without it. For the extreme left, voting no meant voting for peace. But voting yes also meant voting for peace, leaving it up to de Gaulle to arrange a peace settlement. Wording of the text aside, peace was the dominant issue in the election.[32]

Such campaigning on the referendum as took place was lackluster and desultory, as if the organized parties were resigned to the general's having his direct consultation with the people.[33] De Gaulle was obviously bent on making the election a vote of confidence in his leadership. Three times in rapid succession, December 20 and 31, and January 6, he addressed the nation from the Elysée Palace. Calling for a yes vote in his speech of December 20, he exclaimed: "To me whose task is heavy, what support it will provide!"[34] On New Year's Eve he drew a contrast between the dire consequences of a no ballot—"What a blow would thereby be delivered, preventing me from pursuing my task"—and the happy consequences of voting yes: "In this case I would be confirmed and strengthened for serving as guide to the country and for widening the gate of peace and reason."[35]

His election-eve address was a distillate of the Gaullist theory of direct democracy: "Frenchwomen, Frenchmen, you know it is I to whom you are going to respond. For more than twenty years events have willed that I serve as guide to the country in the grave crises we have lived through together. . . . I need, yes, I need! to know what is in your minds and hearts. That is why I turn to you above all intermediaries. In truth—who is not aware of it—this affair is between you and me."[36] A no vote, he made clear, or even an insufficiently enthusiastic yes vote, would leave him no choice but to surrender his office.

Three-fourths of the 20 million voters who went to the polls on the mainland—75.2 percent—voted yes in response to the question posed in the referendum; 24.7 percent voted no. Much discussion ensued as to whether the majority had voted yes to de Gaulle, or yes to self-determination, or yes to peace. Voters probably saw all three as related. De Gaulle was the man who had brought them this far; why should he not be allowed to continue? The general's threat to resign may have helped assure the lopsidedness of the outcome. Had he consulted the voters on some issue other than Algeria, the results might have been more evenly balanced between yeses and noes. But he cleverly posed what amounted to a question of confidence on the one issue on which many voters of the left could not bring themselves to deny him.[37] Whatever their antagonism toward the style and substance of the Fifth Republic in general and the social and economic policies of General de Gaulle in particular, self-determination belonged to their own traditions and conformed to their own thinking about Algeria.

The outcome of the referendum undoubtedly strengthened de Gaulle's hand vis-à-vis his opponents both on the mainland and in Algeria. That the country was squarely behind him in his search for a settlement had been made as plain as anything in politics usually gets. Much of the no vote—that of the Communists—was as much an expression of an urge to have done with the war as the yes vote was.[38] The soldiers and their dreams of an Algeria transformed under French tutelage had almost no support at all.

Dispersing disaffected soldiers did not keep them from plotting against the government. The main organizers of the putsch had all been transferred out of Algeria. Theirs was a familiar list of names. Yves Godard, organizer of the Battle of Algiers and formerly the all-powerful Algiers police chief, had been reassigned to Nevers; Argoud, wire puller of the Week of the Barricades and presiding genius of the putsch, to Metz; Broizat, militant anticommunist Catholic and regimental commander, to Chalôns-sur-Marne; Charles Lacheroy, theorist of *guerre révolutionnaire,* to the Ecole de guerre; Roland Vaudrey, regimental commander, to Paris; Chateau-Jobert, regimental commander and leader of the jump on Port Saïd, to Niamey (Africa). Dufour, former commander of the 1er REP, having made off with the regimental colors in the bizarre and futile hope of avoiding recall to the mainland, was under fortress arrest and awaiting reassignment to Germany. All of these officers were colonels; all of them, save Argoud (who may have wished to be one), were paratroopers.

Broizat, Argoud, Godard, Lacheroy, and Vaudrey took part in a series of clandestine meetings held between January and April 1961 at the Ecole de guerre in Paris. They were joined by Colonel Gardes, the ex-head of the psychological warfare branch, the inevitable General Faure, and Capt. Pierre Sergent, ex-company commander of the 1er REP. With the exception of Faure, who seems to have been along for the ride, and who never made it back to Algiers, these were the officers who organized the putsch.[39]

The conspirators of the Ecole de guerre were six colonels in search of a general. The army would not have followed Faure across the street. Massu was approached, but declined to take part in a revolt against de Gaulle.[40] Salan was the best-known military opponent of the Algerian policy, but he was not well liked in the army (he was distrusted as too much the political operator) and not thought to have done well as commander in chief.[41] For a time, General Edmond Jouhaud was the primary candidate for the leadership. A *pied noir,* he was well connected in Algiers. But he was an air force officer who was not well known in the army, on whose support a putsch would stand or fall.

Challe was the indispensable man. The former commander in chief kept in touch with the military dissidents after he left Algeria in April 1960; but not until a year later, relieved, at his request, of his NATO command and retired from the air force, did he accede to their plans for a putsch. For Challe, the last straw was de Gaulle's press conference of April 11, 1961, when the general did not bother to conceal his impatience with the failure to reach a settlement. "Algeria costs us," de Gaulle remarked, "it's the least one can say, dearer than she brings in." France had nothing to gain from holding on in North Africa. Indeed, its commitments across the Mediterranean having become liabilities, "France would look with the greatest *sang-froid* on a solution such that Algeria would cease belonging to her domain." A solution that might once have seemed disastrous, "we now look on with a perfectly tranquil heart." France would not stand in the way of the Algerians creating their own state, a state "sovereign within and without." In countless ways, he claimed, France had recently shown that the creation of such a state was but the fulfillment of French policy. "In sum, what's all that: it's decolonization—it is a fact: decolonization is in our interest and, consequently, our policy."[42]

The day after de Gaulle's address, his last doubts removed as to the course he must take, Challe met with Jouhaud and General André Zeller, former army chief of staff, who had already joined the colonels. Together they set April 20 as the date for the putsch.[43] The conspirators were in a hurry because they counted on using the thoroughly politicized 1er REP to seize Algiers (not without dissent—some conspirators opposed involving foreign troops in a confrontation between Frenchmen). In the last two weeks of April the regiment was scheduled for rest at its home base of Zéralda, thirty kilometers west of Algiers, whence it could swoop down on a sleeping city. But committing the timetable of the putsch to the whereabouts of the paratroops left many loose ends dangling.

United in opposing de Gaulle, the conspirators were at odds over aims and tactics. There were two factions, and, indeed, two distinct conspiracies. The Challists had had enough of civilians—or perhaps they merely betrayed the average soldier's view of the armed civilian as the symbol of disorder itself. At any rate, theirs was a military operation. They aimed to seize Algiers, to rally the armed forces behind them, to conduct the one last grand offensive that would bring the ALN to its knees, and to hold free elections on the political future of Algeria. They claimed to have no designs against the republic.[44] As an earnest of their good faith and limited intentions, they planned to send all conscripts home from Algeria and engage the ALN with professional soldiers and settler volunteers. Challe always denied that he planned a paratroop assault against the mainland, but someone in his entourage may have thought of resurrecting Operation Resurrection.[45]

General Salan and his friends had other ideas about the practice and purpose of a putsch. The Mandarin, placed on a gilded shelf in late 1958, when he had been named military governor of Paris, had retired from the army in June 1960. He had immediately become outspokenly critical of de Gaulle's Algerian policy. He had tried to establish residence in Algiers, for the purpose of leading opposition to de Gaulle from such a congenial place. When the government forbade the move, Salan repaired to Spain, where he became a pole of attraction to such fugitives from French justice as Pierre Lagaillarde and Jean-Jacques Susini.[46] A self-described fascist, the twenty-six-year-old Susini shortly became the chief theoretician and strategist of the OAS in Algeria. His acute intelligence and his icy blue eyes were the two things that struck most people who met him. His belief in the political virtues of violence would have put this right-wing terrorist of the 1960s at home among the left-wing terrorists who roamed Europe in the 1970s. (As it was, he turned to robbing banks instead.)[47]

As his willingness to listen to the likes of Susini suggested, Salan did not share Challe's aversion to civilians. The Madrid conspirators did not conceive of a rising against the Fifth Republic as strictly a military operation. The army would play the key role in such a rising, to be sure; but the soldiers would be joined by armed civilians. Soldiers and settlers together in defense of *Algérie française* was essentially the strategy of May 13 and of the Week of the Barricades. Only this time the conspirators did not mean to restrain themselves. Salan's circle had no patience with the Challists' conception of a putsch as a temporary suspension of the laws of the republic. Once de Gaulle had left office, he would stay out; a new regime would replace the Fifth Republic.[48]

Had the putsch succeeded in toppling de Gaulle, a showdown between Salan and Challe on what was to happen next could surely not have been avoided. As it was, Madrid was a poor place from which to organize a revolt against the French head of state. Out of sight, Salan was also pretty much out of the minds of the colonels who for months shuttled between North Africa and the mainland in search of a leader. He had to choose between joining a putsch already in motion or not joining at all.

One thing the leadership of the putsch had in common was liabilities. The four generals nominally in command—Challe,

Jouhaud, Salan, Zeller—were all on the retired list. Officers on active duty were sure to ask themselves why they should put their careers at risk for the sake of this superannuated quartet. Moreover, the fate of the conspiracy depended above all on the army's state of mind. The leaders' conception of this state of mind dated from their active-duty years. Salan's, for instance, went back to the end of 1958, only weeks after the officers had withdrawn from the committees of public safety and months before de Gaulle's self-determination speech; Challe's dated from the spring of 1960, only weeks after the Barricades episode. Madrid and even NATO headquarters at Fontainebleau were not good vantage points from which to test the Army of Algeria's mood as it stood in April 1961.

The putsch began auspiciously enough. At two o'clock in the morning of April 22, a Saturday, the 1er REP moved into Algiers and seized nearly without incident (a master sergeant was accidentally shot and killed) the usual strong points and the headquarters of the military and civil administrations. The city awoke to find the military rebels in control.[49]

But the revolt's first day was its best. Most of the units that came over at all came over then. The main support for the conspiracy resided in the paratroop regiments—elements of the Tenth and Twenty-fifth divisions, the spearheads of the Challe offensive. Not all the para regiments rallied to Challe. The Third Regiment of Colonial Paratroops (renamed the Third Regiment of Paratroops of Marine Infantry [3^e R.P.I. Ma.]), for instance, Bigeard's old outfit, remained loyal to the government. But it was one of the few that did. The Fourteenth and Eighteenth regiments of light-infantry paratroops (*chasseurs parachutistes*) left the Constantinois to put themselves at Challe's disposal; the First Regiment of Foreign Legion Infantry moved toward Algiers from the Oranais, the western flank of Algeria.[50]

Outside the para regiments, though, April 22 was a different story. Despite the presence of two air force officers, Challe and Jouhaud, in the leadership of the putsch, the air force had little enthusiasm for the movement. And the navy retained its reputation for always being one revolution behind. A stray naval officer or two joined the putsch, but most shut themselves up ashore or on shipboard and rode out the revolt as they might have ridden out a Mediterranean squall.[51]

On the 23rd, General Salan turned up in Algiers, Jean-Jacques Susini in tow. Lagaillarde had been left behind in Madrid.[52] Colonel Godard, once again a de facto police chief, as well connected as any soldier to the world of settler activism, was already giving the civilians of the embryonic OAS the free run of the city, and this alarmed Challe. The arrival of Salan put at Challe's elbow the man whose views on the tactics and purposes of the revolt were decidedly different from his. Behind the façade of unity, Salan's "politicians" maneuvered for the upper hand over the exponents of a strictly military operation.[53]

The great performance of the crisis—one of the great performances of his career—belonged to General de Gaulle. At eight o'clock on Sunday evening, April 23, he went on radio and television and poured out his scorn and wrath. The ringleaders of the putsch he denounced as "Usurpers—partisan, ambitious, and fanatical—who see and comprehend the nation and the world only through the distortion of their frenzy. . . . In the name of France," he went on, "I order that all means, I say *all* means, be employed everywhere to block the road to these men. . . . I forbid any Frenchman, and first of all any soldier, to carry out any of their orders. . . . The future of the usurpers must be only that for which the rigor of the law destines them. Frenchwomen! Frenchmen! See where France risks going compared with what she was in the process of becoming again. Frenchwomen, Frenchmen, help me!"[54]

De Gaulle's speech made the government seem better prepared to meet the rebels' challenge than it probably was.[55] On Sunday evening, the regime had relatively few experienced forces on hand with which to defend the capital. As if responding to the general's appeal for help, the following afternoon thousands of Parisians went out on a largely spontaneous general strike.[56] Throughout Algeria, conscripts huddled around transistor radios heard the head of state himself not only approve but command the kinds of actions against rebel officers they had already begun to carry out.

On Monday morning, the putsch was dead in the water. Challe had not succeeded in rallying any more units than he began with on Saturday. Officers who had joined the putsch found themselves without troops to command, for conscripts under their orders refused to follow them. Still the rebels held on, evidently hoping for a miracle. By Tuesday noon, even in Algiers, Challe could be certain of the loyalty only of the 1er REP. The other para regiments were wavering.[57]

For bringing the putsch to such a pass, the Gaullists and the left both claimed credit. Both sets of claims rested on the contingent's resistance to the officer corps's rebellion. Resistance took many forms. In the Constantine army corps it was especially inventive. One drafted army doctor lured a rebel major into the infirmary and immobilized him in a full-body cast. Elsewhere in Constantine, the resistance, organized by young Catholic trade unionists, took the form of a sit-down strike. Draftees assumed their usual assignments and refused to budge from them. Radio operators were in an especially good position to bedevil the putschists, as messages got lost and scrambled.[58]

Were the draftees' actions a response to de Gaulle's speech, to the urgings of the leader to use "all means to block the road"? Or was resistance a spontaneous movement of the rank and file, preceding by more than a day the leader's broadcast appeal? Did the famous transistors create the resistance, in short, or did they only legitimize it?

"In Algeria," General de Gaulle wrote in his memoirs, "a

million transistors were tuned in. From then on"—that is, from the moment of his speech—"the revolt met on the spot a passive resistance that became hourly more explicit."[59] According to writers of the left, however, draftees did not await a signal from de Gaulle to begin organizing themselves against the putsch. By the time de Gaulle spoke, they claim, most of the units whose officers had gone over to the rebel side had already refused to join them. The writers concede, though, that the general's speech reassured many of those who had acted on their own against rebellious authority that they were only doing their duty.[60]

What did the resistance accomplish? Was it an iron bar that brought the machinery of the rebellion screeching to a halt? This was the view congenial to the left. Or did the military revolt, never building up sufficient momentum to get anywhere, collapse of its own internal weaknesses? This is the more plausible view.

The conspirators badly miscalculated the mood of the army. Instead of an officer corps passionate in its commitment to *Algérie française,* outraged at de Gaulle's alleged violation of its honor and burning to get even with its betrayer, most were *attentistes,* fence-sitters waiting to see to which side it was more prudent to leap. The Challists later complained that many senior officers, tipped off on the date set for the putsch, arranged to be on leave when the fateful day arrived.[61] The more time Challe spent on the telephone, listening to one general after another evade his appeals for help, the plainer it must have become that his enterprise was doomed.

The ten regiments at Challe's side from the beginning, some eight thousand to ten thousand men, were not enough to bring the cautious off the fence. The conspirators' miscalculation of the army's mood, the failure of their move on Algiers to trigger the chain reaction they expected left them bemused and uncertain. With no alternative to fall back on, they stubbornly persisted in attempting to wheedle from the officer corps a commitment they had counted on winning spontaneously. Pierre Sergent, the fervent Foreign Legion captain, doubted many of them ever really believed in the likelihood of success.[62] To such men, defeat came as a self-fulfilling prophecy.

By April 25 the leaders of the putsch recognized that the end had come. Challe and his followers gave themselves up to the authorities, as their sense of duty required of defeated soldiers. The "politicians"—Salan, Jouhaud, Godard, Paul Gardy,* Argoud, and others—went underground. They resolved to keep on fighting, if not to keep Algeria French, then to wreck the prospects of an *Algérie algérienne*. The failure of the putsch released them to do as they wanted: arm the civilians and embark on a terrorist campaign of their own. From among the politicians came much of the leadership of the OAS.[63]

The 1er REP's vivid sense of theater did not fail it. Down the road to Zéralda lay courts-martial and the disbanding of their regiment, but as the legionnaires were trucked back to camp they sang Edith Piaf's music-hall hit, "Je ne regrette rien." Some of them contrived to blow up the barracks they had built, following Legion tradition, with their own hands. This touch of grand opera brought the putsch to a close.[64]

The general strike and the draftees' passive resistance encouraged the left to take credit for the collapse of the putsch. In the face of such claims, the government tried to minimize the danger the country had faced. *L'Humanité*'s crowing over the "victory" and demanding severe punishments for the putschists and a draconian purge of the army earned it yet another police seizure.[65]

Government spokesmen continued to insist that credit for overcoming the putsch belonged to de Gaulle. According to a

*A retired inspector general of the Foreign Legion.

poll taken a short time after the events of April, about four Frenchmen in ten subscribed to this thesis.[66] But rallying behind the regime was short-lived. In May the deep and prolonged unrest in French agriculture came boiling to the surface in "the most extensive and violent *jacquerie* that modern France has known."[67] Peasants spilled tons of potatoes in crossroads, sacked town halls, and burned effigies of government officials. Tractor-borne demonstrators converged by the thousands on larger towns. Young peasants, it was said, applied in this new war at home lessons they had learned fighting guerrillas in Algeria.[68] Certainly, the disturbances in rural France notified the government that the people were not prepared to put aside their own grievances indefinitely for the sake of meeting the crisis in North Africa. The renewed social agitation of 1960 and 1961 signaled that most Frenchmen believed the danger from Algeria was nearly over.

Punishing the rebels as severely as the left demanded would have stirred resentment in the rest of the officer corps, deepened the army's sense of alienation from the nation and the regime, and tempted to still further adventure those officers guilt-stricken over their failure to join their defeated colleagues. Treating the putschists too leniently might seem a payoff of the soldiers to whom the regime owed its existence, or an admission that the army might still make trouble.

General de Gaulle was determined to remove the trials of the putschists from the hands of ordinary courts-martial, which he blamed for going too easily on the defendants in the Barricades affair. By a decree of April 27, and under the authority of article 16 of the constitution, he established a High Military Tribunal. The tribunal consisted of nine judges—five military and four civilian—drawn from the magistrature, general officers of the armed forces, the Legion of Honor, and the Order of the Liberation, all of whom were to be named by the president. Established to try crimes against state security and military discipline, as well as a catchall "related infractions committed in connection with events in Algeria," the High Military Tribunal received cases referred to it by decree and allowed no appeal from its decisions. The executive, not an examining magistrate, decided whether the facts of a case merited a trial. The government did not retreat from this intrusion into the judicial branch until after the end of the war.[69]

The tribunal met the conflicting demands of political justice by going hard on the leaders and easy on the followers. Unlike the Barricades trial, which became a weeks-long forum for attacks on the regime, the sessions went speedily. Most defendants limited their testimony to explaining the motives behind their actions; by the end of July 1961 nearly all of them had been tried. The stiffest sentences went to those who had not appeared in the courtroom. Generals Salan, Jouhaud, and Gardy and Colonels Argoud, Broizat, Gardes, Godard, and Lacheroy, all of whom went underground rather than give themselves up, were condemned to death *in absentia.* (This judgment was not as severe as it looked; anyone falling into the hands of the French authorities had the right to be retried, as Jouhaud and Salan were. Both escaped the firing squad.)

Those who went home and faced the music were given prison sentences tailored to fit their places in the military hierarchy and the seriousness of their actions.

Challe, Zeller, and General Pierre-Marie Bigot, the air force officer who had gone along with the subterfuge enabling the chief conspirators to make their way from France to Algeria, all received fifteen years. Elie de Noix de Saint-Marc, interim commander of the 1er REP, was sentenced to ten years; the colonels commanding the Fourteenth and Eighteenth Paratroop regiments, to eight. Sentences meted out without suspension ran down to General André Petit's five years. Suspended sentences ranging from five years to one year were imposed on senior officers judged less compromised by their participation in the putsch than the leadership and on such relatively junior officers as company commanders and squad leaders of the 1er REP. Several officers were acquitted of the charges against them.[70]

More than two hundred French officers wound up in prison, serving sentences or awaiting trial for their parts in the putsch. Among this number were some of the best officers in the army, men with long and distinguished records. To ask what such able and honorable men were doing in the dock was to ask to what extent ruination was a fate of their own devising, or to what extent they were the government's victims.[71]

Certainly, defendant after defendant portrayed himself as a victim. Captain Estoup, it will be recalled, described to the court how he had dutifully carried out every unfamiliar and contradictory mission the government had thrust upon him, until its demands strayed too far from conduct he deemed commensurate with honor. It was true that from the outset of the war in Algeria, indeed from the outset of the era of decolonization, the professional soldiers had been made the executants of contradictory and ambiguous policies. The Battle of Algiers was only one such case. The soldiers had been strung along in their view of themselves as the defenders of western civilization in Indochina, as the builders of a new and liberal order in Algeria, first by the Fourth Republic, then by General de Gaulle. Major Saint-Marc, by all accounts the paragon of the honorable soldier, summed up at his trial the feelings of many of his comrades. "Fifteen years of hope," he said, "turned out to be fifteen years of deceit."[72]

If de Gaulle did not betray the army outright, as the military rebels so passionately believed, neither did he offer it a straightforward explanation of the course he had decided to take. Reasons of state may excuse de Gaulle's dissembling and duplicity. Nevertheless he wound up negotiating with the FLN and relinquishing to it the governance of Algeria, actions he explicitly told the soldiers he would not commit. Independence cost the lives of thousands of Algerians the soldiers had sworn to protect, just as they said it would. In

April 1961 de Gaulle had only anger and scorn for the leaders of the putsch. But he recognized years later that "their motives—as I knew and felt—were not entirely base."[73]

If de Gaulle deceived the soldiers, they also deluded themselves. They were not the only men in France who had consciences, as they all too readily allowed themselves to believe. Nor did wearing a military uniform constitute the sole badge of patriotism, as Estoup professed to think. The most disastrous manifestation of the army's collective self-delusion was its conviction that dissent from de Gaulle's Algerian policy left it no recourse but revolt. In truth, there was a remedy at hand far short of defiance, prison, and disgrace. As Major Enrico explained to Captain Valère, any officer who could not in good conscience carry out his government's policy could resign from the army.[74] As de Gaulle told the officers assembled before him on November 23, 1961, at Strasburg, a city chosen to emphasize the army's new preoccupation with the defense of Western Europe, "As soon as the state and the nation have chosen their path, military duty is marked out once and for all. Beyond its rules, there can be, there are only lost soldiers. . . ."[75]

10 Algerian Algeria

The failure of the putsch removed from the French side the last force capable of frustrating de Gaulle's urge to have done with the Algerian war. It was widely believed that the general, having faced down an uprising in his own camp, would speedily reach an agreement with the rebels. Electoral and public-opinion polls had repeatedly shown the overwhelming majority of the French to be squarely behind this goal.[1] No political party had the power, scarcely any had the inclination, to stand in de Gaulle's way. Indeed, no French leader in modern times, save Clemenceau, had to pay less attention to parliamentary opposition and constitutional restraints. The agreement ending the war, when it came, was one for which de Gaulle could justly claim entire responsibility.

But agreement did not come quickly. In May 1961 the French government and the FLN resumed the negotiations broken off at Melun in June 1960. But not until the following March, nearly a year after the collapse of the putsch, did negotiators arrive at a cease-fire and at agreements ending French sovereignty over Algeria.

These months of negotiation were filled with some of the war's most horrifying episodes. OAS gunmen murdered Algerians lying helpless in hospital beds; FLN terrorists shot down European teenagers sunning themselves at a beach. Plastic bombs reaped among settlers and Algerians an indiscriminate harvest, in Algiers and Oran, especially.[2] In the same months, Paris reverberated with explosions. A bomb meant for André Malraux instead blinded a little girl. This outrage brought thousands of Parisians into the streets; hundreds of thousands more, the largest crowds seen in the capital since the days of the Popular Front, came out after eight demonstrators died under a police assault.[3] The last year of the war confirmed what Tocqueville noted in 1848: "In a rebellion, as in a novel, the most difficult part to invent is the end."[4]

The settlers feared that the failure of the putsch meant they were shortly to be thrown to the wolves. Any chance of the army's "tilting" their way in a confrontation between Paris and Algiers seemed gone forever. For the defense of their interests, they could henceforth depend on no one but themselves. They had to resist the government's attempt to abandon them with the only weapons they had at hand; they must respond to FLN terrorism with terrorism of their own. Such reasoning led the overwhelming majority of the settler community to support the OAS.[5] The French government found itself caught between FLN and OAS, negotiating a place in an Algerian Algeria for settlers doing their best to prevent such an Algeria from coming to pass. The terrorism of one extreme served as an excuse for the continuing attacks of the other. Upward the vicious spiral went.

In the last months of 1961 Algiers reverted to the battleground it had been in the first months of 1957. The OAS targets were enemies in the French police, settlers regarded as too liberal in their sympathies, and Algerians who happened in its way. "The OAS Mounts Guard over Algiers," announced tracts scattered in the streets. "The OAS Strikes Whom It Wants When It Wants," warned graffiti scribbled on walls. In banner headlines Parisian newspapers reproduced these minatory slogans.[6]

The impression of omniscience and omnipotence the OAS managed briefly to sustain was false. The Secret Army Organization was a sinister Wizard of Oz. Its terrifying façade concealed a band of activists few in numbers, uncertain in aims, badly divided over tactical issues, ideology, and personality. A French police official who helped break the OAS later wrote: "It was never more than a temporary mosaic of dissimilar, incoherent and often conflicting elements."[7] Most of the writing on the OAS, by insiders and outsiders alike, offers some variation on this judgment.[8]

Founded in Madrid in February 1961 (Pierre Lagaillarde and Jean-Jacques Susini both claimed to have come up with the idea—Susini's is probably the more trustworthy claim), the OAS committed an important murder or two before the putsch, but it did not begin operations in Algeria in earnest until after the army's last gasp.[9] It was in the summer that the ultras and the army activists driven underground by the failure of the putsch put together a semblance of an organization. Until then, Susini later wrote, everyone who had access to a mimeograph machine regarded himself as an OAS propagandist.[10]

The OAS never had more than three thousand members, of whom perhaps a hundred engaged in terrorism. Only the army officers had any previous experience of an underground organization. Many members could not keep a secret; some had a juvenile fascination with passwords and code names and insisted on making the clandestine life even more complicated than necessary.[11] Few had the ruthless efficiency of Roger Degueldre, the Legion deserter who organized in Algiers the Delta commandos, squads of killers who dispatched the police official Gavoury and numerous other victims.[12] In addition to plain men, ill suited to deadly violence, the OAS attracted numerous adventurers and thieves. What happened after the war to a sizable part of its treasury remains to this day a mystery.[13]

Many OAS members declared themselves ready to sacrifice their lives for the sake of *Algérie française,* but few were willing to mute their quarrels of ideology and personality.

Pierre Sergent, who took command of the metropolitan OAS, complained: "Each believes in *his* truth, in *his* solution that he considers unique. Each jealously protects *his* boutique and *his* activists like so many treasures."[14] Even keeping Algeria French was not enough to overcome the ill-feeling between ex-members of the Algerian Communist party (PCA) and integrist Catholics, as antagonistic to "bolshevism" as they were devoted to the Sacred Heart.[15] In its divisions before the common enemy, the OAS resembled the Paris Commune of 1871. And just as the commune could not decide what to do about the government at Versailles, so the OAS could not figure out what course of action, beyond its blind and desperate terrorism, to take against the government of General de Gaulle.

As de Gaulle moved inexorably toward a settlement, the OAS became less selective in its violence. It turned to wrecking what the settlers had built in Algeria, seeking to ruin with scorched-earth tactics a victory the FLN could no longer be denied. The OAS's doomsday schemes included launching a tanker loaded with sixteen thousand liters of gasoline into the Casbah from the heights above, burning down the library of the Faculty of Algiers, and blowing up oil-storage facilities in Oran.[16]

As the fall of 1961 approached, the distance separating the French government and the FLN narrowed rapidly. De Gaulle yielded ground he had previously insisted on defending. He was not one to keep the settlers from sleeping in the bed they were making for themselves. The FLN may have wanted to come to terms before the OAS reduced Algeria to chaos. Neither side had anything to gain from dragging things out, and recognizing that they faced in the OAS a common enemy may have pushed the French and the FLN closer to agreement.

The Melun talks, it will be recalled, broke off inconclusively at the end of June 1960. Neither side betrayed any eagerness to resume them. At the end of December, following de Gaulle's riot-torn trip to Algeria, the French made in Switzerland a secret contact with two representatives of the FLN. More secret talks followed in February and March (these meetings were limited to talks about the possibility of resuming talks; no substantive issues were discussed). On March 30, 1961, the French government and the GPRA announced that talks would presently resume at Evian, near the frontier with Switzerland, to which the Algerian delegates could withdraw for discussions among themselves. But Louis Joxe, who as minister of state for Algeria was to head the French delegation, declared that representatives of Messali Hadj's MNA would also be welcome at the conference table. Apprised that its old enemies were to be allowed into discussions on the future of Algeria, the GPRA abruptly withdrew.

The putsch distracted French attention from the peace talks. On May 10, however, both sides announced that they had agreed to meet at Evian. The French made no mention of talking with anyone but the GPRA. Accepting bilateral discussions meant accepting a bilateral peace settlement. When the French and Algerian delegates convened at Evian on May 20, the search for an agreement began in earnest. Henceforth, even though talks were suspended from time to time, neither side regarded them as adjourned. Broken off at Evian on June 13, discussions were resumed at Lugrin from July 20 through July 28. Secret contacts took place in the last half of October. Notes and texts were handed back and forth in the winter. Between February 12 and 18, 1962, private talks resumed in a government ski lodge in Les Rousses, preparatory to publicly announced negotiations at Evian on March 7. On March 18, French and Algerian delegates signed an agreement ending the war and setting forth the relationship to prevail between France and an independent Algeria.

Serious peace negotiations lasted little more than a year. Talks ending the Korean war dragged on at Panmunjom more than two years. Finding a way out of the second Indo-china war required four-and-a-half years of discussions. Compared with these tedious and labyrinthine efforts, the Algerian settlement was carried out with efficiency and dispatch.

For all of that, reaching a settlement was not easy. Both sides gave ground. The GPRA conceded a little and the French a great deal. De Gaulle's critics think his concessions were both unwise and unnecessary; the severest regard the settlement as a sellout. His admirers think he managed to get the best terms circumstances permitted.[17]

When allowances are made for Bernard Tricot's eagerness to put a good face on a settlement he played a large role in working out, his memoirs remain the best available source on the evolution of the French negotiating position. His account is closely followed here.[18]

At the outset, that is according to the terms de Gaulle laid down in his speech of June 14, 1960, the French envisaged the purpose of talks to be the negotiation of a cease-fire. Since the outbreak of the insurrection, every government had insisted that nothing substantive could be discussed with anyone until after such a cease-fire had been reached. The general still maintained that the political future of Algeria must derive solely from the choice Algerians made in free elections, not from an agreement between the French government and the FLN. But in his press conference of April 11, 1961, de Gaulle announced that he was willing to include in negotiations a discussion of the country's political future.[19] He suggested submitting to the approval of Algerian voters an agreement worked out among all political groups on the scene, including the GPRA.

The implication that he was still looking for a third force may have lessened the impact of de Gaulle's startling change of position. A third force—an Algerian alternative to the FLN—was a will-o'-the-wisp, and probably had been since the early years of the insurrection. The FLN had in Algeria

no serious competitors for power, having done everything it
could to see to that. Political activists who had not been won
over, such as Ferhat Abbas, had been for the most part
eliminated, as attested by the number of Messalistes who
turned up dead on both sides of the Mediterranean. De
Gaulle was too shrewd a political realist not to be aware of
all this. By 1961 his talk of a third force had the look of a
not-very-hopeful bluff: come to the conference table, it said
to the FLN, lest you be squeezed out by someone else. Anyway, private contacts between France and the GPRA
amounted to a tacit acceptance of bilateralism; they suggested that the revolutionaries had nothing to fear from third
forces.[20]

If secret talks established that the GPRA wanted an end
to the war, they also revealed the vagueness of the issues the
revolutionaries were willing to discuss. In their view, sitting
down at the conference table did not necessarily mean getting down to cases. At the end of March 1961, three major
obstacles loomed in the way of a settlement: 1) the status of
Europeans in Algeria; 2) the status of the Sahara; 3) the
relationship between political talks and a cease-fire.[21]

The GPRA wanted to talk first and then stop shooting; the
French sought the opposite. Except for occasional encounters at the frontiers, fighting between the organized armed
forces of the two sides had virtually ceased. But terrorism
continued. The GPRA persisted in seeing the French request
for an interruption of terrorist attacks as an attempt to seize
some sort of advantage, and steadfastly refused to go along
with it. A communiqué issued following the meeting of the
Council of Ministers of March 15 reiterated the government's
desire to see talks on self-determination get under way, but
it made no separate mention, as had always been the practice,
of the need for a cease-fire. Passing the issue over in silence
signaled the GPRA that it could have its way. At the opening
of the first Evian talks, on May 20, France declared a unilat-
eral cease-fire. But FLN terrorism did not cease; it inten-

sified.[22] In stepping up such attacks while peace talks took place, the GPRA as good as proclaimed that the settlers would not be welcome in the new Algeria. Every FLN terrorist became a recruiting sergeant for the OAS.

At Evian it became immediately apparent how distant the two sides were. The GPRA did not stray from the generalities it had been putting out for public consumption. Its delegates seemed ready, on the main points at issue, to hold out for everything or nothing. On two points, especially, they were adamant: the unity of the Algerian territory and the unity of the Algerian people. In other words, they were at odds with the French over the status of the Sahara and that of the European minority.[23]

The French insisted that the great stretch of desert encroaching on the Mediterranean littoral from the south was an entity distinct from Algeria. This distinction, made after the discovery in the Sahara of huge oil and gas reserves, had some foundation in natural history but none in human history. It is true that the Atlas mountains form a barrier separating the Sahara from the coastal plain to the north. Nevertheless, it is equally true that throughout French rule in North Africa, and especially after 1900, the desert expanse and its nomadic tribes had been ruled from Algiers; French administrators had themselves regarded the southern territories as part of Algeria.[24]

At stake between France and the GPRA were not, of course, the sand and rock of the desert, but the riches beneath its surface. French capital (in part) and French technicians had tapped the gas and petroleum reserves that had encouraged French politicians to talk of a France freed at last from imported sources of energy.[25]

At Evian, French negotiators proposed that France share the resources of the Sahara—but not its political control— with the developing countries bordering it, including Algeria, and the tribes thinly scattered on it. Once Algeria had become a full-fledged state, multilateral negotiations would take place on the question of sovereignty over the desert. The GPRA wanted nothing to do with this. It kept insisting that Algeria and the Sahara were one and indivisible.[26] Had this debate taken place in the 1970s, when war had disrupted the flow of Middle Eastern oil and the Organization of Petroleum Exporting Countries sent prices soaring, coming to terms over the Sahara might have been far more difficult. But in 1961 the world supply of petroleum still seemed plentiful and cheap. De Gaulle was too impatient for a settlement to let the Sahara stand in the way. What mattered most, he believed, was that France be assured access to the desert's resources, not that the tricolor continue to fly over it. This position provided a way around the impasse reached at Lugrin.

In a press conference on September 5, 1961, de Gaulle abandoned the effort to make the Sahara a territory distinct from Algeria. Asked for his views on the question of sovereignty over the desert, the general replied that "our line of conduct is that which safeguards our interests and takes realities into account." French interests included the ability to exploit the gas and oil France had discovered, or would discover; the maintenance of landing rights at airfields and transit rights permitting communication with former French territories in black Africa. The realities, he went on, were that "there isn't a single Algerian who doesn't think the Sahara should be part of Algeria"; and that no Algerian government, whatever its relationship with France, would cease demanding sovereignty over the Sahara. As long as its interests in the desert were assured, France was indifferent to the question of sovereignty.[27]

Between Lugrin and de Gaulle's concession on the Sahara, the GPRA underwent a major shake-up. When peace talks reached an impasse, the Algerian negotiators repaired to Tripoli for a lengthy meeting of the GPRA's presiding body, the Conseil national de la République algérienne (CNRA). Negotiations with the French had provoked considerable dissension among the revolutionaries. The general staff of the

Armée de libération nationale, whose influence within the revolutionary movement had grown steadily as fighting in Algeria had diminished, favored taking a tougher line than the GPRA advocated. The ALN did not get its way, but at the end of the meeting the GPRA was differently composed than when the CNRA had convened. The liberals Ferhat Abbas and Ahmed Francis were replaced by the radicals Benyoussef Ben Khedda and Saad Dahlab; some portfolios were reshuffled.[28]

The CNRA apparently believed that remaking the GPRA would improve chances for a settlement. Ferhat Abbas, for one, thought he was dropped for having incurred de Gaulle's displeasure in an incident in Algiers in 1943. Others have suggested that the general had never had a high opinion of the Sétif pharmacist and was not sorry to see him go.[29] It is also true that Abbas and his associates shared the liberal's classic liability: their propensity for compromise made them vulnerable to attacks from the left. Putting the radicals in control of the GPRA was probably intended to obviate second-guessing of the peace negotiators. The French could be more confident that arrangements worked out at the conference table would not be called into question in Tripoli or Tunis. (The ALN general staff maintained its intransigence, but an open split in the ranks of the revolutionaries was avoided until after the Evian agreements had been signed.)[30]

In the end, settling the Algerian war came down to dealing with the issue that had provoked the spilling of so much blood and so many tears. It is virtually certain that in the absence of a large settler community in North Africa, France would never have gone to war to keep Algeria French. No government of the Fourth Republic would have sent hundreds of thousands of draftees merely for the purpose of keeping the French flag flying over a large expanse of territory. Now that the revolutionaries were at last to be conceded what they desired, protecting the settlers remained the government's most pressing and worrisome concern.

The French negotiators had somehow to ensure that a once dominant minority, having incurred the everlasting hatred of some elements of the majority, would be able to lead a tranquil existence in a new Algeria. And adequate guarantees for such an existence had to be negotiated in the face of the minority's attempts at self-immolation. No harder task confronted the negotiators and, as it turned out, none more futile.

At the first Evian meeting, the Algerian negotiators airily assured their French counterparts that the settlers would have nothing to fear in the way of reprisals. But vague assurances of good intentions were unacceptable to the French. Their list of precise guarantees was no less unacceptable to the GPRA—especially the demand for dual citizenship for Europeans who remained in Algeria. Declarations of nondiscrimination and guarantees of civil liberties were one thing; anything as precise as electoral laws, special arrangements for local government, associations for the protection of minority rights, belonged to a sovereign state to grant (or withhold) and ought not to be the subject of negotiations. And the Algerians' declaration that they would respect property "legitimately acquired" was hardly reassuring. The French readily conceded that the way in which the settlers had obtained much of their land would not bear close inspection; still, they were not prepared to leave it to the new Algerian authorities to establish on their own the test of "legitimacy."[31]

Not even within hailing distance of each other at Evian on the status of the settlers, the two delegations moved no closer at Lugrin. As the fall of 1961 approached, the OAS appeared to be succeeding in its effort to narrow the choices confronting the settlers to the suitcase or the coffin. The French government recognized this by quietly making preparations for repatriation. Here was a ticklish issue indeed. For adequate arrangements threatened to stampede the settlers into the exodus the government was working desperately to avoid; while doing nothing to receive thousands of immigrants at once invited chaos on both sides of the Mediterranean if worse came to worst—as finally it did.[32]

Still, the two sides had made progress toward a settlement. De Gaulle's yielding on the Sahara appears to be the breakthrough from which all the rest followed. It is tempting to think he took a hard line on the Sahara only in order to have something important to give away, but no evidence supports such a suggestion. In any event, the French position on other issues also softened or changed shape in the fall of 1961. Changes in language that signified little or nothing to casual observers made a world of difference to insiders.

Until October, de Gaulle said he envisioned the future relationship between France and Algeria as one of "association"—not quite a commonwealth arrangement, but not quite a relationship between sovereign states, either. France, the senior partner in this association, would continue to supply to the junior member the technical expertise and economic assistance provided under the Constantine Plan and would still enjoy certain vestigial rights to the use of defense bases, and so on.

In a brief televised address of October 2, on the occasion of the opening of Parliament (and the lifting of article 16 of the constitution), de Gaulle dropped the customary reference to "association" and spoke instead of "France's cooperation offered to the new Algeria for its life and development. . . ."[33] "Cooperation" implied a remoter relationship between the former colonizing power and the new state. France would not be tutoring a protégé but offering foreign aid to a new nation, from which it could count on little in return.

Previously de Gaulle had always insisted that French aid and assistance to a new Algerian state would be forthcoming only in the event that an "organic cooperation" between settlers and Algerians could be worked out. By this he had

meant that French assistance depended on the settlers enjoy-
ing the guarantees his representatives had set forth at the first
Evian conference. But on October 2 he untied the string he
had attached to assistance and demanded only that the
"community of European origin have its rights and guarantees."[34] Such a phrase hinted that the French might be willing
to agree to less than they had asked for at Evian.

Stalled since Lugrin and the reshuffling of the GPRA,
peace talks got under way again in the second half of October. Plainly eager to reach a settlement before conditions in
Algeria deteriorated into a Hobbesian war of all against all,
the French suggested a secret meeting between three of their
delegates and representatives from the GPRA empowered to
sign a cease-fire agreement.[35]

From February 11 through February 18, 1962, the two sides
met at Les Rousses, in a ski lodge ordinarily at the disposal
of French civil servants and their families (a perquisite of the
kind that may help explain the antagonism in France between civil service and citizenry).

The French delegates—Louis Joxe, Robert Buron, and
Jean de Broglie, all members of the government—were
crammed with their Algerian counterparts into a stuffy,
smoke-filled room. Perhaps such an ambiance promoted
rapid progress. In a week of intense and sometimes acrimoni-
ous debate, the delegates substantially narrowed the ground
of difference on the rights to be accorded Europeans, on the
procedures to be followed at the declaration of a cease-fire,
and on the amount of economic aid France would extend to
Algeria in the first three years following self-determination.[36]

Buron wondered whether the fragile beginnings worked
out in the makeshift conference room at Les Rousses would
ever be able to withstand the tide of events in Algeria, where
"every day the French slaughter a few *maquisards.* Every
day the fellaghas massacre a few French. Every day some
Frenchmen assassinate other Frenchmen in order to delay a
solution we have tried so hard to bring nearer."[37]

The second Evian conference, convened on March 7, built on the foundations laid down at Les Rousses. In the end, the French and the Algerians had relatively little trouble coming to terms on such issues as the arrangements for exercising self-determination and such guarantees that went along with it as amnesty, the freeing of prisoners, the return of exiles, and the presence of foreign observers on election day. The GPRA came round to the position that French sovereignty would end only with the vote on self-determination; it agreed to establish a provisional executive that would rule Algeria between the cease-fire and such time, foreseen as between three and six months, as the vote took place. A High Commissioner named by France was to hold the powers of the republic in Algeria, especially in such matters as defense and the maintenance of order. He would await the results of the election before yielding these powers.

Nor did any major difficulties arise over cultural and technical cooperation. The GPRA agreed to respect property rights already acquired in Algeria by both persons and corporations. Rural property owners affected by any plan of agrarian reform would be fairly compensated for their holdings. Algeria would remain in the franc zone.[38]

But such matters were, and always had been, side issues compared to the two great obstacles that had for so long blocked the path to an agreement. Even after de Gaulle had yielded on the question of sovereignty over the Sahara, negotiators had still to come to terms over the exploitation of the desert's petroleum resources. After hard bargaining, the GPRA agreed to confirm licensing arrangements the French government had already ceded to third parties for the mining and transport of oil and gas; to accord French petroleum companies preferential treatment in the granting of new permits for exploration and exploitation; to undertake no discriminatory measures against such companies.

The heart of the negotiations at the second Evian meeting remained the status of the settlers. To the question, of whom does "the Algerian people" consist, the French and the FLN gave different answers. In the view of the FLN, the Algerian people consisted only of non-Europeans. The settlers could choose to become Algerian citizens within a few years of independence, but if they refused, they would remain foreigners. In either case, their rights with respect to language, religion, and other civil liberties would be respected. The French maintained that Europeans whose roots went deep in Algeria were also Algerians; they should not have to apply for citizenship in the new nation. But the French also recognized the need to keep the settlers supplied with a lifeline back to the home country. Hence, they should enjoy dual citizenship; as long as they stayed in Algeria they had no need, and would not be permitted, to enjoy their rights as French citizens. But after a delay of several years they would be permitted to renounce their Algerian nationality, if they wished, and remain French.

The Algerian delegates insisted on the impossibility of being both French and Algerian: the settlers must choose to be one or the other. Getting nowhere with their proposal for dual citizenship, the French fell back to another position, and this one the FLN accepted. Europeans in Algeria would remain French. But they would immediately enjoy Algerian civil rights and could participate in Algerian political, administrative, and municipal life without having to make any formal request. Within three years of self-determination they could ask to become Algerian citizens. Algeria would cease to regard them as French, and thus would the unity of the Algerian people be preserved. Nothing, however, would keep France from continuing to regard the settlers as French. The old nation and the new one would each treat the settlers by the light of its own laws. A settler who chose to remain in Algeria would be another Algerian. Should he change his mind, and return to France, he would be welcomed as a Frenchman.

The FLN stopped insisting that its vague assurances of

nondiscrimination against settlers were sufficient, and agreed to accord them a special legal status. Europeans would be awarded seats in Algerian public assemblies in proportion to their numbers. The city councils of Oran and Algiers, where most of the settlers were concentrated, would have a European president or vice-president. Rules would be drawn up regarding the participation of Europeans in the administration of justice. They would be permitted to establish an *association de sauvegarde* for the defense of their rights and interests.[39]

On March 18, the agreement reached at Evian, a document of ninety-eight pages, was signed. At noon on March 19, General Charles Ailleret, the French commander in chief in Algeria, and Ben Khedda, president of the GPRA, gave the forces under their commands the order for a cease-fire. As far as the mainland French, the French government, and the leadership of the FLN were concerned, the war was over.

The OAS desperadoes were not yet ready to concede defeat. Quarreling among themselves over their next move, they once more drew on the old tactic of making the army intervene on the side of the settlers. By lobbing mortar shells into the lower Casbah of Algiers, the OAS hoped to provoke revenge-seeking Algerians into attacking European neighborhoods. The French army would be forced to decide between defending the settlers and standing idly by; choosing for the settlers would effectively disrupt the cease-fire. But despite the mortar attacks, the expected Algerian descent on the settler quarters did not take place.[40]

Just as the Casbah had been the FLN's stronghold in the course of the Battle of Algiers, so Bab El Oued, a predominantly working-class neighborhood, became the fortress of the OAS in the last weeks of *Algérie française*. In Bab El Oued lived settlers who had nowhere else to go, men and women who had no savings to speak of, no wealth to send out of the country, no place of refuge awaiting them in France.

On March 23, an incident in Bab El Oued destroyed for good whatever faint hope still existed that the army might come over to their side.

That morning two truckloads of conscripts on patrol in the quarter skidded in an oil slick laid by OAS agents. A hostile crowd surrounded them. Mingling in the crowd and posted on rooftops were roughly a dozen armed OAS agents, and some of the frightened soldiers cocked their weapons. The OAS commando opened fire. In the space of a few seconds, six draftees were killed. Cries of consternation and dismay arose from people who had been jeering the soldiers moments before. Within half an hour of the shooting, gendarmes and zouaves, veterans of riot-control duty—tougher customers than the young men lying dead in the street—surrounded Bab El Oued.

At two-thirty there commenced an afternoon of gunfire more intense than anything seen in the city during the entire course of the war. The rattle of heavy machine guns could be heard over the sound of small arms. Armored vehicles rolled through the streets. Shortly before dusk, fighter planes flew over rooftops, strafing an OAS gun emplacement. The quarter was subjected to the same kind of house-to-house searches the paras had conducted in the Casbah in 1957. The morning's trigger-happy escapade cost Bab El Oued dearly. At least twenty civilians were killed and eighty wounded; the army's casualties were fifteen killed and seventy-one wounded.[41]

As if driven by an irresistible urge for self-destruction, the OAS command called for further resistance to the peace settlement. Early on the morning of March 26, a tract appeared calling for a general strike at two in the afternoon, followed by a rally at the War Memorial at three —the last such rally, as it turned out, in the history of *Algérie française*. At the close of the rally the demonstrators would march to Bab El Oued in honor of the martyrs of March 23. The prefecture of police promptly forbade the march, but the settlers no longer paid attention to the writ of French authorities.

The strike and the rally both passed without incident. Then the demonstrators began moving toward Bab El Oued. They took two routes. A throng of settlers descended the avenue Pasteur. Another large group took the rue d'Isly. A thin line of infantry was positioned across the rue d'Isly near its intersection with Pasteur. Only nine soldiers, eight of whom were Algerians, faced the unfriendly crowd. Behind them, the other group of demonstrators advanced down the avenue Pasteur. Sandwiched between two excited mobs, the thin line was easily broken. As the crowd surged along the rue d'Isly toward Bab El Oued, however, it encountered a much more formidable obstacle—a detachment of booted, helmeted, and armed CRS blocking the way. In no mood to tangle with these street-hardened riot police, the crowd turned around on itself and headed back down the rue d'Isly, away from Bab El Oued, toward the main post office.

The soldiers who had been bypassed had regrouped near the post office. As the crowd reached the intersection of the rue d'Isly and avenue Pasteur, a shot rang out, then a fusillade. The forces at ground level fired from several directions. OAS snipers, or perhaps only armed Europeans (more and more free-lancers were taking to the streets), shot from rooftops, windows, and balconies. Terrified demonstrators dashed for cover against walls and in the doorways of buildings. To the journalist Yves Courrière, flat on his belly in the street, the shooting seemed to go on for hours. It lasted twelve minutes. In the wild confusion, with every armed man shooting at his own set of enemies, more than seventy persons were killed.[42]

Courrière saw in the massacre of the rue d'Isly the death of French Algeria. From the time of the shooting, he thinks, dates the mood of panic and despair that engulfed the settlers and swept them into exodus.[43] The shooting offered final proof, if proof was still needed, that not even to the army could they look for protection. The OAS's boast of striking whom it wanted when it wanted had been exposed as an absurd joke. The incident offered not only a taste of civil war but a presage of anarchy. A day later, on March 27, on the strength of a lead obtained from interrogating a senior officer suspected of sympathies with the OAS, the army tracked Edmond Jouhaud to his headquarters in Oran.[44] On April 20 in Algiers, a double agent named Levansseau put the finger on Salan. The silver hair of which he was so proud dyed an unnatural black, the bemedaled army uniform exchanged for a baggy business suit, a black moustache hiding his mouth, Salan looked more like a seedy traveling salesman than the ex-commander of all French armed forces in Algeria.[45] Bab El Oued left the settlers no place to hide, the arrests of Jouhaud and Salan no one to turn to. Better to get out now, many reasoned, before even worse happened. Better to pack the suitcase than to be stretched out in a coffin.

Getting out did not begin in earnest until April, when French voters overwhelmingly approved the Evian agreements and the Algerian policy of General de Gaulle. Once begun, exodus became a headlong rush to leave. At the airport, the set-piece of revolutionary politics in the late twentieth century played itself out. Clasping small children and such belongings as they had managed to throw together, long lines of refugees shuffled toward airplanes, away from all that was cherished and familiar. Within months, of the million settlers the French army had come to Algeria to protect, fewer than one hundred seventy thousand remained.[46] And soon the army, too, was gone.

The FLN got what it had been fighting for since November 1, 1954: independence for Algeria and control of the apparatus of the new state. France had suffered in Algeria nothing resembling Dien Bien Phu, nor anything like the humiliation of 1940. Nevertheless, in the Evian agreements the French implicitly recognized defeat, surrendered a position maintained in North Africa since a Bourbon monarch reigned in France, an unreformed parliament ruled in England, and Andrew Jackson was President of the United States.

Some thought de Gaulle had been called to office to preserve French rule in Algeria; others believed he had been summoned to make peace. In any event, he wound up conceding the FLN's main demands. Could he have reached such a settlement far sooner than he did? What kept him at war longer than the Fourth Republic had been, only to conclude with the Algerian revolutionaries an agreement that would have driven his predecessors from office? Was he the only politician capable of extricating France from the wreckage of the Algerian adventure, or could someone else have done as well?

There is the opinion that de Gaulle never had a freer hand for reaching a settlement than in 1958. Had he acted soon after he returned to power, he might have salvaged more of the French position than he eventually did.[47] Others believe the need to overcome the French army's resistance to the idea of an Algerian Algeria explains his deliberate pace. Having overmastered the officer corps, he spared it the humiliation of hurrying to a settlement.[48] Still others insist that de Gaulle's stubborn pursuit of impossible solutions needlessly prolonged the war.[49]

The president's admirers see him as the one political figure who had the historical vision, ruthlessness, and courage to remove France from a predicament promising the nation nothing but endless torment.[50] His severest critics regard him as the man who scuttled and ran, denying the protection of the French state to European settlers and the Algerians who had cast their lot with the French, abandoning to a gang of revolutionaries the wealth of the Sahara and dominance of the western Mediterranean.[51] Others lay more stress on vast impersonal forces in bringing on the dénouement of the Algerian drama; they discount the role of heroes, or villains, in history. Sooner or later, they suggest, Algeria would have had its independence of France.[52]

Divining a historical actor's motives is a risky business, especially when the actor is as elusive a figure as Charles de Gaulle. Like Otto von Bismarck, the dominant European of another era, de Gaulle took pains, in the heat of action, to throw everyone off his trail. Like Bismarck, he also took pains, in the calm of his study, to leave the impression that he always knew exactly what he was doing, that he always foresaw the outcome of his policies from a great distance back up the road. His chapter on Algeria is the last place one would expect to find a confession of doubt, indecision, or error.

Yet the portrait of de Gaulle the dissembler can be overdrawn. He was not always eager to conceal his hand. If he believed in the tactical virtues of dissimulation and surprise, he also believed that he owed the French explanations. Long before anyone knew how committing France to self-determination for Algeria would turn out, he was making clear why such a commitment was necessary, why the old relationship with Algeria had to give way to another. De Gaulle cast himself in the role of a history teacher, his father's profession in a Jesuit school in Paris.

The age of empires was over, he declared; France had now to devote its energies to its own modernization. In nearly every major address he delivered between early 1960 and the end of the war, de Gaulle played variations on this theme. Time and again he called on the French to relinquish the past. But never did he denounce imperialism and colonialism as wicked and shameful enterprises. Unlike the left, he did not regard the era of French expansion as the bad old days. "For what France has achieved in this regard and under this form overseas," he said, "she has nothing whatsoever to regret. It is a great human achievement which, in spite of some abuses or mistakes and despite all kinds of low-class demagogues always repeating the same old things, will forever do honor to France."[53] At a stroke he managed to acknowledge the claims of nostalgia and to relegate them to a museum of curiosities from an irretrievable past. "It is entirely natural," he said when he invited the FLN to the Melun talks, "that we feel nostalgia for what the empire was, as we can miss the softness of oil lamps, the splendor of the sailing navy, the charm of the time of horse-drawn carriages."[54]

Colonialism must be renounced not because it was morally reprehensible but because its time had gone. "The spirit [*génie*] of the century," he insisted, "which changes our country, also changes the conditions of its action overseas."[55] The spirit of the century required the French to put their own house in order: "It is a question of transforming our old France into a new country and of marrying her to her times. It is a question of her drawing from it prosperity, power and influence. It is a question of this transformation being our great national ambition."[56]

France must rid itself of external impediments to this great national ambition. In his press conference of April 11, 1961, the occasion on which he first took up the word "decolonization," de Gaulle explained that so vast were the dimensions, and the promise, of internal renovation that France must concentrate at home all the means at its disposal. These means must be channeled into meeting the ferocious "economic, technical and social competition" raging between the "humane regimes" and the "regimes of slavery." The resources France had once poured into its own imperial ventures must now be used to meet the challenges of Soviet imperialism.[57]

In de Gaulle's explanation of the need to reconcentrate efforts on the mainland, external threats mattered far less than internal opportunities. The times offered France a chance to overcome a legacy of economic stagnation and political instability. "Once upon a time there was an old country," de Gaulle said, retelling the fable nearest his heart, "all clad in habits and prudence. Not long ago the most populous, richest and most powerful of those who held the stage, it was, after great misfortunes, as if withdrawn within its shell. While other peoples were growing up around it, it remained stationary. In an age when the power of states depended on their industrial importance, the main sources of energy were stingily meted out to it. It had little coal. It had no petroleum. Its industry suffered from routinism. Its agriculture remained nailed to the spot. Moreover, its population no longer increased, counting, in some years, fewer births than deaths. In the doubt and bitterness that this situation prompted vis-à-vis itself, political, social and religious struggles did not fail to divide it. Finally, two world wars having depleted, destroyed and ravaged it, many in the world wondered whether it would succeed in pulling itself together."[58]

Pull itself together France had done—the general could not resist seeing decline and renewal as variables dependent on whether he was in or out of public life—but only a beginning had been made. Renovation at home left no time, energy, or money for carrying on a colonial war abroad.

Over and over again he drove the point home. On May 8, 1961, on the eve of the first Evian talks, he announced, "In short, this gigantic renewal must be the main business and capital ambition of France."[59] On July 12, between the Evian conference and the Lugrin talks, he declared, "This immense internal effort for power and prosperity determines us to employ our own means at home. This is to say that the enterprise which, not long ago, consisted in assuming the government, the administration, the existence of colonized peoples, is henceforth outdated."[60] On September 5, in the same press conference in which he disclosed France's lack of interest in maintaining sovereignty over the Sahara, he said, "Once again, we are a country in the midst of revolution, which knows the source of prosperity and power is its own development, which needs its means at home in order to carry it out and which does not intend to sink them indefinitely in dead-end tasks."[61] On October 2, he exclaimed, in the opening sentence of a speech: "National renovation! What a huge and formidable undertaking!"[62] In an address on December 29 setting forth the goals of the new year, he said, "In Algeria, France expects that, in one way or another, the present conditions of political, economic, financial, administrative and military engagement which keep her tied to this country, and which, if it remained as it is, would be for her only men and money wasted, when so many tasks call her efforts elsewhere, will come to an end. . . . Finally, and it's the paramount condition of her future, France is resolved to pursue the immense work of her internal renovation."[63]

De Gaulle was given to offering the French choices between calamity and salvation. Sometimes he overdid it, as in the presidential election campaign of 1965, when he presented voters the alternatives of "me or chaos" (after a close squeak in the first round he was reelected). But on the Algerian issue, his either-orism was an effective device. This way, he said, lies economic prosperity, political stability, heightened prestige in the world at large; that way lies stagnation, unrest, and ill opinion. Most of the French probably had little trouble choosing between these alternatives. That the return to sustained economic growth, for which the Fifth Republic always claimed more credit than it deserved, took place in the same years as France fought the war in Algeria was a coincidence on which de Gaulle did not choose to dwell. Plainly he did not care to raise the possibility that the French could simultaneously maintain prosperity and support a low-intensity war (a proposition ultimately fatal to the American presidency of Lyndon Johnson).

National renovation was far more than a gimmick de Gaulle hit upon to explain the need to withdraw from Algeria. It was the central theme of his political career. For all his love of the past, his regal manner, stately prose, and conservative associations (the satirical weekly *Le Canard enchaîné* always portrayed him as the Sun King and his cabinet as courtiers of Versailles), he was essentially a modernizer, a Western version of Kemal Ataturk or Nasser, or maybe a twentieth-century amalgam of Bismarck and Napoleon III.[64] Industrialism and technology, primary agents of historical change, had in de Gaulle's view rendered the old relationship with Algeria as obsolete as these same forces had once made the elaborate fortifications of the Maginot Line.

On numerous occasions he set forth the agenda of national renovation—or modernization—but seldom more completely than in his address of July 12, 1961. Savings must be tapped for investment, the export trade expanded, and new jobs created. In French agriculture, the number of marginally productive peasant holdings must be reduced and their owners provided for; cooperatives must be established; middlemen must be cut from the relationship between producers and consumers. Investment in human capital was as pressing a need as investment in industrial plant. Educational opportunities must be expanded, especially at the secondary and university levels, and facilities greatly increased. Economic growth had been more rapid and intensive in some areas of France than in others, creating regional disparities that must now be reduced. The transportation network linking these areas to each other and to the rest of Europe must be overhauled and the chronic housing shortage overcome.[65]

Such a formidable list of undertakings promised to absorb French energies for a long time to come. In the early 1950s, as France struggled to maintain its hold on Indochina, Pierre Mendès France had repeatedly warned of the necessity of making choices: the nation must decide, he insisted from his deputy's bench, between a colonial war and domestic reform. It could not have both. In 1954 he had liquidated the one in the interests of accomplishing the other, only to find himself confronted with the insurrection in Algeria.[66]

A decade after Mendès first cautioned the French of the

necessity of choice, de Gaulle resumed the theme. The vicissitudes of politics and differences in outlook and temperament had put the general and his former Resistance colleague sharply at odds. But they shared the aim of national renovation; both saw colonialism and its sequels as embodying the grip on France of the dead hand of the past. Insofar as Gaullism and Mendèsism were exhortations to fling off that hand, to "marry France to the century," as de Gaulle liked to put it, they left little to choose between them. One writer of the left detected in the Fifth Republic a strain of "authoritarian Mendesism";[67] he might just as easily have seen in the Mendès France experiment a form of "democratic Gaullism." Important differences of style existed between Mendès and de Gaulle, and in politics, style matters a great deal. But in their views on the French crisis—a generation of economic stagnation, political instability, and war—the man who sent French troops to Algeria closely resembled the man who withdrew them.

"Do you know how you can tell a speech by Jaurès?" Clemenceau is once said to have asked about the great Socialist leader, his archrival in parliamentary debate. "All the verbs are in the future tense."[68] If de Gaulle's verbs were not all in the future tense, much of the explanation of his Algerian policy dealt with the future. If the French economy seemed to be performing well now, lifting the Algerian burden would make its prospects even brighter. Nearly everything that de Gaulle said in this vein could not fail to leave the impression that once the war ended, life on the whole would improve.

The settlers found no comfort in this. Indeed, they found little comfort in anything de Gaulle said during the last two years of the war. The president's explanation of his Algerian policy, tailored for a mainland audience, was to the settlers a pronouncement of impending doom. De Gaulle did little to assuage their fears. On the rare occasions when he spoke directly to them, it was in tones of admonition and reproach.

In his New Year's address of December 31, 1960, he remarked, "I therefore especially invite the community of
French origin of Algeria to decisively tear itself away from
the disorders and chimeras which would cut it off from the
nation and not only accept what the country is going to
decide [in the referendum on self-determination], but to
make of it its business and to seize the new opportunity that
is offered to its abilities and energies."[69] In his speech of
October 2, 1961, he declared: "We adjure the French of Algeria, whatever their regrets for a time gone by, to stay with
France, to contribute their sincere assistance to the birth of
a new Algeria, the one France hopes for, one in which they
shall have a worthy place."[70]

He was always careful to assure the settlers of a welcome
in France, should they find none in the new Algeria, but he
made no other promises. No wonder many settlers came to
interpret the "I have understood you" of June 1958 as signifying "I have taken your measure."

In the Evian agreements, France recognized the right of
Algeria to self-determination and agreed to render economic
assistance to the new Algerian state. De Gaulle described
these measures as the result of policies he had set forth in his
first eighteen months in office, the consequence of three years
of patient searching for a satisfactory conclusion to the war.
What he did not acknowledge was that the purpose of economic aid and the mechanism of self-determination had been
totally transformed—both to the advantage of the FLN.
Elections on self-determination were originally designed to
be held after the FLN had been eliminated as a claimant to
the succession; instead, the FLN wound up controlling the
elections. The Constantine Plan had aimed at winning support from the FLN, not at lending it assistance.

For all his insistence on the need to face realities, de Gaulle
also believed in the need to keep up appearances. He never
conceded that the Evian agreements represented the last
resting place in a measured retreat. De Gaulle's progressive

elimination of the options open before him reminded Bernard Tricot of the closing of a Chinese fan.[71] The search for a third force, and for a cease-fire prior to political talks, effectively ended when he opened bilateral contacts with the FLN; he yielded the idea of maintaining control of the resources of the Sahara in September 1961; hoping for an association between France and Algeria, he settled for cooperation; seeking dual citizenship for the settler minority, he agreed to a formula keeping them French only in the eyes of a French beholder. Having given more ground than he got in return, he pronounced the agreements ending the war the best that circumstances permitted.

Who can gainsay him? He had managed to disentangle France from Algeria. Whatever the complaints lodged by those who had long wished for such an end against the way he had gone about it, he had got the job done; he had succeeded in putting an end to the obsession; he had closed the imperial era; he had set the country on a new course. Conditions may have been more propitious for de Gaulle than they were for his predecessors; letting go of the past may be easier when an economy is expanding than when times are mean and cramped. Nevertheless, ending the war in Algeria was a remarkable feat of political leadership. Perhaps de Gaulle succeeded where others had failed because he alone, of the leadership available, was bold enough—some would say ruthless enough—to disregard the interests of the settlers, to risk sacrificing their position in North Africa for the sake of reaching an agreement with the FLN. He gambled and lost, but the repatriation of the settlers may not have come as a great surprise.

Yet what was gained in the course of the four years de Gaulle took to reach a settlement that could not have been had in 1958? The answer surely is: very little.

The Evian agreements assured France access to the oil and gas of the Sahara and guaranteed the minority rights of settlers who chose to remain. But circumstances made guarantees and assurances fragile things, likely to break when subjected to stress. French access to petroleum depended on the leadership of a poor but ambitious state resisting the temptation to regulate the exploitation and distribution of resources within its sovereign territory. Respect for the settlers' civil rights depended on the capacity for tolerance of a society in the ascendancy after decades of settler rule. Even in the absence of the OAS, the prospects of a minority cast down from its position of supremacy may not have been very good. One-party states elsewhere have established poor records in looking out for minority rights; there is little reason to think the new Algeria would have behaved differently. In the event, its respect for the guarantees of Evian was never put to the test; the settlers removed the problem by removing themselves from Algeria. But the agreements on energy worked out at Evian were a constant source of trouble between the old master of the Sahara and the new. Algeria began with the lion's share of petroleum revenues, but its new government kept insisting on renegotiating some clauses of the Evian agreements and contravening others, and within a decade of independence almost nothing was left of them.[72]

Some observers believed that the end of the conflict in Algeria would provoke endless troubles on the mainland.[73] It was easy to imagine that a remnant of the OAS, its aim of stopping de Gaulle reduced to a blood-soaked fantasy, might set out on a campaign of vengeance and reprisal, picking off one by one a long list of enemies. It was not hard to envisage a mob of half-pay officers, castoffs from a peacetime army, making a formidable nuisance of itself. And officers who remained in the service despite their bitter disappointment in the outcome of the war might be suspect in their loyalty to the regime. It could readily be supposed that one million settlers, cast up as "repatriates" on an alien shore, would hold themselves aloof from the rest of society, heartsick and vengeful, susceptible to the blandishments of a variety of demagogues. At the least, their presence might be expected to evoke among the French the noisy recriminations that had marked the end of other wars.

None of these expectations came to pass. Save for a spectacular attempt on de Gaulle's life in August 1962, the OAS disappeared from sight more quickly than its initials faded from the walls and sidewalks of Paris. Officers retired against their will were quietly absorbed into civilian life; those who remained on active duty embraced the tradition of the army as *La Grande Muette* as if it had never been broken. Displaying the energy for which they had been noted in Algeria, the settlers quickly found a place for themselves in the expanding mainland economy; reclaiming farms that had gone to ruin was characteristic of their activities. If they tended to gather in the south of France, as close as they could get to the remembered North African sun, they were far from being a hard knot of troublemakers. Politically, save for such issues as indemnification for losses suffered in Algeria, they went their separate ways.[74]

Other wars have left on France more tangible evidence of their impact. Spring plowing along the Somme each year turns up a harvest of bomb fragments. Little of value grows in the shell-poisoned earth of the countryside around Verdun. In the twenties and thirties, pitiful husks of men—gassed, maimed, disfigured—scuttling along the sidewalks in their strange wheeled contraptions served constantly to remind passersby of what had happened on the Marne, along the Chemin-des-Dames, and at Verdun. The Algerian war left few such reminders.

With respect to psychic wounds, the war of 1914–18 remains for the French the Great War. Draining the strength, sapping the will of combatants and noncombatants alike, it left France victorious but exhausted, obsessed with preventing a recurrence of the nightmare and fearful that it could not. The losing effort in Algeria, by contrast, demanded no such emotional involvement from most of the French and left no such hangover. They knew the end of the war marked the end of a phase in their history, however much some may have regretted it. Beyond a shadow of a doubt, they knew that French troops would never again be sent to fight in French territory overseas.

Nearly every village in France has a monument naming the village men who died in the Great War. In the aggregate, these monuments announce the decimation of the male population. In this respect, the impact of the war in Algeria on the French bears no comparison to that of the war of 1914–18. In the eight years of the Algerian war, 17,456 French soldiers died.[75] In ten months at Verdun, 162,308—nearly ten times as many—were killed.[76] In one week of May 1871, at least 20,000 French were killed in the street fighting that ended the Paris Commune.[77] Almost twice as many French soldiers —32,000—died in the Crimea in 1854–56.[78]

It was the Algerians who suffered the heavy losses, although the extent of their suffering is not clear and perhaps never will be. One hundred forty-one thousand are calculated to have been victims of their fellow revolutionaries; sixteen thousand Algerian civilians to have died at the hands of the FLN; another fifty thousand are estimated to have been spirited away and presumably killed. These are the French figures; they add up to roughly two hundred seven thousand. Algerian estimates of Algerian dead vary from three hundred thousand to the government's claim of one million.[79]

To these numbers must be added the *harkis,* the Algerian auxiliaries who signed on with the French, only to be left in the lurch at independence. Some made their way to the mainland, but for the most part they died the horrible deaths many French soldiers had predicted for them. Estimates of their losses vary from thirty thousand to one hundred fifty thousand.[80] More Algerians may have died as *harkis* than served as guerrillas in the FLN. Even if these figures are put aside as falling in the category of postindependence reprisals, not wartime losses, the FLN killed more Algerians in the course of the war for independence than it did Frenchmen.

The losses the FLN inflicted on the French—and seventeen thousand is a great many lives, no matter how small a figure it may be made to seem in comparison with the great bloodlettings of the twentieth century—divided the French less than the casualties they inflicted on the Algerians. Or at least less than certain kinds of casualties. The French army's methods in Algeria became an issue sooner than the French government's aims did. And France's recent past, the experience of occupation and resistance, memories of the SS and the Gestapo, impassioned the debate over the army's methods. Politicians who had resisted the Nazis found themselves identified with them, and soldiers who believed they had nothing to be ashamed of had the name of Captain Dreyfus flung in their faces.

It was the issue of torture, more than any other, that goaded governments of the Fourth Republic into attacking civil liberties, especially with respect to freedom of the press. A regime too weak to respect its own laws earned the contempt of the victims of repression without winning the support of the army its actions were meant to shield.

The debate on torture clarified some issues and muddied others, including the question of responsibility. Attacking the paras for their conduct in the Battle of Algiers, for instance, distracted attention from the question of who had decided the city must at all costs be rid of terrorism. And it obscured the fact that every army interrogator derived his authority from the Special Powers Law the National Assembly had overwhelmingly approved.

The debate at least drew attention to the question whether it was possible to fight a "war of the shadows" except by such dark and terrible means. Their negative responses gave antiwar radicals and theorists of *guerre révolutionnaire* one ground of agreement. But the radicals had eyes only for the victims of torture, the theorists only for its practitioners. From similar arguments they drew different conclusions, one side calling for an end to the war, the other side defending its continuance. Caught between them were critics of the war who recognized the predicaments of the soldiers and defenders of the army, who understood the yearnings of the terrorists. Such men of two minds as Pierre-Henri Simon strove to keep the moral absolutism of the extremes from ripping the republic apart.

It was not moral absolutism that finally destroyed the republic, but its inability to reach an accommodation with Algerian nationalism without losing the support of the French army. Having campaigned in the elections of 1956 on a pledge to shorten the war, the organized left, Socialists in the lead, intensified it instead. Bent on taking a new path, Pflimlin and his parliamentary associates ran head on into the army. So it fell to Charles de Gaulle to bring about a settlement. He was no more successful than his predecessors at accommodating the nationalists without alienating the army. But he was able to survive challenges his predecessors could not have, partly because of institutional changes, partly because of the passage of time, partly because of the force of his will and personality, and partly, perhaps, because no alternative as attractive to as many different people any longer waited in the wings. Once he concluded that independence was the price of disentanglement, he did not hesitate, as his predecessors had done, to give the nationalists nearly everything they wanted.

As far as the vast majority of the French were concerned, the importance of the settlement lay not in what it retained for France in Algeria, but in what it restored to the mainland. France was at peace after twenty-three years of war. The last conscripts to serve in Algeria had been born under the German Occupation. The fathers of some of them had taken part in the debacle of 1940. And many professional soldiers went from fighting in Europe to Indochina to Algeria with scarcely a break between. For six years every household in France with a son of draft age had faced the likely prospect of seeing him off to Marseilles and thence to North Africa for the duration of his military service. While most came home safe and sound, some did not, and no parents could help fearing their son might be among this number. For eliminating such fears, the independence of Algeria probably seemed a small price to pay.

If the settlement restored peace to the mainland, it also restored a measure of tranquillity. The resolution of the Algerian crisis did bring other conflicts to the fore; some had scarcely abated throughout the course of the war. But none of these conflicts involved issues over which the French could easily contemplate killing each other. None of them raised such passionate voices hurling against their enemies such grave charges; none made such claims to public attention, to the exclusion of all else, as the Algerian war did. The new conflicts were part of the give-and-take of a democratic society; for a time the war in Algeria had seemed to threaten the existence of that society. If the danger was not always as great as some observers maintained—some put "the brink of civil war" to the same mischief as the little boy put the wolf —in 1962 both the danger and the cries of danger ceased. On the subject of Algeria a great silence fell over the land.

Notes

Unless otherwise noted, the place of publication is Paris.

CHAPTER I

1 Pierre Rouanet, *Pierre Mendès France au pouvoir* (1965), pages 375–76.

2 *Le Monde,* November 2, 1954.

3 Pierre Leulliette, *Saint Michel et le dragon; souvenirs d'un parachutiste* (1961), pages 9–15.

4 Marcel Bigeard, *Pour une parcelle de gloire* (1975), page 50; Jacques Pâris de Bollardière, *Bataille d'Alger; bataille de l'homme* (1972), pages 52–53; Jean-Jacques Servan-Schreiber, *Lieutenant en Algérie* (1957), page 113; Raoul Girardet, *La Crise militaire française* (1964), page 185; Jean Planchais, *Malaise de l'armée* (1958), page 13.

5 Jean-Raymond Tournoux, *Secrets d'état* (1961), page 21.

6 Vincent Monteil, *Les Officiers* (1964), page 164; Georgette Elgey, *Histoire de la IVᵉ République,* vol. 2, *La République des contradictions, 1951–1954* (1965), pages 432 n., 444.

7 Planchais, *Malaise,* page 10.

8 "L'Armée française: passé, présent, conditionnel," *Esprit* 18 (May 1950): 777; Bollardière, *Bataille,* page 64; Henri Navarre, *L'Agonie d'Indochine* (1958), page 319; Girardet, *Crise militaire,* pages 163–64; Monteil, *Les Officiers,* page 146; Jean Planchais and Jacques Nobécourt, *Une Histoire politique de l'armée,* vol. 2, *De de Gaulle à de Gaulle, 1940–1967* (1967), pages 265–66.

9 Pierre-Henri Simon, *Portrait d'un officier* (1958), pages 109–10.

10 V. N. Giap, *Guerre du peuple; armée du peuple* (1968), page 40.

11 The main writings on *guerre révolutionnaire,* cited in all the works on the subject, are "La guerre révolutionnaire," special number of *Revue militaire d'information,* February–March 1957; [Commandant] Jacques Hogard, "Guerre révolutionnaire ou révolution dans l'art de la guerre," *Revue de défense nationale* 12 (December 1956): 1497–1513;

"L'Armée française devant la guerre révolutionnaire," *Revue de défense nationale* 13 (January 1957): 77–79; "Le soldat dans la guerre révolutionnaire," *Revue de défense nationale* 13 (February 1957): 211–26; Colonel Némo, "La guerre dans le milieu social," *Revue de défense nationale* 12 (May 1956): 605–28; Col. Charles Lacheroy, "La Guerre révolutionnaire," in *La Défense nationale* (1958), 307–30. The best of the many scholarly books on *guerre révolutionnaire* is Peter Paret, *French Revolutionary Warfare from Indochina to Algeria; The Analysis of a Political and Military Doctrine* (New York, 1964).

12 Several recent books stress how ancient are the techniques of guerrilla warfare: J. Bowyer Bell, *The Myth of the Guerrilla* (New York, 1971); Chalmers Johnson, *Autopsy on People's War* (Berkeley and Los Angeles, 1973); Walter Laqueur, *Guerrilla* (Boston, 1976).

13 Quoted in Planchais, *Malaise,* page 74.

14 Paret, *French Revolutionary Warfare,* page 29.

15 Douglas Johnson, "Algeria: Some Problems of Modern History," *Journal of African History* 5 (1964): 233; Frederick A. de Luna, *The French Republic under Cavaignac 1848* (Princeton, 1969), pages 285–88; Pierre Nora, *Les Français d'Algérie* (1961), pages 84–87.

16 H. Isnard, *La Vigne en Algérie,* 2 vols. (Gap, 1954); Edmund S. Morgan, *American Slavery, American Freedom; The Ordeal of Colonial Virginia* (New York, 1975), pages 108–11.

17 Georges Iver, "La Conquête et la colonisation de l'Algérie," *Histoire et historiens de l'Algérie* (1931), pages 304–5; Dorothy Good, "Notes on the Demography of Algeria," *Population Index* 28 (January 1961): 6–9.

18 H. Isnard, "La Viticulture algérienne: erreur économique?" *Revue africaine* (1956): 457–73; Samir Amin, *The Maghreb in the Modern World* (London, 1970), page 36.

19 Clifford Geertz, *The Social History of an Indonesian Town* (Cambridge, Mass., 1965), page 3.

20 Robert Descloîtres, *L'Algérie des bidonvilles; le tiers monde dans la cité* (1961); Pierre Bourdieu, *The Algerians,* trans. Alan C. M. Ross (Boston, 1962), pages 163–64.

21 The foregoing statistics are drawn from Jean Pelletier, *Alger 1955; Essai d'une géographie sociale* (1959).

22 Alexis de Tocqueville, *Oeuvres complètes,* vol. 3, *Ecrits et discours politiques* (1962), page 151.

23 Roger Le Tourneau, *Evolution politique de l'Afrique du nord musulmane* (1962), page 308.

24 Jacques Berque, *Le Maghreb entre deux guerres* (1962), pages 358–60.

25 Bruno Etienne, *Les Problèmes juridiques des minorités européennes au maghreb* (1968), page 55.

26 Berque, *Le Maghreb,* page 70.
27 Robert M. Utley, *Frontier Regulars; The United States Army and the Indian* (New York, 1973), page 3.
28 Samir Amin, *L'Economie du maghreb,* vol. 1, *La Colonisation et la décolonisation* (1966), pages 154–55.
29 Louis Chevalier, *Le Problème démographique nord-africain* (1947); Dorothy Good, "Notes on the Demography of Algeria," pages 3–32; Louis Henry, "Perspectives relatives à la population musulmane de l'Afrique du nord," *Population* 2 (1947): 267–80; Léon Tabah, "La Population algérienne: croissance, niveau de vie, investissements," *Population* 11 (1956): 429–60.
30 Club Jean Moulin, *Deux pièces du dossier Algérie* (1962), pages 103–6; René Gendarme, *L'Economie de l'Algérie* (1959), page 202.
31 Charles-Robert Agéron, *Les Algériens musulmans et la France, 1871–1914,* 2 vols. (1968).
32 *Ibid.,* vol. 2, pages 569–76.
33 Berque, *Le Maghreb,* page 244.
34 William B. Quandt, *Revolution and Political Leadership; Algeria, 1954–1968* (Cambridge, Mass., 1969), pages 25–42.
35 Charles-André Julien, *L'Afrique du nord en marche; nationalismes musulmanes et souveraineté française,* 3rd ed. (1972), page 104.
36 Quandt, *Revolution and Political Leadership,* pages 38–39; Le Tourneau, *Evolution politique,* page 327; Jean-Claude Vatin, *L'Algérie politique; histoire et société* (1974), pages 199–214.
37 Interview with the author, June 24, 1973.
38 Charles-André Julien calls the last chapter of his *L'Afrique du nord en marche,* "La Politique des occasions perdues," pages 342–52; Vincent Confer, *France and Algeria; The Problems of Civil and Political Reform, 1870–1920* (Syracuse, 1966).
39 In the early 1830s, one deputy remarked to his parliamentary colleagues, "As far as I am concerned, I would give up Algiers any day for a shack on the Rhine." Quoted in Herbert Lüthy, "The Crisis of French Colonialism," *Atlantic Monthly,* May 1956, page 61. This point of view persisted down to the outbreak of insurrection in 1954.
40 No single book adequately tells this enormous story, but on the disaster of 1940, Marc Bloch, *Strange Defeat; A Statement of Evidence Written in 1940* (New York, 1968) remains unsurpassed; on the Free French, Charles de Gaulle, *Mémoires de guerre,* 3 vols. (1954–59) is indispensable; and on Vichy, Robert O. Paxton, *Vichy France; Old Guard and New Order* (New York, 1972) is the best book in any language.
41 Jean Lacouture, *Cinq hommes et la France* (1961), page 289; Ferhat Abbas, *La Nuit coloniale* (1962), page 152.

42 Lacouture, *Cinq hommes,* pages 290–91.

43 *Ibid.,* page 291.

44 Abbas, *Nuit coloniale,* pages 154–57; Manfred Halpern, "The Algerian Uprising of 1945," *The Middle East Journal* 2 (1948): 191–202; Laurent Theis and Philippe Ratte, *La Guerre d'Algérie ou le temps des méprises* (1974), page 48; Jean-Claude Vatin claims the PPA went to the demonstration looking for trouble, *L'Algérie politique* pages 276–78; Quandt's informants told him that Messali Hadj and some members of his party were preparing for armed insurrection in the spring of 1945; Messali canceled the badly organized rising after issuing an order to begin, *Revolution and Political Leadership,* pages 51–52.

45 Charles-Robert Agéron, "L'insurrection de 1871 en Algérie," in *Politiques coloniales au Maghreb* (1973), pages 219–30.

46 C. Vann Woodward, *The Strange Career of Jim Crow* (New York, 1955), page 119; Alain de Sérigny, *Echos d'Alger,* vol. 2, *L'Abandon, 1946–1962* (1974), page 17.

47 Julien, *L'Afrique du nord,* page 265.

48 Thomas Oppermann, *Le Problème algérien: données historiques, politiques, juridiques* (1961), pages 75–78.

49 Colette and Francis Jeanson, *L'Algérie hors la loi* (1955), pages 277–90; Oppermann, *Problème,* pages 79–93.

50 Oppermann, *Problème,* page 95; Julien, *L'Afrique du nord,* pages 278–79; Robert Aron, ed., *Les Origines de la guerre d'Algérie* (1962), pages 259–87.

51 Quandt, *Revolution and Political Leadership,* pages 60–61.

52 Yves Courrière, *La Guerre d'Algérie,* vol. 1, *Les Fils de la Toussaint* (1968), pages 85–86.

53 Quandt, *Revolution and Political Leadership,* pages 90–91; Mohamed Boudiaf, *La Préparation du premier novembre* (1976).

54 Aron, *Les Origines,* page 314; Serge Bromberger, *Les Rebelles algériens* (1958), page 20; Courrière, *Fils de la Toussaint,* page 77; Mohamed Harbi, *Aux Origines du FLN; la scission PPA-MTLD* (1975); Mohamed Lebjaoui, *Vérités sur la révolution algérienne* (1970), page 27.

55 Quandt, *Revolution and Political Leadership,* pages 66–86.

56 Aron, *Les Origines,* page 311; Bromberger, *Les Rebelles,* pages 21–22; Courrière, *Fils de la Toussaint,* pages 106–9; Lebjaoui, *Vérités,* page 11; Philippe Tripier, *Autopsie de la guerre d'Algérie* (1972), pages 46–47.

57 Quandt, *Revolution and Political Leadership,* page 93.

58 Courrière, *Fils de la Toussaint,* pages 101–3, 246–48.

59 Ethnographers showed far more interest in the inhabitants of the Aurès than did the French administration. Jean Servier happened to be doing field research in the mountains when the insurrection broke out.

He described his experiences in *Dans l'Aurès sur les pas des rebelles* (1955).

60 Two biographies of Mendès are Rouanet, *Mendès France*, and Alexander Werth, *The Strange History of Pierre Mendès-France and the Great Conflict over French North Africa* (London, 1957).

61 The best book on the politics of the Fourth Republic remains Philip M. Williams, *Crisis and Compromise: Politics in the Fourth Republic* (London, 1964). One bedside gathering was a colloquium published as Edward M. Earle et al., *Modern France: Problems of the Third and Fourth Republics* (Princeton, 1951). Herbert Lüthy's *France Against Herself* (New York, 1955) is a Swiss journalist's provocative appraisal.

62 The journalist Jacques Fauvet, who became editor-in-chief of *Le Monde,* described the National Assembly this way in an article written for the *New York Times Magazine* of November 17, 1957, reprinted in John E. Talbott, ed., *France Since 1930* (New York, 1972), pages 118–26.

63 "Travail sur l'Algérie (octobre 1841)," *Oeuvres complètes,* vol. 3, page 213. In the last years of the Second Empire, Prévost-Paradol elaborated the same theme in *La France nouvelle* (1868), pages 413–15.

64 The theme made its way into primary and secondary schoolbooks: Manuela Semidei, "De l'Empire à la décolonisation à travers les manuels scolaires français," *Revue française de science politique* 16 (February 1966): 59–61; Georges Hardy, *Histoire sociale de la colonisation française* (1953), page 255; Henri Hauser, "Greater France," *Foreign Affairs* 2 (1923): 228; Raoul Girardet, *L'Idée coloniale en France* (1972), pages 31–39.

65 An excellent brief discussion of Mendèsism is to be found in Stanley Hoffmann, *Decline or Renewal? France Since the 1930s* (New York, 1974), pages 96–98. Peter Gourevitch, "Political Skill: A Case Study," *Public Policy* 14 (1965): 239–76.

66 Williams, *Crisis and Compromise,* pages 45–46.

67 Philippe Devillers and Jean Lacouture, *End of a War: Indochina 1954* (New York, 1969), page 301.

68 Lüthy, *France Against Herself,* page 455.

69 D. K. Fieldhouse, *Economics and Empire 1830–1914* (Ithaca, 1973), pages 198–210.

70 Werth, *Strange History,* pages 109–19.

71 Fieldhouse, *Economics and Empire,* pages 110–18, 278–85; Jean Ganiage, *L'Expansion coloniale de la France sous la Troisième République* (1968), pages 66–80, 105–8, 243–76.

72 Quoted in Werth, *Strange History,* page 110.

73 Hoffmann, *Decline or Renewal,* page 98.

74 Claude Estier, *La Gauche hebdomadaire, 1914–1962* (1962), pages 181–206. Françoise Giroud, for many years editor of *L'Express,* has published a volume of memoirs: *I Give You My Word* (Boston, 1974); so has Jean Daniel, who was the magazine's chief correspondent on the war in Algeria: *Le Temps qui reste; essai d'autobiographie professionnelle* (1973).

75 One of his books is called *Choisir* (1974).

CHAPTER 2

1 Quoted in Pierre Rouanet, *Pierre Mendès France au pouvoir* (1965), page 476.

2 William B. Quandt, *Revolution and Political Leadership: Algeria, 1954–1968* (Cambridge, Mass., 1969), page 94; Michael K. Clark, *Algeria in Turmoil; A History of the Rebellion* (New York, 1959), page 109; Laurent Theis and Philippe Ratte, *La Guerre d'Algérie ou le temps des méprises* (1974), page 69.

3 Quandt, *Revolution and Political Leadership,* page 93.

4 Yves Courrière, *La Guerre d'Algérie,* vol. I, *Les Fils de la Toussaint* (1968), page 254.

5 Philippe Tripier, *Autopsie de la guerre d'Algérie* (1972), page 73.

6 Courrière, *Fils de la Toussaint,* page 254.

7 Marcel Fèvre, *Petite suite algérienne de guerre et chirurgie* (1957), pages 32, 34.

8 Edgar O'Ballance, *The Algerian Insurrection, 1954–1962* (London, 1967), pages 49–50.

9 C. A. de Cherrière, "Les Débuts de l'insurrection algérienne," *Revue de défense nationale* 12 (1956): 1457.

10 Jacques Chevallier, *Nous, les algériens* (1958), page 126.

11 *Ibid.,* page 127; *Le Monde,* November 16, 1954.

12 Pierre Mendès France, *Choisir* (1974), page 93; Pierre Leulliette, *Saint Michel et le dragon; souvenirs d'un parachutiste* (1961), pages 11–15.

13 Quoted in Rouanet, *Mendès France,* page 383.

14 *Le Monde,* November 14, 1954.

15 Rouanet, conversation with Mendès France, *Mendès France,* page 532.

16 "Jacques Soustelle," *Contemporary Review,* no. 1118 (February 1959), pages 88–90; Jacques Soustelle, *Vingt-huit ans de gaullisme,* 2nd ed. (1971), especially pages 9–112; Fernand Braudel includes Soustelle in the innermost circle of *Annalistes* in the foreword to Traian Stoianovich, *French Historical Method; The Annales Paradigm* (Ithaca, 1976), page

13; Jean Chauvel, *Commentaire,* vol. 2, *D'Alger à Berne (1944–1952),* (1972), pages 19–20.

17 Jacques Fauvet, *La IVe République* (1959), page 285.

18 *L'Express,* January 29, 1955; also *France observateur,* January 27, 1955.

19 *L'Année politique 1955,* page 180.

20 Tillion's Resistance activities are described in Martin Blumenson, *The Vildé Affair* (Boston, 1977), *passim,* and her years in a German concentration camp in her own book, *Ravensbrück,* trans. Gerald Satterwhite (New York, 1975).

21 Jacques Soustelle, *Aimée et souffrante Algérie* (1956), pages 30–52.

22 *Ibid.,* pages 73–94.

23 *France observateur,* May 19, 1955 and June 23, 1955; Ya'akov Firestone, "The Doctrine of Integration with France among the Europeans of Algeria," *Comparative Political Studies* 4 (1971): 177–204.

24 Germaine Tillion, *L'Afrique bascule vers l'avenir; l'Algérie en 1957 et autres textes* (1961), page 43.

25 Robert Descloîtres, *L'Algérie des bidonvilles; le tiers monde dans la cité* (1961).

26 Quandt, *Revolution and Political Leadership,* pages 66–68.

27 *L'Aurore,* January 26, 1955.

28 Quoted in Fauvet, *IVe République,* page 285.

29 Alexander Werth, *The Strange History of Pierre Mendès-France and the Great Conflict over French North Africa* (London, 1957), pages 168–77; Philip M. Williams, *Crisis and Compromise; Politics in the Fourth Republic* (London, 1964), pages 419–21.

30 Fauvet, *IVe République,* pages 291–93.

31 Soustelle, *Vingt-huit ans de gaullisme,* page 115.

32 Alistair Horne, *A Savage War of Peace; Algeria, 1954–1962* (New York, 1978), pages 103–4.

33 Tripier, the former intelligence officer, provides a description of FLN organization in *Autopsie,* pages 73–75, annexes 10–13; Alf Andrew Heggoy, *Insurgency and Counterinsurgency in Algeria* (Bloomington, Ind., 1972), pages 107–29.

34 Quandt, *Revolution and Political Leadership,* pages 95–96.

35 Tripier, *Autopsie,* pages 70–80; Clark, *Turmoil,* pages 135–40, 163–80; Yves Courrière, *La Guerre d'Algérie,* vol. 2, *Le Temps des léopards* (1969), pages 41–46.

36 Tripier, *Autopsie,* page 79.

37 *Ibid.,* pages 77–78; Heggoy, *Insurgency,* pages 85–106.

38 Soustelle, *Aimée et souffrante,* page 224.

39 Tripier, *Autopsie,* page 78.

40 The Algerian writer and teacher Mouloud Feraoun recorded in his diary the indifference of his compatriots to the proselytizing of the FLN. His diary is a moving account of the evolution of a man caught in the middle—Algerian by birth, French by education, both French and Algerian by culture. He eventually came to support the FLN's aims. Feraoun was murdered by the OAS in early 1962. *Journal, 1955–1962* (1962). In his dilemma as a man in the middle he resembled Albert Camus.

41 *Le Monde,* August 25, 1955. The figures on victims of the FLN are Tripier's in *Autopsie,* page 75; the figures on victims of the French army are from Clark, a French sympathizer who also gives a detailed account of the massacre, *Turmoil,* pages 172–82; Courrière, *Temps des léopards,* pages 183–91; Horne, *Savage War,* pages 119–23.

42 François Sarrazin [pseud. Vincent Monteil], "L'Algérie, pays sans loi," *Esprit* 23 (September–December 1955): 1664.

43 *L'Express,* March 16, 1956.

44 Quoted in *L'Express,* December 3–4, 1955 (*L'Express* had temporarily become a daily newspaper).

45 Clark's *Turmoil,* the work of an American war correspondent, shares with Tripier's *Autopsie,* the book of an intelligence expert, the view that the Soustelle Plan distracted the government's attention from military operations. That the French government moved too slowly with too little force is also the view of O'Ballance, *The Algerian Insurrection,* pages 51–53.

46 The phrase became the subject of bitter mockery, just as "police action" did during the Korean war. In his comment on the phrase, Paul Mus provided the epigraph—and the title—of this book. *Guerre sans visage; lettres commentées du sous-lieutenant Emile Mus* (1961), page 14.

47 Arnold Fraleigh, "The Algerian Revolution as a Case Study in International Law," in *The International Law of Civil War,* ed. Richard Falk (Baltimore, 1971), pages 179–243.

48 Clark, *Turmoil,* page 143. Geoffrey Barraclough and Rachel F. Wall, *Survey of International Affairs 1955–1956* (London, 1960), page 34.

49 *L'Année politique 1955,* pages 226–27.

50 *L'Express,* December 24–25, 1955. Jean Planchais and Jacques Nobecourt, *Histoire politique de l'armée,* vol. 2, *De de Gaulle à de Gaulle, 1940–1967* (1967), page 299.

51 *L'Année politique 1955,* pages 233, 275; André Beaufre, *The Suez Expedition 1956,* trans. Richard Barry (London, 1969), page 40; Clark, *Turmoil,* page 199.

52 Jean-Paul Benoit, "Chronologie de la guerre d'Algérie," *La Nef,* nos. 12–13 (October 1962–January 1963); *L'Express,* October 22–23 and November 19, 1955.

53 Jean Gardt and Claude Roque, *Service militaire pourquoi?* (1960), pages 47–48; *L'Express,* September 17, 1955.

54 "Une Jeunesse en guerre," *Esprit* 26 (May 1958): 791–97; Pierre Belleville, "La Guerre et la 'gauche,' " *Perspectives socialistes,* no. 39–40 (August–September 1960), page 57.

55 Maurienne, "Notre génération et l'expérience algérienne," *Partisans,* no. 6 (September–October 1962), pages 16–17; Jean-Pierre Vittori, *Nous, les appelés d'Algérie* (1977) is based on interviews with 300 former conscripts.

56 Roger Barberot, *Malaventure en Algérie avec le général Pâris de Bollardière* (1957), pages 51–60, 69–73; Courrière, *Temps des léopards,* page 316.

57 *L'Express,* October 18 and December 12, 1955.

58 Jean-Jacques Servan-Schreiber, *Lieutenant en Algérie* (1957), page 70.

CHAPTER 3

1 Maurice Duverger, François Goguel, and Jean Touchard, eds., *Les Elections du 2 janvier 1956* (1957), pages 3–13.

2 *L'Express,* December 16, 1955.

3 Jacques Fauvet, "D'une election à l'autre," in *Les Elections du 2 janvier,* page 21.

4 Alexander Werth, *The Strange History of Pierre Mendès-France and the Great Conflict over French North Africa* (London, 1957), pages 256–65.

5 Georges Dupeux, "Les plates-formes des partis," in *Les Elections du 2 janvier,* pages 49–66.

6 The best book on Poujade is Stanley Hoffmann, *Le Mouvement Poujade* (1956).

7 Mattei Dogan, "Les Candidats et les élus," in *Les Elections du 2 janvier,* pages 425–66.

8 Joseph Kraft, *The Struggle for Algeria* (New York, 1961), page 147.

9 Mollet, who died in 1976, has yet to find a biographer.

10 Jacques Fauvet, *La IVe République* (1959), page 310.

11 Yves Courrière, *La Guerre d'Algérie,* vol. 2, *Le Temps des léopards* (1969), pages 264–73. Courrière's study is remarkable for its detail, but the words he has put in the mouths of his chief actors and the thoughts he has put in their minds must be read with a grain of salt.

12 Fauvet, *IVe République*, page 310.

13 *L'Express*, February 8 and 11–12, 1956; Michael K. Clark, *Algeria in Turmoil; A History of the Rebellion* (New York, 1959), pages 279–84; Courrière, *Temps des léopards*, pages 274–76; Alistair Horne, *A Savage War of Peace; Algeria, 1954–1962* (New York, 1978), pages 147–50.

14 Jean-Raymond Tournoux, *Secrets d'état* (1961), page 90; Morland, Barangé, Martinez [pseud.], *Histoire de l'organisation de l'armée secrète* (1964), pages 57–62. These three pseudonyms conceal the identities of three extremely well-informed French police officials, according to some sources—or the identity of *one* extremely well-informed police official, according to other sources.

15 Kraft, *Struggle,* pages 153–54; Robert Buron, *Les Dernières années de la IVe République* (1968), pages 177–78; Fauvet, *IVe République,* page 316.

16 Courrière, *Temps des léopards,* pages 277–83; François G. Dreyfus, *Histoire des gauches en France, 1940–1974* (1975), page 164; Roger Quilliot, *La SFIO et l'exercice du pouvoir* (1972), pages 613–14.

17 Quilliot, *La SFIO,* pages 617–19.

18 Walter LaFeber, *America, Russia, and the Cold War, 1945–1975,* 3rd ed. (New York, 1976), pages 243–45. LaFeber gives as sources on the Tonkin Gulf incident, U.S. Congress, Senate Committee on Foreign Relations, *The Gulf of Tonkin, The 1964 Incidents,* 90th Cong., 2nd sess. (Washington, D.C., 1968); *The Pentagon Papers* as published by *The New York Times* (New York, 1971), pages 234–42, 258–79.

19 Yves Godard, *La Bataille d'Alger,* vol. 1, *Les Paras dans la ville* (1972), pages 77–78. Colonel Godard was one of the organizers of the Battle of Algiers.

20 Arlette Heymann, *Les Libertés publiques et la guerre d'Algérie* (1972), page 26.

21 *Programme et action du gouvernement en Algérie; mesures de pacification et réformes* (Algiers, 1956), page 83; Thomas Oppermann, *Le Problème algérien; données historiques, politiques, juridiques* (1961), pages 166–67.

22 *L'Année politique 1956,* pages 31–35; "Pouvoirs 'spéciaux,' " *Les Temps modernes,* no. 123 (1956), pages 1345–53; William G. Andrews, *French Politics and Algeria* (New York, 1962), pages 70–74; Jacques Fauvet, *Histoire du parti communiste français,* vol. 2 (1965), pages 276–77; François Fejtö, *The French Communist Party and the Crisis of International Communism* (Cambridge, Mass., 1967), pages 46–48.

23 *L'Express,* March 16 and April 27, 1956; *Le Monde,* April 27, 1956.

24 "Qui démoralise l'armée?" *Temps modernes,* no. 123 (1956), page 1535.

25 *Le Monde,* April 5, 1956.

26 Tripier, *Autopsie,* page 149.

27 Gabriel Bonnet, *Les Guerres insurrectionnelles et révolutionnaires de
    l'antiquité à nos jours* (1958), pages 254–55; Clark, *Turmoil,* pages
    306–8; Alf Andrew Heggoy, *Insurgency and Counterinsurgency in
    Algeria* (Bloomington, Ind., 1972), pages 189–90; George Armstrong
    Kelly, *Lost Soldiers; The French Army and Empire in Crisis, 1947–1962*
    (Cambridge, Mass., 1965), pages 127, 176–77.

28 Many conscripts who served in the *quadrillage* complained of bore-
    dom. François Denoyer, *Quatre ans de guerre en Algérie; lettres d'un
    jeune officier* (1962), pages 57, 84, 169–70; Jean-Yves Alquier et al.,
    Ceux d'Algérie; Lettres de rappelés précédées d'un débat (1957), pages
    35, 39, 43.

29 John Steward Ambler, *Soldiers Against the State; The French Army in
    Politics* (New York, 1968), page 375.

30 The paratroops were especially identified with the siege of Dien Bien
    Phu. Bernard Fall, *Hell in a Very Small Place: The Siege of Dien Bien
    Phu* (Philadelphia, 1966); Tournoux, *Secrets d'état,* page 77.

31 The doctrine of *guerre révolutionnaire* and its appeal to veterans of
    Indochina is described in Chapter 1, pages 5–8.

32 *Paris-Presse,* July 14–15, 1957; *Le Figaro,* July 15, 1957; *L'Aurore,* July
    15, 1954; *L'Humanité,* July 14 and 15, 1954; *Le Figaro,* July 13–14, 1957;
    July 14 and 15, 1958; July 14, 1959; July 13, 14, and 15, 1960; July 14, 15, and
    16, 1961; July 14, 15, and 16, 1962.

33 J. M. Domenach, "La République, son armée et sa politique," *Esprit,*
    May 1954, page 749.

34 Ward Just, *Military Men* (New York, 1971), page 135; Gilles Perrault,
    Les Parachutistes (1961), pages 14–21; Gideon Aran, "Parachuting,"
    American Journal of Sociology 80 (July 1974): 124–53. I owe this
    reference to Prof. Joshua A. Fishman.

35 Pierre Leulliette, *St. Michael and the Dragon; Memoirs of a Para-
    trooper,* trans. John Edmonds (Boston, 1964), page 49. On the rite of
    passage in another "outsider" role: John Van Maanen, "Observations
    on the Making of Policemen," *Human Organization* 32 (Winter 1973):
    407–18. I owe this reference to Prof. Robert Darnton.

36 Just, *Military Men,* page 135.

37 *Le Monde,* February 28, 1963.

38 Leulliette, *St. Michael,* page 1.

39 Christiane Fournier, *Nous avons encore des héros* (1957), page 206. The
    uniform reminded the novelist Graham Greene of a different animal:
    "Anywhere in the world when I see two men dicing I am back in the
    streets of Hanoi or Saigon or among the blasted buildings of Phat
    Diem; I see the parachutists, protected like caterpillars by their strange

markings, patrolling by the canals. . . . ." *The Quiet American* (New York, 1956), page 179. Copies of the leopard uniform were a best-selling item in the toy section of Paris department stores in the Christmas season of 1960. Jean Feller, *Le Dossier de l'armée française: le guerre de cinquante ans* (1966), page 401.

40 Alain Jacob, *D'une Algérie à l'autre* (1963), page 18. The ultra leader Pierre Lagaillarde, for example, himself a former paratrooper, was photographed wearing the uniform during the rising of May 13, 1958, and the "Week of the Barricades" of January 1960. He and other defendants charged in that episode tried to wear the *tenue léopard* at their trial. Janet Flanner (Genêt), *Paris Journal, 1944–1965* (New York, 1965), page 460.

41 Marcel Bigeard, *Pour une parcelle de gloire* (1975); André Cochinal, "Le Lion qu'on ne met pas en cage: Bigeard," *Carrefour,* February 25, 1958; Roger Trinquier, *Le Coup d'état du 13 mai* (1962), pages 68–77 (Trinquier succeeded Bigeard as commander of the Third Regiment of Colonial Paratroops); Jacques Massu, *La Vraie Bataille d'Alger* (1971), pages 111–12.

42 *Le Monde,* April 30, 1958.

43 Georges Buis, *La Grotte* (1961), page 50.

44 Maurice Duverger, *Demain la République* (1958), page 118; P. Carpentier, "L'Armée après six ans de guerre," *Perspectives socialistes,* August–September 1960, page 30.

45 The phrase is Philip Williams's. See "The Army and Its Putsch," *Wars, Plots and Scandals in Postwar France* (Cambridge, 1970), page 93.

46 Williams, *Wars, Plots and Scandals,* pages 193–94.

47 I have relied on Ambler's translation in *Soldiers Against the State,* pages 382–83. Ambler has an interesting discussion of the paratroops, *ibid.,* pages 374–84. The prayer is also to be found in Perrault, *Les Parachutistes,* page 157.

48 Howard S. Becker, *Outsiders: Studies in the Sociology of Deviance,* rev. ed. (New York, 1973), especially pages 37–39, 79–100.

49 Marcel Bigeard and Marc Flament, *Aucune bête au monde* (1959), unpaginated.

50 Horne subscribes to this view in *Savage War,* pages 161–64.

51 Paul Ely, *Mémoires,* vol. 2 (1969), page 86; Jacques Soustelle, *Aimée et souffrante Algérie* (1956), pages 20–22; Courrière, *Temps des léopards,* pages 403–6.

52 Dreyfus, *Histoire des gauches,* page 16; Christian Pineau, foreign minister at the time of Suez, *1956: Suez* (1976), especially pages 81–89; Quilliot, *La SFIO,* pages 661–64; Henri Azeau, *Le Piège de Suez* (1964) emphasizes the French point of view; Hugh Thomas, *The Suez Affair,*

rev. ed. (London, 1970), pages 53–55. The following paragraphs are based on Thomas's excellent account.

53 André Beaufre, *The Suez Expedition 1956*, trans. Richard Barry (London, 1969), pages 144–48.

54 Ambler, *Soldiers Against the State*, page 306; Courrière, *Temps des léopards*, page 430; Tournoux, *Secrets d'état*, page 149.

55 Thomas, *Suez Affair*, page 184.

56 Horne, *Savage War*, pages 159–61; Robert Merle, *Ahmed Ben Bella*, trans. Camilla Sykes (New York, 1967), page 110; Pineau, *1956: Suez*, page 140, all take the view that the capture of Ben Bella and his colleagues altered the course of the war. Other views are to be found in Clark, *Turmoil*, pages 347–53; Elie Kedourie, "The Retreat from Algeria," *Times Literary Supplement*, April 21, 1978, page 448; Kraft, *Struggle*, pages 157–59; William B. Quandt, *Revolution and Political Leadership: Algeria, 1954–1968* (Cambridge, Mass., 1969), page 105.

57 Jo W. Saxe, "The Economics of Algeria," *The Banker* 107 (October 1957): 653–61; (November 1957) 728–38; "Les Conséquences économiques et financières de la guerre d'Algérie," *Cahiers de la République*, no. 12 (March–April 1958), pages 25–51; "Note sur le coût de la guerre et du développement de l'Algérie," *Cahiers de la République*, no. 13 (May–June 1958), pages 72–85.

58 Serge Adour [pseud. Gérard Belorgey], "En Algérie: de l'utopie au totalitarisme," *Le Monde*, October 31–November 6, 1957. This important and insightful series of articles describes the progressive disillusionment of a recent graduate of the Ecole nationale d'administration, training ground in France of a presumptive administrative and political elite. The quotation is from the installment of November 6.

59 Daniel Ligou, *Histoire du socialisme en France (1871–1961)* (1962), pages 610–21; Dreyfus, *Histoire des gauches*, pages 169–70; Duncan MacRae, "Intraparty Divisions and Cabinet Coalitions in the Fourth French Republic," *Comparative Studies in Society and History* 5 (1963): 164–211; Philip M. Williams, *Crisis and Compromise; Politics in the Fourth Republic* (London, 1964), page 91; Quilliot, *La SFIO*, pages 729–39.

60 Jean Lacouture, *Un sang d'encre* (1974), page 178.

61 Harvey G. Simmons, *French Socialists in Search of a Role* (Ithaca, 1970), pages 38–52.

62 *Ibid.*, pages 53–73.

63 Quoted in Dreyfus, *Histoire des gauches*, page 219.

64 Michel Crouzet, "La Bataille des intellectuels français," *La Nef*, nos. 12–13 (October 1962–January 1963), page 53.

65 Geneviève Bugnod and Irène Eddi, "Le Parti communiste français et

la question algérienne du 1er novembre 1954 au 13 mai 1958," Mémoire de maîtrise, Université de Paris I, 1972.

66 The critical literature on the Communist party's role in the Algerian war is as large as the friendly literature. Among the former is Jean Baby, *Critique de base; le parti communiste français entre le passé et l'avenir* (1960), pages 100–122; David Caute, *Communism and the French Intellectuals* (London, 1964), pages 210–11; Fejtö, *French Communist Party*, pages 40–48; Edgar Morin, *Autocritique* (1970); Paul Clay Sorum, *Intellectuals and Decolonization in France* (Chapel Hill, 1977), pages 160–63; Williams, *Crisis*, page 93. A defense of the party is to be found scattered throughout two of the five volumes of memoirs of Jacques Duclos, its perennial second-in-command: *Mémoires*, vol. 4, *Dans la mêlée* (1971), and vol. 5, *Et la lutte continue, 1959–1969* (1973). The party sets forth its official views on the war in Monique Lafon, ed., *Le Parti communiste français dans la lutte contre le colonialisme* (1962). An interesting scholarly case for the party's position is made by Irwin Wall, "The French Communists and the Algerian War," *Journal of Contemporary History* 12 (1977): 521–43.

67 Simone de Beauvoir, *La Force des choses* (1963), page 457.

CHAPTER 4

1 William B. Quandt, *Revolution and Political Leadership: Algeria, 1954–1968* (Cambridge, Mass., 1969), pages 99–101, 103–6. Serge Bromberger, *Les Rebelles algériens* (1958), pages 142–43.

2 Available evidence is ambiguous. Michael K. Clark, who is unsympathetic to the FLN, cites a document found on the body of a "rebel chief" stating as an aim of the strike "To provide the experience necessary for the general insurrection." *Algeria in Turmoil; A History of the Rebellion* (New York, 1959), page 315. A rehearsal, however, is not a performance, and no one supporting the view that an insurrection was intended has brought forth evidence more conclusive than this. Jacques Massu, *La Vraie Bataille d'Alger* (1971), page 89; Alain de Sérigny, *Echos d'Alger*, vol. 2, *L'Abandon, 1946–1962* (1974), page 223; Philippe Tripier, *Autopsie de la guerre d'Algérie* (1972), page 128; Mouloud Feraoun, *Journal, 1955–1962* (1962), page 189. Feraoun noted in his diary for January 16, 1957, rumors he had heard of a forthcoming insurrectional strike. Yves Godard, whom some see as the real organizer of the French side of the battle, wrote that the settlers believed the FLN intended an insurrection. But he and Lacoste regarded such an uprising as suicidal and therefore unlikely. *La Bataille d'Alger*, vol. 1,

Les Paras dans la ville (1972), pages 224–27. Godard, one of the most
able and controversial commanders on the French side, died before he
could finish a projected trilogy on the war. Yacef Saadi, *Souvenirs de la
Bataille d'Alger* (1961), pages 30–31; Mohamed Lebjaoui, *Bataille
d'Alger ou bataille d'Algérie* (1972), page 35; *France observateu*, February
7, 1957, all present the view that the FLN never intended an
insurrection. Yves Courrière, *La Guerre d'Algérie*, vol. 2, *Le Temps des
léopards* (1969), page 449, also gives details on the planning of the strike
and sees the FLN's aims as mainly propagandistic.

3 Tripier, *Autopsie,* pages 128–32.

4 Richard Cobb, "The Beginning of the Revolutionary Crisis in Paris,"
A Second Identity (Oxford, 1969), page 154.

5 Bromberger, *Les Rebelles,* pages 142–43.

6 *Ibid.,* page 146; "Une note de Monsieur Paul Teitgen," in Pierre
Vidal-Naquet, ed., *La Raison d'état* (1962), page 191. Teitgen was
secretary-general of police in Algiers.

7 Bromberger, *Les Rebelles,* pages 153–56; Tripier, *Autopsie,* pages 131–
34; Roger Trinquier, *Le Coup d'état du 13 mai* (1962), page 31; Jean-
Claude Vatin, *L'Algérie politique; histoire et société* (1974), pages 266–
67.

8 Bromberger, *Les Rebelles,* pages 152–53; Godard, *Les Paras,* page 273.

9 Yacef Saadi, *Souvenirs,* pages 19–20.

10 Bromberger, *Les Rebelles,* pages 140, 149–50; Yacef Saadi, *Souvenirs,*
pages 8–9; Roger Trinquier, *Modern Warfare,* trans. Daniel Lee (New
York, 1964), page 15.

11 Bromberger, *Les Rebelles,* pages 162–64, 167–68; Tripier, *Autopsie,*
pages 133–36.

12 Quandt, *Revolution and Political Leadership,* pages 105–6.

13 Bromberger, *Les Rebelles,* page 161.

14 Pierre Leulliette, *Saint Michel et le dragon; souvenirs d'un parachutiste*
(1961), page 306; Yacef Saadi, *Souvenirs,* pages 17–18; Germaine Tillion,
Les Ennemis complémentaires (1960), pages 31–67.

15 Bromberger, *Les Rebelles,* page 166; Courrière, *Temps des léopards,*
pages 399–400.

16 Bromberger, *Les Rebelles,* page 164.

17 Tripier, *Autopsie,* annex 9.

18 "Déposition du procureur-général Reliquet, 5 juillet 1960," in Vidal-
Naquet, *Raison d'état,* page 270.

19 Godard, *Les Paras,* page 257; Teitgen note, Vidal-Naquet, *Raison
d'état,* page 195.

20 Alistair Horne, *A Savage War of Peace: Algeria, 1954–1962* (New York,
1978), page 187.

21 *Programme et action du gouvernement en Algérie; mesures de pacifica-tion et réformes* (Algiers, 1956), page 83.

22 Massu, *Vraie Bataille,* pages 87–105.

23 Reporters on the scene judged the strike at the outset to be 90 percent to 99 percent effective, *France observateur,* January 31 and February 7, 1957; *L'Express,* February 1, 1957; *The New York Times,* January 29, 1957. Leulliette, *Saint Michel,* page 315, and Godard, *Les Paras,* page 250, concurred. Within forty-eight hours, though, the *New York Times* correspondent regarded the army's measures as notably effective. *New York Times,* January 31 and February 6, 1957.

24 Godard, *Les Paras,* page 237.

25 The enormous scholarly literature on guerrilla warfare may soon be equaled by the growing literature on terrorism. Recent studies include Walter Laqueur, *Guerrilla* (Boston, 1976); Chalmers Johnson, *Autopsy on People's War* (Berkeley and Los Angeles, 1973); Walter Laqueur, "Interpretations of Terrorism: Fact, Fiction and Political Science," *Journal of Contemporary History* 12 (1977): 1–42; H. Edward Price, Jr., "The Strategy and Tactics of Revolutionary Terrorism," *Comparative Studies in Society and History* 19 (1977): 52–56; Martha Crenshaw Hutchinson, *Revolutionary Terrorism; The FLN in Algeria* (Stanford, 1978); J. Bowyer Bell, *Transnational Terrorism* (Washington, D.C., 1975); Paul Wilkinson, *Political Terrorism* (London, 1974).

26 "Une Note du colonel Trinquier et du R. P. Delarue," in Vidal-Naquet, *Raison d'état,* page 118; Leulliette, *Saint Michel,* page 302; Pierre Sergent, *Je ne regrette rien* (1972), page 228.

27 Teitgen note, in Vidal-Naquet, *Raison d'état,* pages 197–99; "Le Rapport de maître Maurice Garçon (12 juin 1957)," *ibid.,* page 154; Massu, *Vraie Bataille,* pages 102–4; Pierre Vidal-Naquet, *La Torture dans la République* (1973), pages 51, 57.

28 Marcel Bigeard, *Pour une parcelle de gloire* (1975), page 281; Trinquier, *Coup d'état,* pages 32–37; Tripier, *Autopsie,* pages 137–38.

29 Bigeard, *Pour une parcelle de gloire,* page 280.

30 Leulliette describes these roundups in *Saint Michel,* pages 303–5.

31 Trinquier describes the techniques of interrogation in *Modern Warfare,* pages 43–51.

32 This is Massu's thesis in *Vraie Bataille.*

33 The text of the Special Powers Law and related decrees are printed in *Programme et action du gouvernement en Algérie,* page 64ff.

34 Teitgen note, in Vidal-Naquet, *Raison d'état,* pages 186–202.

35 Leulliette describes the interrogation methods of the company to which he belonged in *Saint Michel,* pages 307–13.

36 The disappearances of suspects arrested in the course of the Battle of

Algiers have generated an endless controversy. That disappearances took place, no one has bothered to deny; at issue have been their number and the explanations put forth to account for them. The most celebrated disappearance, taken up by critics of the war as a symbol of all the rest, was that of Maurice Audin: Pierre Vidal-Naquet, *L'Affaire Audin* (1958), and the following chapter of this book. The number of disappearances most commonly cited by war critics is 3,024, the figure established by Paul Teitgen, who as secretary-general of police had charge of keeping track of *assignations à résidence.* Teitgen's typescript record is reproduced in Courrière, *Temps des léopards,* opposite page 289. Courrière later inexplicably gives the figure as 3,994 (page 517), and this is the number Godard attacks as a gross exaggeration in *Les Paras,* pages 431–37.

37 These matters are discussed in the following chapter.

38 Tripier, *Autopsie,* pages 141–42.

39 Yacef Saadi, *Souvenirs,* pages 116–17; Tripier, *Autopsie,* page 142.

40 Vatin, *L'Algérie politique,* pages 272, 299; Quandt, *Revolution and Political Leadership,* page 106.

41 The paras became the idols of the settler press: *L'Echo d'Alger,* January 2, 3, 4, 5, 20–21, 24, and 25, February 5, 9, 12, 14, 16, 17–18, 22, 23, and 24–25, March 1, 1957, and so on.

42 *Carrefour,* December 26, 1956; April 2 and June 18, 1958.

43 Albert-Paul Lentin, *L'Algérie des colonels; journal d'un témoin, juin–octobre 1958* (1958), page 42.6

CHAPTER 5

1 Albert-Paul Lentin, *Algérie entre deux mondes,* vol. 1, *Le Dernier quart d'heure* (1963), pages 83–84; François Mauriac, *Bloc-Notes, 1952–1957* (1958) [a collection of Mauriac's weekly columns in *L'Express*], page 310; *France observateur,* March 28, 1957; *Le Monde,* March 26, 1957; Jean Planchais and Jacques Nobécourt, *Une Histoire politique de l'armée,* vol. 2, *De de Gaulle à de Gaulle, 1940–1967* (1967), page 310; FJ [Francis Jeanson?], *Esprit* 25 (1957): 815; "Le Rapport de maître Maurice Garçon (12 juin 1957)," in Pierre Vidal-Naquet, ed., *La Raison d'état* (1962), pages 158–59. An equally mysterious and controversial death was that of Ben M'Hidi, member of the Comité de coordination et d'exécution (CCE) captured and interrogated in the course of the Battle of Algiers. As in the case of Boumendjel, the army claimed Ben M'Hidi had committed suicide, the army's critics that he had been murdered. Bruno Etienne points out that at least seven

versions of how Ben M'Hidi met his death have been published: "Lectures d'une guerre," *Annuaire de l'Afrique du nord* 11 (1972): 924.

2 Cahiers du Témoignage chrétien, 38, *De la Pacification à la répression: le dossier Jean Muller* (1957), page 19.

3 *Ibid.,* unpaginated preface.

4 The letter that precipitated the "Bollardière Affair" appeared in *L'Express,* March 29, 1957.

5 Comité résistance spirituelle, *Des Rappelés témoignent* (1957); Robert Bonnaud, "La Paix des Nementchas," *Esprit* 25 (1957): 580–92; "Les Jeunes soldats devants les tortures," *Les Temps modernes* 136 (1957).

6 Georges Suffert, "Rumeurs," *Esprit* 25 (1957): 819.

7 Simone de Beauvoir, *La Force des choses* (1963), page 126; Jean-Marie Domenach, "Démoralisation de la nation," *Esprit* 25 (1957): 577; *Des Rappelés témoignent,* page 1 [unpaginated].

8 All these themes recur in *Des Rappelés témoignent,* perhaps the most accessible compilation of reservists' accounts. The testimony of individuals, such as that of Robert Bonnaud in "La Paix des Nementchas," is scattered throughout the periodical press of the antiwar left. *Les Temps modernes,* for instance, published among others, G. M. Mattéi, "Jours kabyles (notes d'un rappelé)," nos. 137–38 (1957), pages 138–59; X . . . "Journal de campagne," nos. 137–38 (1957), pages 160–73; Jacques Pucheu, "Un an dans les Aurès," no. 139 (1957), pages 433–47; Jean-Luc Tahon, "En 'pacifiant' l'Algérie," nos. 147–48 (1958), pages 2094–2112; Jean-Philippe Talbo-Bernigaud, "Zones interdites," no. 177 (1961), pages 709–26.

9 *Des Rappelés témoignent,* page 27.

10 *Ibid.,* page 13.

11 *Ibid.,* page 71.

12 Bonnaud, "Paix des Nementchas," pages 591–92.

13 Jean-Jacques Servan-Schreiber, *Lieutenant en Algérie* (1957).

14 Paul Zweig, *Three Journeys: An Automythology* (New York, 1976), page 114.

15 Beauvoir, *Force,* pages 125–26.

16 The phrase is Gordon Wright's: "The Dreyfus Echo: Justice and Politics in the Fourth Republic," *Yale Review* 48 (1959): 354–73; Victor Brombert, "Toward a Portrait of the French Intellectuals," *Partisan Review* 27 (1960): 481–85; Paul Clay Sorum, *Intellectuals and Decolonization in France* (Chapel Hill, 1977), pages 113–29.

17 *France observateur,* January 13, 1955.

18 Robert O. Paxton, *Vichy France; Old Guard and New Order* (New York, 1972). No comparable synthesis on the Resistance has yet been written. An excellent recent book on an important dimension of that

experience is H. R. Kedward, *Resistance in Vichy France: A Study of Ideas and Motivation in the Southern Zone* (Oxford, 1978).

19 Michael J. Arlen, *Living-Room War* (New York, 1966).

20 Simone de Beauvoir delineated the boundaries of this world in a volume of her memoirs: "I spent the first twenty years of my life in a big village which went from the Lion of Belfort to the rue Jacob, from the boulevard Saint-Germain to the boulevard Raspail: I still live there." *Force,* page 132.

21 Laurent Theis and Philippe Ratte, *La Guerre d'Algérie ou le temps des méprises* (1974), page 51; Pierre Vidal-Naquet, "Face à la raison d'état," *Partisans* 5 (July-August 1962): 165; personal communication to author, June 1973.

22 "Opération bonne conscience," *Esprit* 25 (1957): 244.

23 *L'Express,* November 13, 1954; January 8 and 15, 1955.

24 Jacques Massu, *La Vraie Bataille d'Alger* (1971), page 227.

25 The preceding two paragraphs rely on Servan-Schreiber, *Lieutenant en Algérie.*

26 Michel-Antoine Burnier, *Choice of Action; The French Existentialists on the Political Front Line,* trans. Bernard Murchland (New York, 1968), page 31.

27 Jean-Paul Sartre, "Le Colonialisme est un système," *Les Temps modernes,* no. 123 (1956), page 1386.

28 Preface to Frantz Fanon, *The Wretched of the Earth,* trans. Constance Harrington (New York, 1968), page 22; Sartre's position has elicited considerable comment: David Caute, *Communism and the French Intellectuals* (New York, 1964), page 256; Saul Bellow, "Writers and Literature in American Society," in *Culture and Its Creators: Essays in Honor of Edward Shils,* ed. Joseph Ben-David and Terry N. Clark (Chicago, 1977), pages 189–90; Raymond Aron, *History and the Dialectic of Violence: An Analysis of Sartre's Critique de la raison dialectique* (New York, 1975).

29 Mauriac, *Bloc-Notes,* page 311.

30 Adrien Dansette, *Histoire religieuse de la France contemporaine,* rev. ed. (1965); Andre Latreille and René Rémond, *Histoire du catholicisme en France* (1965); René Rémond, *Les Catholiques, le communisme et les crises, 1929–39* (1960); Françoise Kempf, "Les Catholiques français," in *Les Eglises chrétiennes et la décolonisation,* ed. Marcel Merle (1967), pages 147–215.

31 Jean-Louis Loubet del Bayle, *Les Non-conformistes des années 30* (1969), pages 121–82.

32 Pierre-Henri Simon, *Contre la torture* (1957), pages II–12.

33 *Ibid.,* pages 98–99.
34 Pierre-Henri Simon, *Portrait d'un officier* (1958), page 115.
35 *Ibid.,* page 141.
36 *Ibid.,* page 169.
37 This is the theme elaborated in Pierre Vidal-Naquet, *La Torture dans la République* (1972).
38 Otto Kirchheimer, *Political Justice* (Princeton, 1961), page 322.
39 Jacques Duquesne, *L'Algérie ou la guerre des mythes* (1958), page 41.
40 Raoul Girardet, *L'Idée coloniale en France* (1972), page 241; Pierre Boudot, *L'Algérie mal enchaînée* (1961), page 80.
41 *L'Express,* March 29, 1957.
42 Jacques Pâris de Bollardière, *Bataille d'Alger; bataille de l'homme* (1972), pages 19–60.
43 *France observateur,* April 11, 1957.
44 Yves Courrière gives details on the Faure incident, *La Guerre d'Algérie,* vol. 2, *Le Temps des léopards* (1969), pages 430–39.
45 Massu, *Vraie Bataille,* pages 227–28.
46 Bollardière, *Bataille,* page 95; *France observateur,* April 11, 1957; Mauriac, *Bloc-Notes,* page 310; Vidal-Naquet, *Raison d'état,* page 131; Roger Quilliot, *La SFIO et l'exercice du pouvoir* (1972), pages 686–87.
47 René-William Thorp, *Vues sur la justice* (1962), pages 144–46; *France observateur,* May 9, 1957.
48 *The Economist,* July 27, 1957.
49 Arlette Heymann, *Les Libertés publiques et la guerre d'Algérie* (1972), pages 228–39; Burnier, *Choice of Action,* pages 114, 120n.
50 "Comment s'effectue une saisie," *France observateur,* March 13, 1958.
51 Heymann, *Libertés publiques,* page 63.
52 *France observateur,* May 3, 1957; Philip M. Williams and Martin Harrison, *Politics and Society in de Gaulle's Republic,* 2nd ed. (London, 1971), page 41.
53 Pierre Vidal-Naquet, *L'Affaire Audin* (1958).
54 A fuller account of the Audin Affair is to be found in John Talbott, "The Strange Death of Maurice Audin," *The Virginia Quarterly Review* 52 (1976): 224–42, from which the following is drawn. The article is based on interviews conducted in the summer of 1973, correspondence with participants in the affair, and the files of *Le Monde.*
55 *Le Monde,* December 14, 1957.
56 John Ardagh, *The New French Revolution* (London, 1968), page 432.
57 Vidal-Naquet, *La Torture,* pages 170–78.

CHAPTER 6

1 William G. Andrews, *French Politics and Algeria* (New York, 1962), pages 75–87; Philip M. Williams, *Crisis and Compromise: Politics in the Fourth Republic* (London, 1964), page 56.

2 Andrews, *French Politics,* pages 136–59.

3 *Ibid.,* pages 159–63; Jacques Fauvet, *La IVe République* (1959), pages 334–39.

4 George Dangerfield, *The Strange Death of Liberal England* (New York, 1935), pages 74–138, 333–63; *idem, The Damnable Question; A Study in Anglo-Irish Relations* (Boston, 1976), pages 28–90; Nicholas Mansergh, *The Irish Question, 1840–1921,* 3rd ed. (London, 1975), pages 135–228.

5 A detailed account of the Bazooka Affair is Morland, Barangé, Martinez [pseud.], *Histoire de l'organisation de l'armée secrète* (1964), pages 77–86. A participant in the Bazooka episode—and an inveterate Algiers plotter—was Joseph Ortiz, *Mes Combats* (1964), pages 36–41. The views of the intended victim of the bazooka shell are in Raoul Salan, *Mémoires: Fin d'un empire,* vol 3, *Algérie française* (1972), pages 100–144. Salan alleges that Michel Debré was mixed up in the attempt on Salan's life as part of a bizarre and complicated scheme for returning General de Gaulle to power. This widely circulated allegation has never been tested in court. Neither the Fourth nor the Fifth Republic ever showed any eagerness to get to the bottom of the Bazooka Affair.

6 Ya'akov Firestone, "The Doctrine of Integration with France Among the Europeans of Algeria," *Comparative Political Studies* 4 (1971): 177–204.

7 The best study of the SAS to have appeared thus far is Alf Andrew Heggoy, *Insurgency and Counterinsurgency in Algeria* (Bloomington, Ind., 1972), pages 188–211, which rests on the memoirs and reports of SAS officers.

8 The army activists are discussed in Chapter 1, pages 3–6.

9 Philip M. Williams and Martin Harrison, *Politics and Society in de Gaulle's Republic,* 2nd ed. (London, 1961), pages 43–44; Fauvet, *IVe République,* pages 339–40.

10 Joseph Kraft, *The Struggle for Algeria* (New York, 1961), pages 165–67.

11 Salan, *Algérie française,* pages 241–51, 255–64.

12 Michael K. Clark, *Algeria in Turmoil: A History of the Rebellion* (New York, 1959), pages 363–68; Alistair Horne, *A Savage War of Peace: Algeria, 1954–1962* (New York, 1978), pages 249–50.

13 Kraft, *Struggle,* pages 167–68.

14 Williams and Harrison, *De Gaulle's Republic,* pages 44–45; Fauvet, *IVe République,* pages 342–43.

15 Clark, *Turmoil,* page 369; Yves Courrière, *La Guerre d'Algérie,* vol. 3, *L'Heure des colonels* (1970), pages 300–301.

16 Philip M. Williams, "Death of the Fourth Republic: Murder or Suicide?" *Wars, Plots and Scandals in Postwar France* (Cambridge, 1970), pages 134–36. This remains the best brief account of the May 13 crisis and is heavily relied upon for what follows. Jean Ferniot, *De Gaulle et le 13 mai* (1965), pages 130–47, 241–48. Ferniot's is the best of the many books on the crisis.

17 Robert O. Paxton, *Vichy France; Old Guard and New Order* (New York, 1972), page 233.

18 Courrière, *L'Heure des colonels,* pages 270–73.

19 Among the accounts of participants or observers are Pascal Arrighi, *La Corse: atout décisif* (1958); Raymond Dronne, *La Révolution d'Alger* (1958); Alain de Sérigny, *La Révolution du 13 mai* (1958); Dominique Pado, *Le 13 mai: histoire secrète d'une révolution* (1958); Paul Gerin, *L'Algérie du 13 mai* (1958); Merry and Serge Bromberger, *Les 13 complots du 13 mai* (1958); Albert-Paul Lentin, *L'Algérie des colonels* (1958); Jacques Massu, *Le Torrent et la digue* (1972); Raoul Salan, *Algérie française;* Roger Trinquier, *Le Coup d'état du 13 mai* (1962); Jean-Raymond Tournoux, *Secrets d'état* (1960).

20 Kraft, *Struggle,* pages 178–83, is a good description of events. "The GG [Gouvernement général]," Kraft remarks, "is one of the most easily defended public buildings in the world." Colonel Roger Trinquier, commander of the Third Regiment of Colonial Paratroops (Bigeard's old outfit), the officer formally in charge of defending the building, gives his version of events in *Le Coup d'état du 13 mai,* pages 89–123. Trinquier, partly owing to his role in the Battle of Algiers, had close ties with settler activists. Other accounts are Clark, *Turmoil,* pages 373–77; Courrière, *L'Heure des colonels,* pages 309–18; Ferniot, *De Gaulle et le 13 mai,* pages 239–49; Brombergers, *13 complots,* pages 163–75.

21 Williams, *Wars, Plots and Scandals,* pages 140–41.

22 *Ibid.,* page 141.

23 *Ibid.,* page 142; Brombergers, *13 complots,* pages 221–23, 228–30.

24 Massu, *Le Torrent et la digue,* pages 42–54, 69.

25 Tournoux, *Secrets d'état,* pages 242–44.

26 Charles de Gaulle, *Mémoires d'espoir,* vol. 1, *Le Renouveau* (1970), page 57; Georgette Elgey, *Histoire de la IVᵉ République,* vol. 2, *La République des contradictions* (1968), page 451; Françoise Giroud, *Si je mens* (1973), page 215; Jean Planchais, *Le Malaise de l'armée* (1958), page 12; letter to the author, October 1975.

27 Tournoux, *Secrets d'état,* pages 341–42.

28 Williams, *Wars, Plots and Scandals,* page 144; Salan, *Algérie française,* pages 311–13.

29 Kraft, *Struggle,* page 189; Ferniot, *De Gaulle et le 13 mai,* pages 311–12.

30 The statement is reprinted in Charles de Gaulle, *Discours et messages,* vol. 3, *Avec le renouveau, 1958–1962* (1970), page 3. This is the "official" collection of de Gaulle's utterances.

31 George Armstrong Kelly, *Lost Soldiers: The French Army and Empire in Crisis, 1947–1962* (Cambridge, Mass., 1965), pages 215–16.

32 Soustelle's account is in *Vingt-huit ans de gaullisme,* 2nd ed. (1971), pages 141–44; Ferniot, *De Gaulle et le 13 mai,* pages 343–59.

33 De Gaulle, *Avec le renouveau,* pages 4–10.

34 Williams, *Wars, Plots and Scandals,* pages 147–48.

35 *Ibid.,* page 148; Kraft, *Struggle,* page 201.

36 Kraft, *Struggle,* page 192.

37 Horne, *Savage War,* page 295, is the latest to take this view.

38 Writing from Paris in the midst of the crisis, Janet Flanner suggested that the Communists, despite their threats to fight in the streets against de Gaulle's return to power, were more likely to call for strikes—if they chose to oppose him at all. *Paris Journal, 1944–1965* (New York, 1965), page 369. Jules Moch, the minister of the interior, told the American reporter Edmund Taylor, "In the face of anything like a real uprising, the government was completely helpless. I was sure that we could not count on the army, . . . and only part of the police could be relied on. As to the dream nourished by some of basing the defense of the Republic on the working class, the information available to me convinced me that the workers as a whole were not prepared to put up any effective resistance against a military coup. They were divided in their sentiments and a great many of them were more afraid of the Communists than of de Gaulle. The truth is that it was almost impossible last week to find any French republicans who were really prepared to die for the defense of a regime which every one criticized and thought needed reformation." "The Democratic Parties and the General," *The Reporter,* June 26, 1958.

39 Fauvet, *IVᵉ République,* pages 352–53; Ferniot, *De Gaulle et le 13 mai,* pages 397–404, and Kraft, *Struggle,* page 192, are inclined to think Operation Resurrection was a bluff. Williams and Harrison, *De Gaulle's Republic,* page 71; Williams, *Wars, Plots and Scandals,* page 156; Clark, *Turmoil,* page 420; Tournoux, *Secrets d'état,* page 337, all think the army meant business. The Brombergers, *13 complots,* pages 308–11, believe the soldiers were divided among themselves as to whether or not they were bluffing. Pierre Viansson-Ponté thinks the army saved its reputation by not attempting to pull off such a ludicrous plan as Operation Resurrection. *Histoire de la République gaullienne,* vol. 1, *La Fin d'une époque: mai 1958–juillet 1962* (1970), page 56.

40 Ferniot, *De Gaulle et le 13 mai,* page 338.
41 A detailed account of the planning of Operation Resurrection is in Brombergers, *13 complots,* pages 303–12. Massu gives his version of its origins, *Le Torrent et la digue,* pages 122–25, 135. Salan did not think much of the plan and hints that he thought of it mainly as a bluff, *Algérie française,* page 346.
42 Arrighi, *La Corse: atout décisif.* A deputy and *Algérie française* activist, Arrighi gives a slightly overheated account of the seizure of his native island. Williams, *Wars, Plots and Scandals,* pages 148–51.
43 Williams, *Wars, Plots and Scandals,* page 151.
44 "To many others besides myself," Robert Buron wrote in his diary, "General de Gaulle, who seemed 12 days ago to be a threat to the regime, and then, until yesterday, as a possible arbiter, indeed a recourse in the case of an impasse, today looks to be the sole possible protector of the Republic against the enterprises of the factious." *Les Dernières Années de la IVe République; carnets politiques* (1968), page 245.
45 Kraft, *Struggle,* pages 194–95.
46 Ferniot, *De Gaulle et le 13 mai,* pages 434–35; Williams, *Wars, Plots and Scandals,* pages 154–55; Brombergers, *13 complots,* pages 369–72.
47 De Gaulle, *Avec le renouveau,* page 11.
48 Williams, *Wars, Plots and Scandals,* page 155.
49 This was the view of Jules Moch. Jean-Raymond Tournoux, *Le Tourment et la fatalité* (1974), page 16.
50 Trinquier, *Coup d'état,* pages 180–82, 188–90.
51 Williams, *Wars, Plots and Scandals,* page 156.
52 Soustelle, *Vingt-huit ans,* page 146.
53 De Gaulle, *Le Renouveau,* pages 24–33.
54 André Dulac, *Nos Guerres perdues* (1968), pages 87–89.
55 Speech of June 8, 1962, *Avec le renouveau,* page 421.
56 Taylor, "The Democratic Parties and the General," *The Reporter,* June 26, 1958.
57 Williams, *Wars, Plots and Scandals,* page 157.
58 Jean-Marie Domenach, "Democratic Paralysis in France," *Foreign Affairs* 37 (October 1958): 33; Jean Poperen, *La Gauche française; le nouvel âge* (1972), pages 52–53.
59 Quoted in Brombergers, *13 complots,* page 393, and in nearly every account of the May 13 crisis.
60 *Le Monde,* May 29, 1958.
61 Ferniot, *De Gaulle et le 13 mai,* pages 461–66.
62 Brombergers, *13 complots,* pages 420–25; Tournoux, *Secrets d'état,* page 395; *L'Année politique 1958,* pages 538–39.

63 Jean-Paul Buffelan, *Le Complot du 13 mai 1958 dans le Sud-ouest* (1966), pages 143–44.
64 Jean-Raymond Tournoux, *Jamais dit* (1971), page 182n.
65 Williams, *Wars, Plots and Scandals,* pages 159–60.
66 Simone de Beauvoir, *La Force des choses* (1963), page 168.

CHAPTER 7

1 The literature on de Gaulle is enormous and still growing. In 1972 the Institut Charles de Gaulle published a bibliography—*Liste des ouvrages publiés en France sur le général de Gaulle*—running from Antomarchi, Xavier, *Le Général raconte aux enfants* (1969), to Wurmser, André, *De Gaulle et les siens* (1947). The best biography is also one of the shortest: Jean Lacouture, *De Gaulle* (1965), rev. ed. (1971). A full-dress scholarly biography remains to be done. The sheer volume of sources for what Lacouture calls "gaullology" is daunting.
2 An interesting study of the relationship between the two men is Jean-Raymond Tournoux, *Pétain et de Gaulle* (1964).
3 Charles de Gaulle, *Mémoires de guerre,* vol. 1, *L'Appel* (1954), page 61.
4 Antoine Argoud, *La Décadence, l'imposture et la tragédie* (1974); Raoul Salan, *Mémoires: Fin d'un empire,* vol. 4, *L'Algérie, de Gaulle et moi* (1974); Alain de Sérigny, *Echos d'Alger,* vol. 2, *L'Abandon, 1946–1962* (1974).
5 Pierre Mendès France, "Charles de Gaulle," in *La Vérité guidait leur pas* (1976), pages 194–207, a reprinting of an assessment Mendès France wrote for *Le Monde* on the occasion of de Gaulle's death in November 1970.
6 Henri Claude, *Gaullisme et grand capital* (1960), pages 148–49, 208–11.
7 Among his most notable—and uncritical—admirers was François Mauriac, *De Gaulle* (1964), especially pages 289–345.
8 Simone de Beauvoir, *La Force des choses* (1963), page 159.
9 Léo Hamon, *De Gaulle dans la République* (1958). The following paragraphs draw on the whole book, but especially pages 49–61.
10 *Ibid.,* page 59.
11 Charles de Gaulle, *Mémoires d'espoir,* vol. 1, *Le Renouveau* (1970), pages 48–50.
12 Xavier Yacono, *Les Etapes de la décolonisation française* (1971), page 53. The Brazzaville speech is printed in Charles de Gaulle, *Discours et messages,* vol. 1, *Pendant la guerre; juin 1940–janvier 1946* (1970), page 372.
13 D. Bruce Marshall, *The French Colonial Myth and Constitution-Making in the Fourth Republic* (New Haven, 1973), page 102.

14 Quoted in Philippe Devillers and Jean Lacouture, *End of a War; Indochina 1954* (New York, 1969), page 14.

15 De Gaulle, *Discours et messages,* vol. 2, *Dans l'attente, 1946–1958* (1970), page 265.

16 *Ibid.,* page 331.

17 *Ibid.,* page 80.

18 *Ibid.,* page 81.

19 *Ibid.,* pages 106–9.

20 *Ibid.,* page 133.

21 Edmond Michelet, *Querelle de la fidelité* (1971), pages 101–2; Roger Stéphane and J. M. Darbois, *Mémoires de votre temps* (1967), page 264; Christian Pineau, *1956: Suez* (1976), page 26; Jean-Raymond Tournoux, *Jamais dit* (1971), pages 189–90; Rosenberg is quoted in Laurent Theis and Philippe Ratte, *La Guerre d'Algérie ou le temps des méprises* (1974), page 208.

22 *France observateur,* March 6, 1958.

23 Anthony Hartley, *Gaullism; The Rise and Fall of a Political Movement* (New York, 1971), page 165n; Olivier Guichard, for many years de Gaulle's private secretary and press spokesman, interviewed in *L'Express,* June 29, 1970.

24 Robert Buron, *Carnets politiques de la guerre d'Algérie* (1965), pages 67–68.

25 De Gaulle, *Discours et messages,* vol. 3, *Avec le renouveau, 1958–1962* (1970), page 3.

26 In a computer-assisted study of de Gaulle's public vocabulary, Jean-Marie Cotteret and René Moreau discovered that *état* ("state") was among the general's favorite (most frequently uttered) words. The others were: *La France, le pays, la République, le monde, le peuple, la nation, le progrès, la paix, l'avenir. Le Vocabulaire du général de Gaulle* (1969), page 7.

27 De Gaulle, *Avec le renouveau,* pages 13–15.

28 De Gaulle, *Dans l'attente,* page 10.

29 De Gaulle, *Avec le renouveau,* page 10.

30 John Talbott, "French Public Opinion and the Algerian War: A Research Note," *French Historical Studies* 9 (Fall 1975): 359–60.

31 Bernard Tricot, *Les Sentiers de la paix: Algérie, 1958–1962* (1972), pages 35–49. Named in June 1958 assistant to René Brouillet, head of the secretariat-general for Algerian Affairs, Tricot shortly became de Gaulle's chief adviser on Algeria. His memoirs are an invaluable source on the evolution of the general's Algerian policy. Yves Courrière, *La Guerre d'Algérie,* vol. 3, *L'Heure des colonels* (1970), page 445.

32 Courrière, *L'Heure des colonels,* pages 441–42; Alistair Horne, *A Savage War of Peace; Algeria, 1954–1962* (New York, 1978), pages 309–10.

33 Salan describes his brusque treatment at de Gaulle's hands in *Mémoires: Fin d'un empire*, vol. 4, *L'Algérie, de Gaulle et moi* (1974), pages 184–98; De Gaulle's assessment of Salan: "In short, there was something slippery and inscrutable in the character of this capable, clever and in some respects beguiling figure which seemed to me to accord ill with the certitude and rectitude demanded by a high and honorable responsibility." *Memoirs of Hope: Renewal and Endeavor*, trans. Terence Kilmartin (New York, 1971), pages 52–53.

34 Maurice Challe, *Notre Révolte* (1968), pages 91–117, 150–51.

35 Stanley Hoffmann, "Vietnam: An Algerian Solution?" *Foreign Policy*, no. 2 (1971), page 27.

36 Challe, *Notre Révolte*, pages 91–144; Courrière, *L'Heure des colonels*, pages 460–75, 517–22; Edgar O'Ballance, *The Algerian Insurrection, 1954–1962* (London, 1967), pages 131–43.

37 Philippe Tripier, *Autopsie de la guerre d'Algérie* (1972), pages 316–39.

38 *Ibid.*, pages 421–33; Challe, *Notre Révolte*, pages 146–48.

39 Martha Crenshaw Hutchinson, *Revolutionary Terrorism; The FLN in Algeria* (Stanford, 1978), pages 131–53; De Gaulle, *Le Renouveau*, page 79.

40 Tricot, *Sentiers*, pages 30–31; Germaine Tillion, *L'Afrique bascule vers l'avenir; l'Algérie en 1957 et autres textes* (1961).

41 Tricot, *Sentiers*, pages 67–79; Samir Amin, *L'Economie du maghreb*, vol. 1, *La Colonisation et la décolonisation* (1966), pages 213–19; Jean-Claude Vatin, *L'Algérie politique; histoire et société* (1974), pages 288–90.

42 De Gaulle, *Avec le renouveau*, page 56.

43 *Ibid.*

44 William B. Quandt, *Revolution and Political Leadership: Algeria, 1954–1968* (Cambridge, Mass., 1969), pages 134–38.

45 Charles Morazé, *Le Général de Gaulle et la République* (1972), page 71.

46 *Le Renouveau*, page 74.

47 Raymond Aron, "The Fifth Republic," *Encounter* 11 (December 1958): 17.

48 Michelet, *Querelle de la fidelité*, page 121.

49 *L'Express*, January 28, 1960.

50 Tricot, *Sentiers*, pages 48, 69.

51 De Gaulle, *Avec le renouveau*, page 88.

52 *Le Monde*, August 14, 1959.

53 Tricot, *Sentiers*, pages 107–10.

54 De Gaulle, *Le Renouveau*, page 78.

55 De Gaulle, *Avec le renouveau*, pages 117–22.

CHAPTER 8

1 Quoted in Jean-Raymond Tournoux, *Jamais dit* (1971), pages 206–8. A photograph of the manuscript letter is included in an unpaginated "iconographical album" at the back of the book. The senior officer is not identified. It could have been any one of a number of generals unhappy with de Gaulle's Algerian policy, from Maurice Challe on down.

2 Roy Macridis and Bernard E. Brown, *The De Gaulle Republic* (Homewood, Ill., 1960), page 322.

3 John Talbott, "French Public Opinion and the Algerian War: A Research Note," *French Historical Studies* 9 (Fall 1975): 359–60.

4 Robert Buron, *Carnets politiques de la guerre d'Algérie* (1965), page 128.

5 Hubert Beuve-Méry, *Onze ans de règne* (1974), page 192. This is a collection of the front-page editorials that the founder and former editor-in-chief of *Le Monde* signed "Sirius."

6 Pierre Viansson-Ponté, *Histoire de la République gaullienne*, vol. 1, *La Fin d'une époque, mai 1958–juillet 1962* (1970), page 180; Morland, Barangé, Martinez [pseud.], *Histoire de l'organisation de l'armée secrète* (1964), pages 149–50.

7 Massu gives his version of the incident in *Le Torrent et la digue* (1972), pages 292–313. De Gaulle makes only a passing and rather indulgent reference to Massu's indiscretion. *Mémoires d'espoir*, vol. 1, *Le Renouveau* (1970), page 83.

8 Yves Courrière, *La Guerre d'Algérie*, vol. 3, *L'Heure des colonels* (1970), pages 567–74. Joseph Ortiz, *Mes Combats* (1964). The most detailed account of the Week of the Barricades remains Merry and Serge Bromberger, Georgette Elgey, and Jean-François Chauvel, *Barricades et colonels, 24 janvier 1960* (1960), the work of four journalists who covered the war.

9 *Le Monde*, January 21, 1960.

10 Pierre Sergent, *Ma Peau au bout de mes idées* (1967), page 192.

11 Ortiz, *Mes Combats*, pages 159–62; Courrière, *L'Heure des colonels*, pages 578–83; Viansson-Ponté, *La Fin d'une époque*, pages 255–58.

12 Brombergers et al., *Barricades, passim;* Viansson-Ponté, *La Fin d'une époque*, page 258.

13 Argoud's memoirs, as their title suggests, are in the manner of a diatribe against de Gaulle: *La Décadence, l'imposture et la tragédie* (1974); the Comité Audin published his deposition given in a closed courtroom at the Barricades trial as *Sans Commentaire* (1961); Roger

Barberot, *Malaventure en Algérie avec le général Pâris de Bollardière* (1957), pages 140–41; Alain Jacob, *D'une Algérie à l'autre* (1963), pages 72–83; Ortiz, *Mes Combats,* pages 132–33; Pierre Sergent, *La Bataille* (1968), page 78. Argoud appears in Jean-Jacques Servan-Schreiber's *Lieutenant en Algérie* (1957) as the disillusioned idealist "Major Marcus." Alain Jacob, correspondent in Algeria for *Le Monde,* recalled watching Argoud enter an office in the ministry of defense on the rue Saint Dominique in Paris. "Take a good look," said a friend of Argoud to Jacob, "there goes the First Consul."

14 Maurice Challe, *Notre Révolte* (1968), pages 155–56; Edward Behr, *The Algerian Problem* (London, 1961), pages 168–69. Behr covered the war for *Time* magazine. Paul Delouvrier, an old friend, had shared with him some weeks before the Week of the Barricades his growing fears of the collusion between settlers and senior army officers (page 165). Behr was an eyewitness to the events of January 24–30.

15 Brombergers et al., *Barricades,* pages 243–44; Courrière, *L'Heure des colonels,* pages 587–91; Alistair Horne, *A Savage War of Peace; Algeria, 1954–1962* (New York, 1978), page 363; George Armstrong Kelly, *Lost Soldiers; The French Army and Empire in Crisis, 1947–1962* (Cambridge, Mass., 1965), pages 270–71.

16 Behr, *Algerian Problem,* pages 168–72; Challe, *Notre Révolte,* pages 157–58; Horne, *Savage War,* page 363; Kelly, *Lost Soldiers,* page 371; Paul Ribeaud, *Barricades pour un drapeau* (1960), pages 74–79; Raoul Salan, *Mémoires: Fin d'un empire,* vol. 4, *L'Algérie, de Gaulle et moi* (1974), pages 235–36; Viansson-Ponté, *La Fin d'une époque,* page 259.

17 Behr, *Algerian Problem,* pages 173–74; Challe, *Notre Révolte,* pages 161–62.

18 De Gaulle, *Avec le renouveau,* pages 162–66.

19 Ortiz, *Mes Combats,* pages 254–55.

20 Sergent, *Ma Peau,* page 198; Jean Planchais, "La Cassure de l'armée," *La Nef,* no. 33 (February–April 1968), page 119.

21 Jacques Soustelle, *Vingt-huit ans de gaullisme,* 2nd ed. (1971), pages 220–23.

22 Bernard Tricot, *Les Sentiers de la paix: Algérie, 1958–1962* (1972), pages 141–43, 155–57.

23 *L'Express,* March 10, 1960; Tricot, *Sentiers,* page 162.

24 Tricot, *Sentiers,* page 158.

25 *Ibid.,* page 157.

26 Horne, *Savage War,* pages 376–77.

27 Tricot, *Sentiers,* page 161.

28 Quoted in *ibid.,* pages 163–64.

29 The difficulty of distinguishing true messages from false is the theme of Roberta Wohlstetter, *Pearl Harbor; Warning and Decision* (Stanford, 1962).

30 *Le Monde,* February 26, 1960.

31 Michel-Antoine Burnier, *Choice of Action; The French Existentialists on the Political Front Line,* trans. Bernard Murchland (New York, 1968), page 108; Simone de Beauvoir, *La Force des choses* (1963), pages 130–31.

32 Courrière, *L'Heure des colonels,* pages 382–400; Francis Jeanson, *Sartre dans sa vie* (1974), page 213.

33 Arnaud was arrested and charged with failing to report to the authorities the whereabouts of a known fugitive. He claimed the journalist's privilege of not revealing his sources, a claim the courts refused to uphold. An account of Jeanson's press conference and Arnaud's trial is set forth in Arnaud, *Mon Procès* (1961).

34 The foregoing paragraphs rely on Francis Jeanson, *Notre guerre* (1961).

35 Michel Crouzet, "La Bataille des intellectuels français," *La Nef,* nos. 12–13 (October 1962–January 1963), pages 54–55.

36 In eight years of war, fifty-six young men went to jail for refusing military service. Maurienne, "Notre génération et l'expérience algérienne," *Partisans,* no. 6 (September–October 1962), page 25.

37 "Incidents of Desertion, Fiscal Years 1959 through 1975," Office of the Assistant Secretary of Defense, Manpower and Reserve Affairs, typescript.

38 Renée G. Kasinsky, *Refugees from Militarism; Draft-Age Americans in Canada* (New Brunswick, N.J., 1976), page 294. Lawrence M. Baskir and William A. Strauss put the number of exiles in Canada at thirty thousand. *Reconciliation After Vietnam; A Program of Relief for Vietnam Era Draft and Military Offenders* (Notre Dame, 1977), page 136.

39 Automobile accidents in France claimed more French casualties in the years 1954–1962 than the war in Algeria did. Horne, *Savage War,* page 538.

40 Richard D. Challener, *The French Theory of the Nation in Arms* (New York, 1955).

41 Jeanson, *Notre guerre,* page 50.

42 Daniel Blanc, *Après les armes, citoyens* (1962), page 23; Viviane Isambert-Jamati, "Rémarques sur le service militaire," *Revue française de sociologie* 2 (1961): 100–105; Laurence Wylie, *Village in the Vaucluse,* rev. ed. (New York, 1964), pages 55–133, especially 123–24.

43 Jean-Pierre Cattelain, *L'Objection de conscience* (1973), pages 53–55; Philip M. Williams and Martin Harrison, *Politics and*

Society in de Gaulle's Republic, 2nd ed. (London, 1971), page 288.

44 Noël Favrelière, *Le Désert à l'aube* (1960). In 1973 Favrelière's book was republished under the less lyrical title *Le Déserteur.*

45 Maurice Maschino, *L'Engagement* (1961), page 112, for both quotations in the paragraph. The preceding paragraphs rely on *L'Engagement.*

46 One such young man was Michel Biran, who wrote a valuable account of his experiences in Algeria: "Deuxième classe en Algérie," *Perspectives socialistes,* no. 4 (November 1961), entire issue.

47 Guy Pedroncini, *Les Mutineries de 1917* (1967).

48 François Maspero, ed., *Le Droit à l'insoumission; "le dossier des 121"* (1961), page 16. *Le Monde,* September 5, 1961, noted the appearance of the Manifesto but did not print it.

49 Maspero, *Dossier des 121,* page 18.

50 Maspero, *Dossier des 121,* lists the signers, pages 18–20. Michel Contat and Michel Rybalka, *Les Ecrits de Sartre* (1970), page 359n.

51 Maurice Nadeau, "Pourquoi nous sommes parmis les '121,' " *Les Lettres nouvelles* 9 (1960): 7.

52 Interview of the author with a signer of the Manifesto, June 27, 1973.

53 Beauvoir, *Force,* pages 392–93; *L'Express,* October 18, 1960; *The New York Times,* September 29 and October 18, 1960.

54 Letter to the editor, *The New York Times,* October 2, 1960.

55 Maspero, *Dossier des 121,* pages 40–42.

56 Marcel Péju, ed., *Le Procès du réseau Jeanson* (1961). Teitgen's testimony appears on pages 102–5; Sartre's letter, on pages 116–19.

57 Jean-Marc Théolleyre, *Ces Procès qui ébranlèrent la France* (1967), pages 144–93; Péju, *Procès du réseau Jeanson,* pages 231–32.

58 Janet Flanner (Genêt), *Paris Journal, 1944–1965* (New York, 1965), page 456. The column is dated November 2, 1960.

59 Jules Roy, *The War in Algeria,* trans. Richard Howard (New York, 1961), page 117.

60 *Ibid.,* page 89.

61 Quoted in Maspero, *Dossier des 121,* page 135.

62 Quoted in Maschino, *L'Engagement,* page 46.

63 *Ibid.,* page 48.

64 *L'Humanité,* October 3, 1960.

65 *L'Express,* April 28, June 16, June 23, and October 6, 1960; Burnier, *Choice of Action,* page 133n.

66 *Combat,* October 10, 1960.

67 Cited in *Dossier des 121,* pages 139–40.

68 Paul Ricoeur, "L'Insoumission," *Esprit* 28 (1960): 1600–1604.

69 K. S. Karol, "Un entretien avec Jean-Paul Sartre: jeunesse et guerre d'Algérie," *Vérité-Liberté,* July–August 1960; Crouzet, "Bataille . . .," *La Nef,* page 62.

70 Albert O. Hirschman, *Exit, Voice and Loyalty* (Cambridge, Mass., 1970).

71 *Ibid.*, page 1.

72 *Ibid.*, page 30.

73 *Ibid.*, page 78.

74 *Ibid.*, page 98.

75 Robert Bonnaud, "Un an après le manifeste des 121," *Vérité-Liberté*, October 1961; reprinted in *Itinéraires* (1962).

CHAPTER 9

1 Charles de Gaulle, *Discours et messages,* vol. 3, *Avec le renouveau, 1958–1962* (1970), pages 240, 258, 263, 268.

2 The earliest—and still the best—book on the putsch is Jacques Fauvet and Jean Planchais, *Le Fronde des généraux* (1961). In the most recent account, Jacques Rouvière, *Le Putsch d'Alger* (1976), the military revolt has taken on the romantic afterglow that lost causes often generate.

3 Yves Courrière, *La Guerre d'Algérie,* vol. 4, *Les Feux du désespoir* (1971), pages 186–205; Morland, Barangé, Martinez [pseud.], *Histoire de l'organisation de l'armée secrète* (1964), pages 191–97.

4 Pierre Viansson-Ponté, *Histoire de la République gaullienne,* vol. 1, *La Fin d'une époque, mai 1958–juillet 1962* (1970), pages 346–47; Yves Courrière, "Le Putsch des généraux," *Historia,* no. 293 (April 1971), page 34; George Armstrong Kelly, *Lost Soldiers: The French Army and Empire in Crisis, 1947–1962* (Cambridge, Mass., 1965), page 312.

5 Fauvet and Planchais, *Fronde,* pages 46–47; Charles de Gaulle, *Mémoires d'espoir,* vol. 1, *Le Renouveau,* page 67; Kelly, *Lost Soldiers,* page 315; Pierre Sergent, *Ma Peau au bout de mes idées* (1967), page 244.

6 Maurice Challe, *Notre Révolte* (1968), pages 91–144; Yves Courrière, *La Guerre d'Algérie,* vol. 3, *L'Heure des colonels* (1970), pages 472–75; Alistair Horne, *A Savage War of Peace: Algeria, 1954–1962* (New York, 1978), pages 330–38; Edgar O'Ballance, *The Algerian Insurrection, 1954–1962* (London, 1967), pages 131–43; Philippe Tripier, *Autopsie de la guerre d'Algérie* (1972), pages 314–43.

7 Pierre Bourdieu, *The Algerians,* trans. Alan C. M. Ross (Boston, 1962), pages 163–84; Michel Cornaton, *Les Regroupements de la décolonisation en Algérie* (1967); Armand Frémont, "Un petit regroupement des hautes plaines constantinoises," *Cahiers de sociologie économique,* no. 4 (1961), pages 93–105; Jules Roy, *The War in Algeria,* trans. Richard Howard (New York, 1961), pages 50–52.

8 Tripier, *Autopsie,* is the most accessible source of statistics on FLN losses as recorded by the French, especially pages 664–65.

9 Georges Buis, *La Grotte* (1961), page 305.

10 *Ibid.,* page 78.

11 *Ibid.,* page 83.

12 *Ibid.,* pages 273–74.

13 *Ibid.,* page 317.

14 Challe, *Notre Révolte,* pages 167–68.

15 Bernard Tricot, *Les Sentiers de la paix: Algérie, 1958–1962* (1972), pages 166–73.

16 *Ibid.,* page 173.

17 Courrière, *Feux du désespoir,* page 100.

18 Tricot, *Sentiers,* pages 175–76.

19 De Gaulle, *Avec le renouveau,* page 229.

20 Challe, *Notre Révolte,* page 170; Tripier, *Autopsie,* page 454.

21 Tricot, *Sentiers,* page 176.

22 Courrière, *Feux du désespoir,* pages 104–10; Tripier, *Autopsie,* pages 455–56.

23 Tricot, *Sentiers,* page 178.

24 Maurice Cottaz, ed., *Les Procès du putsch d'Alger et du complot de Paris* (1962), pages 78–83.

25 Challe, *Notre Révolte,* page 151.

26 Rouvière, *Putsch d'Alger,* pages 78–80.

27 De Gaulle, *Avec le renouveau,* page 165.

28 Jean-Marie Domenach, "The French Army in Politics," *Foreign Affairs* 39 (1961): 193; Jean Planchais, "La Cassure de l'armée," *La Nef,* no. 33 (February–April 1968), page 119.

29 De Gaulle, *Avec le renouveau,* page 260.

30 *Le Monde,* November 17, 1960.

31 The text is to be found in François Goguel, ed., *Le Référendum du 8 janvier 1961* (1962), pages 109–10.

32 Jacques Kayser, "La Presse," in *Le Référendum,* page 75.

33 Jean and Monica Charlot, "La Campagne," in *Le Référendum,* pages 37–60.

34 De Gaulle, *Avec le renouveau,* page 266.

35 *Ibid.,* page 269.

36 *Ibid.,* page 275.

37 François Goguel, "Les Circonstances," in *Le Référendum,* page 33.

38 Jean and Monica Charlot, "La Campagne," in *Le Référendum,* pages 58–59.

39 Viansson-Ponté, *La Fin d'une époque,* page 347.

40 André Zeller, *Dialogues avec un général* (1974), page 212; Jacques Massu, *Le Torrent et la digue* (1972), pages 362–64.

41 Claude Paillat, *Vingt Ans qui déchirent la France*, vol. 2, *La Liquidation* (1972), page 584.

42 De Gaulle, *Avec le renouveau*, pages 288–92.

43 Challe, *Notre Révolte*, page 188; Fauvet and Planchais, *Fronde*, page 54; Zeller, *Dialogues*, page 219.

44 Challe, *Notre Révolte*, pages 188–93.

45 Philip M. Williams, "The Army and Its Putsch," *Wars, Plots and Scandals in Postwar France* (Cambridge, 1970), page 198.

46 Salan ended his memoirs with his retirement from the army. He has nothing to say of the putsch. Fauvet and Planchais, *Fronde*, pages 27–34; Jean Ferrandi, *600 Jours avec Salan et l'OAS* (1969), pages 13–120. Ferrandi was Salan's aide-de-camp.

47 Courrière, *L'Heure des colonels*, pages 478–80; Roland Gaucher, *Les Terroristes* (1965), page 356; Alain Jacob, *D'une Algérie à l'autre* (1963), pages 50–52; Albert-Paul Lentin, *Algérie entre deux mondes*, vol. 1, *Le Dernier quart d'heure* (1963), page 90; Gilles Mermoz, "Connaissance de l'OAS," *Ecrits de Paris*, November 1962, page 61; Joseph Ortiz, *Mes Combats* (1964), page 109; Jean-Jacques Susini, *Histoire de l'OAS* (1963), pages 16–19.

48 Planchais and Fauvet, *Fronde*, pages 176–79.

49 Robert Buron, *Carnets politiques de la guerre d'Algérie* (1965), pages 131–35. Minister of public works, Buron arrived in Algiers on official business a few hours before the outbreak of the putsch. Courrière, *Feux du désespoir*, pages 296–301; Planchais and Fauvet, *Fronde*, pages 79–120; Pierre Sergent, *Je ne regrette rien* (1972), pages 377–92. Sergent's jeep led the 1er REP into Algiers.

50 Fauvet and Planchais, *Fronde*, pages 121–24.

51 Challe had charge of rallying support. The commander who had done so much to make the war a war of movement committed a serious and possibly fatal mistake. Instead of flying around Algeria, as he had done as commander in chief, he tied himself to the telephone. Shut up inside the office he had commandeered, he became a telephone solicitor for high-ranking enlistments in the putsch, wheedling the help of men he had once commanded.

52 Gaucher, *Terroristes*, page 298.

53 Viansson-Ponté, *La Fin d'une époque*, page 357. Ferrandi, *600 Jours*, pages 130–34; Morland, Barangé, Martinez, *Histoire de l'organisation de l'armée secrète*, pages 227–44.

54 De Gaulle, *Avec le renouveau*, pages 307–8.

55 Kelly, *Lost Soldiers*, pages 319–20, 322. Some public figures–André

Malraux was one–could not resist striking heroic attitudes. Elements of the left demanded to be armed from government arsenals. This demand hadn't the slightest chance of being heeded.

56 Horne, *Savage War*, page 456.
57 Fauvet and Planchais, *Fronde*, pages 209–36.
58 Interview of the author with an organizer of the conscripts' resistance, July 1971; Daniel Blanc, *Après les armes, citoyens* (1962), page 69. Zeller thought the extent of resistance had been exaggerated, *Dialogues*, pages 257–58.
59 De Gaulle, *Memoirs of Hope: Renewal and Endeavor*, trans. Terence Kilmartin (New York, 1971), page 108.
60 Henri Azeau, *Révolte militaire; Alger, 22 avril 1961* (1961), pages 175–80.
61 Zeller, *Dialogues*, page 231.
62 Pierre Sergent, *La Bataille* (1968), page 31.
63 Challe, *Notre Révolte*, page 64; Courrière, *Feux des désespoir*, pages 355–61; Ferrandi, *600 Jours*, pages 135–36; Sergent, *Ma Peau*, pages 277–78.
64 Janet Flanner (Genêt), *Paris Journal, 1944–1965* (New York, 1965), page 483; Sergent, *Je ne regrette rien*, pages 398–400.
65 Jacques Duclos, *Mémoires*, vol. 6, *Et la lutte continue* (1972), pages 134–35; *L'Année politique 1961*, pages 58–61.
66 "La Vie politique de september 1960 à mai 1961," *Sondages* (1961), pages 25–28.
67 Gordon Wright, *Rural Revolution in France; The Peasantry in the Twentieth Century* (Stanford, 1964), page 167.
68 *Ibid.*, pages 167–68.
69 De Gaulle, *Le Renouveau*, page 117; Yves-Frédéric Jaffré, *Les Tribunaux d'exception, 1940–1962* (1962), pages 231–32; Jean-Marc Théolleyre, *Ces Procès qui ébranlèrent la France* (1967), *passim;* Tricot, *Sentiers*, pages 151–52; Philip M. Williams and Martin Harrison, *Politics and Society in de Gaulle's Republic* (London, 1971), pages 264–65.
70 Fauvet and Planchais provide a full list of sentences meted out to participants in the putsch, *Fronde*, pages 259–60.
71 Williams, "The Army and Its Putsch," *Wars, Plots and Scandals*, pages 200–201.
72 Quoted in Kelly, *Lost Soldiers*, pages 325–26. An edited transcript of the trial of most of the putschists (the four leaders were tried separately) is Cottaz, *Les Procès du putsch d'Alger* (1962).
73 De Gaulle, *Memoirs of Hope*, page 111.
74 Buis, *La Grotte*, page 83.
75 De Gaulle, *Avec le renouveau*, page 371.

CHAPTER 10

1 François Goguel, ed., *Le Référendum du 8 janvier 1961* (1962); John Talbott, "French Public Opinion and the Algerian War: A Research Note," *French Historical Studies* 9 (Fall 1975): 358–61.

2 Paul Henissart, *Wolves in the City; The Death of French Algeria* (New York, 1971), is a general account of European terrorism and the struggle against it. Events in Oran have been the subject of a French doctoral thesis: Régine Goutalier, "L'OAS en Oranie," thèse de 3e cycle, Université d'Aix-Marseille I, 1975.

3 Pierre Viansson-Ponté, *Histoire de la République gaullienne*, vol. I, *La Fin d'une époque, mai 1958–juin 1962* (1970), pages 441–42, gives both sides of the Charonne metro affair. The Communists accused the police of deliberately using excessive force in their handling of an anti-OAS demonstration; the authorities accused the Communists of provoking the police into the charge that left eight demonstrators crushed to death or suffocated at the entrance of the Charonne metro station. The Communists made their allegations in "La Vérité sur la sanglante répression du 8 février, 1962," *France nouvelle,* supplement of March 21–27, 1962. Morland, Barangé, and Martinez raise the possibility that the OAS had planted troublemakers in the crowd, *Histoire de l'organisation de l'armée secrète* (1964), pages 386–87. Robert Buron complained of the government's clumsiness in the handling of anti-OAS demonstrations and feared such actions might jeopardize the peace talks then in progress, *Carnets politiques de la guerre d'Algérie* (1965), page 188.

4 Quoted in David Goldey, "The Events of May 1968," in Philip M. Williams, *French Politicians and Elections, 1951–1969* (Cambridge, 1970), page 257.

5 Francine Dessaigne, *Journal d'une mère de famille pied-noir* (1962), pages 161, 237–38; Jean Lacouture, "Le Drame algérien: sept ans bientôt," *France Forum,* October 1961, page 17; Morland, Barangé, Martinez, *Histoire de l'organisation de l'armée secrète,* pages 199–200.

6 Georges Ras, a Lille journalist who joined the OAS, describes the secret army's propaganda apparatus, such as it was, in Laurent Theis and Philippe Ratte, *La Guerre d'Algérie ou le temps des méprises* (1974), pages 272–73.

7 Morland, Barangé, Martinez, *Histoire de l'organisation de l'armée secrète,* page 11.

8 François Duprat, *Les Mouvements d'extrême droite en France depuis 1944* (1972), pages 106–7; Jean Ferrandi, *600 Jours avec Salan et l'OAS*

(1969), page 9; Roland Gaucher, *Les Terroristes* (1965), page 314; George Armstrong Kelly, *Lost Soldiers; The French Army and Empire in Crisis, 1947–1962* (Cambridge, Mass., 1965), page 344; Alain Jacob, *D'une Algérie à l'autre* (1963), page 163; Jean-Jacques Susini, *Histoire de l'OAS* (1963), pages 92–93; Xavier Yacono, *Les Etapes de la décolonisation française* (1971), page 115.

9 Robert Buchard, *Organisation armée secrète, février–14 décembre 1961* (1963), pages 9–10; Gaucher, *Terroristes,* page 295; Morland, Barangé, Martinez, *Histoire de l'organisation de l'armée secrète,* page 202; Susini, *OAS,* pages 16–18. Whatever Lagaillarde had to do with founding the OAS, he did not participate in its activities but sat out the rest of the war in Madrid.

10 Susini, *OAS,* page 76.

11 Yves Courrière, *La Guerre d'Algérie,* vol. 4, *Les Feux du désespoir* (1971), pages 440–41.

12 Henissart, *Wolves,* pages 166–69.

13 Interview of the author with a journalist who covered the war, July 1971. Several French filmmakers in the 1960s equated the OAS with gangsterism. J. Daniel, *Guerre et cinéma* (1972), page 353.

14 Pierre Sergent, *La Bataille* (1968), page 37.

15 Claude Mouton, *La Contrerévolution en Algérie* (1972), is the collaborative work of the friends of Robert Martel, the activist farmer of the Mitidja. They believed themselves to have participated in the OAS on behalf of God, Christ, and the Virgin Mary, and regarded the putsch as the work of Masonic provocateurs: page 476. David Gordon thought the "OAS had no clear ideology beyond a vague proto-fascist anti-republicanism and anti-gaullism, although two of the more extreme members, Argoud and Susini, were self-declared fascists." *The Passing of French Algeria* (London, 1966), page 69. Susini discussed ideological divisions in *OAS,* pages 190–91. Edmond Jouhaud, who led the OAS in Oran, claimed he never thought of himself as anything but a republican, *Le Procès Edmond Jouhaud* (1962), page 89.

16 Courrière, *Feux du désespoir,* page 622; Henissart, *Wolves,* includes between pages 224 and 225 a photograph of the burning oil tanks.

17 Alfred Grosser provides a succinct discussion of what he calls "the stages and the methods" of the evolution of de Gaulle's Algerian policy. *French Foreign Policy under De Gaulle,* trans. Lois Ames Pattison (Boston, 1967), pages 37–46.

18 Bernard Tricot, *Les Sentiers de la paix: Algérie, 1958–1962* (1972).

19 De Gaulle, *Avec le renouveau,* pages 293–94.

20 Stanley Hoffmann, "Vietnam: An Algerian Solution?" *Foreign Policy,* no. 2 (Spring 1971), page 4; *idem, Decline or Renewal? France since the 1930s* (New York, 1974), pages 292–93.

21 Tricot, *Sentiers*, pages 229–30.
22 *Ibid.*, page 247; Philippe Tripier, *Autopsie de la guerre d'Algérie* (1972), page 537.
23 Tricot, *Sentiers*, pages 252, 257–63.
24 Thomas Oppermann, *Le Problème algérien; données historiques, politiques, juridiques* (1961), pages 23–28.
25 Jean Lartéguy, *Sahara, an I* (1958), lays stress on the immense benefits France will derive from holding onto the desert.
26 Tricot, *Sentiers*, page 261.
27 De Gaulle, *Avec le renouveau*, pages 340–41.
28 William B. Quandt, *Revolution and Political Leadership: Algeria, 1954–1968* (Cambridge, Mass., 1969), pages 143–45.
29 Jean Lacouture, *De Gaulle* (1971), page 117.
30 Quandt, *Revolution and Political Leadership*, page 145.
31 Tricot, *Sentiers*, pages 250–56.
32 *Ibid.*, page 303.
33 De Gaulle, *Avec le renouveau*, page 350.
34 *Ibid.*
35 Tricot, *Sentiers*, pages 283–86.
36 Buron, *Carnets politiques*, pages 191–235.
37 *Ibid.*, page 235.
38 *Ibid.*, pages 248–63.
39 The preceding paragraphs rely on Buron, *Carnets politiques*, pages 248–63, and Tricot, *Sentiers*, pages 287–300.
40 Yves Courrière, *La Guerre d'Algérie*, vol. 1, *Les Fils de la Toussaint* (1968), pages 14–15.
41 The paragraphs on Bab El Oued rely on Courrière, *Feux du désespoir*, pages 564–70; *idem, Fils de la Toussaint*, pages 17–20; Henissart, *Wolves*, pages 336–41.
42 Courrière, *Fils de la Toussaint*, pages 20–25; *idem, Feux du désespoir*, pages 573–81.
43 Courrière, *Fils de la Toussaint*, page 25.
44 Henissart, *Wolves*, pages 345–47.
45 Ferrandi, *600 Jours*, pages 286–88; Henissart, *Wolves*, pages 380–85.
46 Courrière, *Fils de la Toussaint*, page 25. The Algerian government estimates that between 75,000 and 100,000 Europeans now live in Algeria, of whom 60,000 to 70,000 are French. Of the French, 10,000 are permanent residents who chose to remain in Algeria after independence. According to figures published on September 9, 1979, in the parliamentary debates section of the French *Journal Officiel*, 42,570 Frenchmen living in Algeria had registered with the French consulate general; an additional 2,278 had not registered. I owe this information to S. T. Debagha, minister counselor, Embassy of the Democratic and

Popular Republic of Algeria, letter to the author, December 19, 1979; and to André Baeyens, director, Press and Information Service, French Embassy, letter to the author, December 3, 1979.

47 Roy Macridis and Bernard E. Brown, *The De Gaulle Republic* (Homewood, Ill., 1960), page 322.

48 Grosser, *French Foreign Policy,* page 40.

49 Pierre Mendès France, "Charles de Gaulle," *Le Vérité guidait leur pas* (1976), pages 199–200; Raymond Aron, "The General and the Tragedy," *Encounter,* August 1962, pages 22–23.

50 Louis Terrenoire, *De Gaulle et l'Algérie; témoignage pour l'histoire* (1964), page 252. Alistair Horne, *A Savage War of Peace: Algeria, 1954–1962* (New York, 1978), page 548.

51 These views can be found in the memoirs of most of the leading defenders of *Algérie française,* among them Antoine Argoud, *La Décadence, l'imposture et la tragédie* (1974); Raoul Salan, *Mémoires: Fin d'un empire,* vol. 4, *L'Algérie, de Gaulle et moi* (1974); Alain de Sérigny, *Echos d'Alger,* vol. 2, *L'Abandon, 1946–1962* (1974).

52 Charles-Robert Ageron, *Histoire de l'Algérie contemporaine,* 4th ed. (1970), pages 115–16.

53 De Gaulle, *Avec le renouveau,* page 291.

54 *Ibid.,* page 228.

55 *Ibid.,* page 227.

56 *Ibid.,* page 225.

57 *Ibid.,* page 292.

58 *Ibid.,* page 224.

59 *Ibid.,* page 314.

60 *Ibid.,* pages 327–29.

61 *Ibid.,* page 339.

62 *Ibid.,* page 349.

63 *Ibid.,* pages 375–76.

64 Peter Larmour, "De Gaulle and the New France," *The Yale Review* 55 (1966): 500–520.

65 De Gaulle, *Avec le renouveau,* pages 327–29.

66 Chapter 1 and notes discuss Mendès and his government, pages 28 ff.

67 Pierre Chaulieu, "Perspectives de la crise française," *Socialisme ou barbarie* (1958), page 50.

68 J. Hampden Jackson, *Clemenceau and the Third Republic* (New York, 1962), page 103.

69 De Gaulle, *Avec le renouveau,* page 268.

70 *Ibid.,* page 386.

71 Tricot, *Sentiers,* page 364.

72 Etienne Mallarde, *L'Algérie depuis* (1975), is a critical view of Algeria

since independence. Other studies include Bruno Etienne, *L'Algérie: cultures et révolution* (1977); J. Leca and Jean-Claude Vatin, *L'Algérie politique; institutions et régimes* (1975); Jean-Claude Vatin, *L'Algérie politique; histoire et société* (1974).

73 Philip M. Williams, "Vietnam: America's Algeria?" in *Wars, Plots and Scandals in Postwar France* (Cambridge, 1970), page 218.

74 Pierre Baillet, "L'Intégration des rapatriés d'Algérie en France," *Population* 30 (1975): 303–14; Jane Kramer, "Profiles: Pieds-Noirs," *The New Yorker,* November 25, 1972, pages 52–108.

75 Horne, *Savage War,* page 538.

76 Alistair Horne, *The Price of Glory: Verdun 1916* (New York, 1963), pages 327–28.

77 Roger L. Williams, *The French Revolution of 1870–1871* (New York, 1969), page 151.

78 Agatha Ramm, "The Crimean War," in *The New Cambridge Modern History,* vol. 10, *The Zenith of European Power,* ed. J. P. T. Bury, (Cambridge, 1960), page 485.

79 Horne, *Savage War,* page 538.

80 *Ibid.*

Selected Bibliography

The bibliography includes the sources I found most useful in writing this book. The notes contain everything to which I had occasion to refer. Unless otherwise noted, the place of publication is Paris. Two important books appeared too late for me to be able to benefit from their contributions to an understanding of the war: Tony Smith, *The French Stake in Algeria, 1945–1962* (Ithaca, 1978); and Hervé Hamon and Patrick Rotman, *Les Porteurs de valise: la résistance française à la guerre d'Algérie* (1979).

Abbas, Ferhat. *La Nuit coloniale.* 1962.

Agéron, Charles-Robert. *Les Algériens musulmans et la France, 1871–1914.* 2 vols. 1968.

———. *Histoire de l'Algérie contemporaine.* 4th ed. 1970.

———. *Politiques coloniales au Maghreb.* 1973.

Alleg, Henri. *La Question.* 1958.

Alquier, Jean-Yves, et al. *Ceux d'Algérie; Lettres de rappelés précedées d'un débat.* 1957.

Ambler, John Steward. *Soldiers Against the State; The French Army in Politics.* New York, 1968.

Amin, Samir. *L'Economie du maghreb.* 2 vols. 1966.

———. *The Maghreb in the Modern World.* London, 1970.

Andrews, William G. *French Politics and Algeria.* New York, 1962.

Argoud, Antoine. *La Décadence, l'imposture et la tragédie.* 1974.

Arnaud, Georges. *Mon Procès.* 1961.

Aron, Robert, ed. *Les Origines de la guerre d'Algérie.* 1962.

Arrighi, Pascal. *La Corse: atout décisif.* 1958.

Azeau, Henri. *Le Piège de Suez.* 1964.

———. *Révolte militaire; Alger, 22 avril 1961.* 1961.

Barberot, Roger. *Malaventure en Algérie avec le général Pâris de Bollardière.* 1957.

Beaufre, André. *The Suez Expedition 1956.* Translated by Richard Barry. London, 1969.

Beauvoir, Simone de. *La Force des choses.* 1963.

Behr, Edward. *The Algerian Problem.* London, 1961.

Bell, J. Bowyer. *The Myth of the Guerrilla.* New York, 1971.

———. *Transnational Terrorism.* Washington, D.C., 1975.

Berque, Jacques. *Le Maghreb entre deux guerres.* 1962.

Beuve-Méry, Hubert. *Onze ans de règne.* 1974.

Bigeard, Marcel. *Pour une parcelle de gloire.* 1975.

Bigeard, Marcel, and Flament, Marc. *Aucune bête au monde.* 1959.

Blanc, Daniel. *Après les armes, citoyens.* 1962.

Bollardière, Jacques Pâris de. *Bataille d'Alger; bataille de l'homme.* 1972.

Boudiaf, Mohamed. *La Préparation du premier novembre.* 1976.

Bourdieu, Pierre. *The Algerians.* Translated by Alan C. M. Ross. Boston, 1962.

Bromberger, Merry and Serge. *Les 13 complots du 13 mai.* 1958.

Bromberger, Merry and Serge; Elgey, Georgette; and Chauvel, Jean-François. *Barricades et colonels, 24 janvier 1960.* 1960.

Bromberger, Serge. *Les Rebelles algériens.* 1958.

Buchard, Robert. *Organisation armée secrète, février–14 décembre 1961.* 1963.

Buffelan, Jean-Paul. *Le Complot du 13 mai 1958 dans le Sud-ouest.* 1966.

Bugnod, Geneviève, and Eddi, Irène. "Le Parti communiste français et la question algérienne du 1er novembre 1954 au 13 mai 1958." Mémoire de maîtrise, Université de Paris I, 1972.

Buis, Georges. *La Grotte.* 1961.

Burnier, Michel-Antoine. *Choice of Action; The French Existentialists on the Political Front Line.* Translated by Bernard Murchland. New York, 1968.

Buron, Robert. *Carnets politiques de la guerre d'Algérie.* 1965.

———. *Les Dernières années de la IVe République; carnets politiques.* 1968.

Cahiers du Témoignage chrétien. *De la Pacification à la repression: le dossier Jean Muller.* 1957.

Caute, David. *Communism and the French Intellectuals.* London, 1964.

Challe, Maurice. *Notre Révolte.* 1968.

Cherrière, C. A. "Les Débuts de l'insurrection algérienne." *Revue de défense nationale* 12 (1956), 1450–62.

Chevalier, Louis. *Le Problème démographique nord-africain.* 1947.

Chevallier, Jacques. *Nous, les algériens.* 1958.

Clark, Michael K. *Algeria in Turmoil; A History of the Rebellion.* New York, 1959.

Claude, Henri. *Gaullisme et grand capital.* 1960.

Club Jean Moulin. *Deux pièces du dossier Algérie.* 1962.

Comité Audin. *Sans Commentaire.* 1961.

Comité résistance spirituelle. *Des Rappelés témoignent.* 1957.

Confer, Vincent. *France and Algeria; The Problems of Civil and Political Reform, 1870–1920.* Syracuse, 1966.

Cornation, Michel. *Les Regroupements de la décolonisation en Algérie.* 1967.

Cottaz, Maurice, ed. *Les Procès du putsch d'Alger et du complot de Paris.* 1962.

Courrière, Yves. *La Guerre d'Algérie.* 4 vols. 1968–72.

Crouzet, Michel. "La Bataille des intellectuels français." *La Nef,* nos. 12–13 (October 1962–January 1963), pages 46–66.

Daniel, Jean. *Le Temps qui reste; essai d'autobiographie professionnelle.* 1973.

Dansette, Adrien. *Histoire religieuse de la France contemporaine.* Rev. ed. 1965.

Denoyer, François. *Quatre ans de guerre en Algérie; lettres d'un jeune officier.* 1962.

Descloîtres, Robert. *L'Algérie des bidonvilles; le tiers monde dans la cité.* 1961.

Dessaigne, Francine. *Journal d'une mère de famille pied-noir.* 1962.

Devillers, Philippe, and Lacouture, Jean. *End of a War; Indochina 1954.* New York, 1969.

Dreyfus, François G. *Histoire des gauches en France, 1940–1974.* 1975.

Dulac, André. *Nos Guerres perdues.* 1968.

Duquesne, Jacques. *L'Algérie ou la guerre des mythes.* 1958.

Duverger, Maurice; Goguel, François; and Touchard, Jean, eds. *Les Elections du 2 janvier 1956.* 1957.

Elgey, Georgette. *Histoire de la IVe République.* 2 vols. 1965–68.

Ely, Paul. *Mémoires.* Vol. 2. 1969.

Etienne, Bruno. *L'Algérie: cultures et révolution.* 1977.

———. *Les Problèmes juridiques des minorités européennes au maghreb.* 1968.

Fauvet, Jacques. *Historie du parti communiste français.* 2 vols. 1965.

———. *La IVe République.* 1959.

Fauvet, Jacques, and Planchais, Jean. *Le Fronde des généraux.* 1961.

Favrelière, Noël. *Le Désert à l'aube.* 1960.

Fejtö, François. *The French Communist Party and the Crisis of International Communism.* Cambridge, Mass., 1967.

Feraoun, Mouloud. *Journal, 1955–1962.* 1962.

Ferniot, Jean. *De Gaulle et le 13 mai.* 1965.

Ferrandi, Jean. *600 Jours avec Salan et l'OAS.* 1969.

Fieldhouse, D. K. *Economics and Empire 1830–1914.* Ithaca, 1973.

Firestone, Ya'akov. "The Doctrine of Integration with France among the Europeans of Algeria." *Comparative Political Studies* 4 (1971): 177–204.

Flanner, Janet (Genêt). *Paris Journal, 1944–1965.* New York, 1965.

Fraleigh, Arnold. "The Algerian Revolution as a Case Study in International Law." In *The International Law of Civil War,* edited by Richard Falk, pages 179–243. Baltimore, 1971.

France. *Programme et action du gouvernement en Algérie; mesures de pacification et réformes.* Algiers, 1956.

Gardt, Jean, and Roque, Claude. *Service militaire pourquoi?* 1960.

Gaucher, Roland. *Les Terroristes.* 1965.

Gaulle, Charles de. *Discours et messages,* vols. 2 and 3. Vol. 2, *Dans l'attente, 1946–1958.* Vol. 3, *Avec le renouveau, 1958–1962.* 1970.

──────. *Mémoires d'espoir.* Vol. 1. 1970.

──────. *Mémoires de guerre.* Vol. 1. 1954.

Geertz, Clifford. *The Social History of an Indonesian Town.* Cambridge, Mass., 1965.

Gendarme, René. *L'Economie de l'Algérie.* 1959.

Giap, V. N. *Guerre du peuple; armée du peuple.* 1968.

Girardet, Raoul. *La Crise militaire française.* 1964.

──────. *L'Idée coloniale en France.* 1972.

Giroud, Françoise. *I Give You My Word.* Boston, 1974.

Godard, Yves. *La Bataille d'Alger.* Vol. 1. 1972.

Goguel, François, ed. *Le Référendum du 8 janvier 1961.* 1962.

Good, Dorothy. "Notes on the Demography of Algeria." *Population Index* 28 (January 1961): 3–31.

Gordon, David. *The Passing of French Algeria.* London, 1966.

Goutalier, Régine. "L'OAS en Oranie." Thèse de 3e cycle, Université d'Aix-Marseille I, 1975.

Grosser, Alfred. *French Foreign Policy under De Gaulle.* Translated by Lois Ames Pattison. Boston, 1967.

La Guerre révolutionnaire. *Revue militaire d'information.* February–March 1957. Special number.

Halpern, Manfred. "The Algerian Uprising of 1945." *The Middle East Journal* 2 (1948): 191–202.

Hamon, Léo. *De Gaulle dans la République.* 1958.

Harbi, Mohamed. *Aux Origines du FLN; la scission PPA-MTLD.* 1975.

Hartley, Anthony. *Gaullism; The Rise and Fall of a Political Movement.* New York, 1971.

Heggoy, Alf Andrew. *Insurgency and Counterinsurgency in Algeria.* Bloomington, Ind., 1972.

Henissart, Paul. *Wolves in the City; The Death of French Algeria.* New York, 1971.

Henry, Louis. "Perspectives relatives à la population musulmane de l'Afrique du nord." *Population* 2 (1947): 267–80.

Heymann, Arlette. *Les Libertés publiques et la guerre d'Algérie.* 1972.

Hirschman, Albert O. *Exit, Voice and Loyalty.* Cambridge, Mass., 1970.

Hoffmann, Stanley. *Decline or Renewal? France Since the 1930s.* New York, 1974.

Hogard, Jacques. "Guerre révolutionnaire ou révolution dans l'art de la guerre." *Revue de défense nationale* 12 (December 1956): 1497–1513.

———. "L'Armée française devant la guerre révolutionnaire." *Revue de défense nationale* 13 (January 1957): 77–79.

———. "Le Soldat dans la guerre révolutionnaire." *Revue de défense nationale* 13 (February 1957): 211–26.

Horne, Alistair. *A Savage War of Peace; Algeria, 1954–1962.* New York, 1978.

Hutchinson, Martha Crenshaw. *Revolutionary Terrorism; The FLN in Algeria.* Stanford, 1978.

Isnard, H. *La Vigne en Algérie.* 2 vols. Gap, 1954.

———. "La Viticulture algérienne: erreur économique?" *Revue africaine* (1956), 457–73.

Jacob, Alain. *D'une Algérie à l'autre.* 1963.

Jeanson, Colette and Francis. *L'Algérie hors la loi.* 1955.

Jeanson, Francis. *Notre guerre.* 1961.

Johnson, Chalmers. *Autopsy on People's War.* Berkeley and Los Angeles, 1973.

Julien, Charles-André. *L'Afrique du nord en marche; nationalismes musulmanes et souveraineté française.* 3rd ed. 1972.

Just, Ward. *Military Men.* New York, 1971.

Kelly, George Armstrong. *Lost Soldiers; The French Army and Empire in Crisis, 1947–1962.* Cambridge, Mass., 1965.

Kraft, Joseph. *The Struggle for Algeria.* New York, 1961.

Lacheroy, Charles. "La Guerre révolutionnaire." In *La Défense nationale,* pages 307–30. 1958.

Lacouture, Jean. *Cinq hommes et la France.* 1961.

———. *De Gaulle.* Rev. ed. 1971.

Laqueur, Walter. *Guerrilla.* Boston, 1976.

Larmour, Peter. "De Gaulle and the New France." *Yale Review,* 55 (1966): 500–520.

Lebjaoui, Mohamed. *Bataille d'Alger ou bataille d'Algérie.* 1972.

———. *Vérités sur la révolution algérienne.* 1970.

Lentin, Albert-Paul. *L'Algérie des colonels; journal d'un témoin, juin-octobre 1958.* 1958.

————. *Algérie entre deux mondes.* Vol. I. *Le Dernier quart d'heure.* 1963.

Le Tourneau, Roger. *Evolution politique de l'Afrique du nord musulmane.* 1962.

Leulliette, Pierre. *Saint Michel et le dragon; souvenirs d'un parachutiste.* 1961.

Loubet del Bayle, Jean-Louis. *Les Non-conformistes des années 30.* 1969.

Lüthy, Herbert. *France Against Herself.* New York, 1955.

Mallarde, Etienne. *L'Algérie depuis.* 1975.

Marshall, D. Bruce. *The French Colonial Myth and Constitution-Making in the Fourth Republic.* New Haven, 1973.

Maschino, Maurice. *L'Engagement.* 1961.

Maspero, François, ed. *Le Droit à l'insoumission; "le dossier des 121."* 1961.

Massu, Jacques. *Le Torrent et la digue.* 1972.

————. *La Vraie Bataille d'Alger.* 1971.

Mauriac, François. *Bloc-Notes, 1952–1957.* 1958.

————. *De Gaulle.* 1964.

Merle, Marcel, ed. *Les Eglises chrétiennes et la décolonisation.* 1967.

Michelet, Edmond. *Querelle de la fidelité.* 1971.

Monteil, Vincent. *Les Officiers.* 1964.

Morland, Barangé, Martinez [pseud.]. *Histoire de l'organisation de l'armée secrète.* 1964.

Mus, Paul, ed. *Guerre sans visage; lettres commentées du sous-lieutenant Emile Mus.* 1961.

Navarre, Henri. *L'Agonie d'Indochine.* 1958.

Nora, Pierre. *Les Français d'Algérie.* 1961.

O'Ballance, Edgar. *The Algerian Insurrection, 1954–1962.* London, 1967.

Oppermann, Thomas. *Le Problème algérien; données historiques, politiques, juridiques.* 1961.

Ortiz, Joseph. *Mes Combats.* 1964.

Paret, Peter. *French Revolutionary Warfare from Indochina to Algeria; The Analysis of a Political and Military Doctrine.* New York, 1964.

Paxton, Robert O. *Vichy France; Old Guard and New Order.* New York, 1972.

Péju, Marcel, ed. *Le Procès du réseau Jeanson.* 1961.

Pelletier, Jean. *Alger 1955; Essai d'une géographie sociale.* 1959.

Pineau, Christian. *1956: Suez.* 1976.

Planchais, Jean. *Malaise de l'armée.* 1958.

Planchais, Jean, and Nobécourt, Jacques. *Une Histoire politique de l'armée.* 2 vols. 1967.

Poperen, Jean. *Le Gauche française; le nouvel âge.* 1972.

Quandt, William B. *Revolution and Political Leadership; Algeria, 1954–1968.* Cambridge, Mass., 1969.

Quilliot, Roger. *La SFIO et l'exercice du pouvoir.* 1972.

Rouanet, Pierre. *Pierre Mendès-France au pouvoir.* 1965.

Rouvière, Jacques. *Le Putsch d'Alger.* 1976.

Roy, Jules. *The War in Algeria.* Translated by Richard Howard. New York, 1961.

Saadi, Yacef. *Souvenirs de la Bataille d'Alger.* 1961.

Salan, Raoul. *Mémoires: Fin d'un empire.* 4 vols. 1971–74.

Semidei, Manuela. "De l'Empire à la décolonisation à travers les manuels scolaires français." *Revue française de science politique* 16 (February 1966): 56–86.

Sergent, Pierre. *Je ne regrette rien.* 1972.

———. *La Bataille.* 1968.

———. *Ma Peau au bout de mes idées.* 1967.

Sérigny, Alain de. *Echos d'Alger.* 2 vols. 1972–74.

Servan-Schreiber, Jean-Jacques. *Lieutenant en Algérie.* 1957.

Servier, Jean. *Dans l'Aurès sur les pas des rebelles.* 1955.

Simmons, Harvey G. *French Socialists in Search of a Role.* Ithaca, 1970.

Simon, Pierre-Henri. *Contre la torture.* 1957.

———. *Portrait d'un officier.* 1958.

Sorum, Paul Clay. *Intellectuals and Decolonization in France.* Chapel Hill, 1977.

Soustelle, Jacques. *Aimée et souffrante Algérie.* 1956.

———. *Vingt-huit ans de gaullisme.* 2nd ed. 1971.

Susini, Jean-Jacques. *Histoire de l'OAS.* 1963.

Tabah, Léon. "La Population algérienne: croissance, niveau de vie, investissements." *Population* 11 (1956): 439–60.

Talbott, John. "The Myth and Reality of the Paratrooper in the Algerian War." *Armed Forces and Society* 3 (Fall 1976): 69–86.

———. "French Public Opinion and the Algerian War: A Research Note." *French Historical Studies* 9 (Fall 1975): 354–61.

———. "Terrorism and the Liberal Dilemma: The Case of the 'Battle of Algiers.' " *Contemporary French Civilization* 2, no. 2 (Winter 1978): 177–89.

———. "The Strange Death of Maurice Audin." *The Virginia Quarterly Review* 52 (1976): 224–42.

Terrenoire, Louis. *De Gaulle et l'Algérie; témoignage pour l'histoire.* 1964.

Theis, Laurent, and Ratte, Philippe. *La Guerre d'Algérie ou le temps des méprises.* 1974.

Théolleyre, Jean-Marc. *Ces Procès qui ébranlèrent la France.* 1967.

Thomas, Hugh. *The Suez Affair.* Rev. ed. London, 1970.

Tillion, Germaine. *L'Afrique bascule vers l'avenir; l'Algérie en 1957 et autres textes.* 1961.

———. *Les Ennemis complémentaires.* 1960.

Tocqueville, Alexis de. *Ecrits et discours politiques.* Vol. 3 in *Oeuvres complètes.* 1962.

Tournoux, Jean-Raymond. *Jamais dit.* 1971.

———. *Secrets d'état.* 1961.

———. *Le Tourment et la fatalité.* 1974.

Tricot, Bernard. *Les Sentiers de la paix: Algérie, 1958–1962.* 1972.

Trinquier, Roger. *Le Coup d'état du 13 mai.* 1962.

———. *Modern Warfare.* Translated by Daniel Lee. New York, 1964.

Tripier, Philippe. *Autopsie de la guerre d'Algérie.* 1972.

Vatin, Jean-Claude. *L'Algérie politique; histoire et société.* 1974.

Viansson-Ponté, Pierre. *Histoire de la République gaullienne,* vol. 1, *La Fin d'une époque: mai 1958–juillet 1962.* 1970.

Vidal-Naquet, Pierre. *L'Affaire Audin.* 1958.

———. *La Torture dans la République.* 1973.

———, ed. *La Raison d'état.* 1962.

Vittori, Jean-Pierre. *Nous, les appelés d'Algérie.* 1977.

Wall, Irwin. "The French Communists and the Algerian War." *Journal of Contemporary History* 12 (1977): 521–43.

Werth, Alexander. *The Strange History of Pierre Mendès-France and the Great Conflict over French North Africa.* London, 1957.

Paul Wilkinson. *Political Terrorism.* London, 1974.

Williams, Philip M. *Crisis and Compromise; Politics in the Fourth Republic.* London, 1964.

———. *Wars, Plots and Scandals in Postwar France.* Cambridge, 1970.

Williams, Philip M., and Harrison, Martin. *Politics and Society in de Gaulle's Republic.* 2nd ed. London, 1971.

Wright, Gordon. "The Dreyfus Echo: Justice and Politics in the Fourth Republic." *Yale Review* 48 (1959): 354–73.

Yacono, Xavier. *Les Etapes de la décolonisation française.* 1971.

Zeller, André. *Dialogues avec un général.* 1974.

I took soundings for the years 1954–1962 in the periodicals listed below.

L'Année politique	*Le Figaro*	*Paris-Presse*
The Economist	*France observateur*	*Les Temps modernes*
Esprit	*L'Humanité*	*The New York Times*
L'Express	*Le Monde*	*Vérité-Liberté,* 1960–61

Index

298

A NOTE ABOUT THE AUTHOR

John Talbott is professor of history at the University of California at Santa Barbara, where he has taught since 1971. Born in Grinnell, Iowa, in 1940, he received his B.A. degree from the University of Missouri and his M.A. and Ph.D. degrees from Stanford University. He is the author of *The Politics of Educational Reform in France, 1918–1940* (1969), and the editor of *France Since 1930* (1972). In 1975–6 he was a Fellow of the Institute for Advanced Study in Princeton and a National Endowment for the Humanities Fellow. His reviews have appeared in the *Los Angeles Times*, the Chicago *Tribune*, *Books & Arts*, *The New York Review of Books*, the Washington *Post, Smithsonian,* and various scholarly journals.

A NOTE ON THE TYPE

The text of this book was set via computer-driven cathode ray tube in Video Times Roman, an adaptation of a face called Times Roman, designed by Stanley Morison for *The Times* (London), and first introduced by that newspaper in 1932.

Among typographers and designers of the twentieth century, Stanley Morison had a strong forming influence, as typographical adviser to the English Monotype Corporation, as a director of two distinguished English publishing houses, and as a writer of sensibility, erudition, and keen practical sense.

Composed, printed and bound by
The Haddon Craftsmen, Inc., Scranton, Pennsylvania.